# OUR HOLY FAITH

OUR HOLY FAITH

BOOK SIX

# KING OF KINGS

TAN Books
Gastonia, North Carolina

Originally published in 1959 as *Our Holy Faith Book VI: Our Faith: God's Great Gift* by Bruce Publishing Company and reprinted in 1998 by The Neumann Press.

Nihil Obstat:
John A. Schulien, S.T.D.
Censor Librorum

Imprimatur:
W Albert G. Meyer
Archbishop of Milwaukee
April 18, 1959

This TAN Books edition has been re-typeset and enhanced with additional content and revisions, including modernized language and updates to the practices of the Catholic Church. Catechism questions and answers have been replaced with the TAN edition of *The Third Council of Baltimore: Baltimore Catechism 1–4*.

Scripture quotes are adapted from the Douay-Rheims 1899 American Edition.

Content revisions and updates by Elisa Torres

Interior design by Caroline Green and David Ferris
Cover design by www.davidferrisdesign.com

ISBN: 978-1-5051-1925-1

Published in the United States by
TAN Books
PO Box 269
Gastonia, NC 28053
www.TANBooks.com

Printed in the United States of America

# Contents

# Publisher's Note

The original editions of the Our Holy Faith series textbooks were published between 1959 and 1964. They were compiled by many different authors over the course of several years. Consequently, the texts varied in their organization from year to year, with similar sections appearing with different names throughout the series and often in varying sequences.

For greater ease of use and consistency, we have reorganized each book so that the Catechism lessons, tests, and other exercises are placed at the end of each relevant chapter or lesson. We have also included answer keys for your convenience in the back of each book.

While the teachings in the original editions remain relevant due to the enduring truths of our Faith, it was necessary to update other aspects in order to more accurately reflect the Church today. These new editions have been revised to incorporate some of the changes to the practices of the Catholic Church.

To the extent possible, we have adapted the text to reflect both the ordinary and extraordinary forms of the Mass and liturgical calendars. In addition to these updates, we have inserted, where relevant to the text, traditional prayers and quotes from the Bible, the Catechism, and the saints.

This new Our Holy Faith series is faithful to the work of the original authors. It honors the fundamental and unchanging truths of the Catholic Church and is heavily influenced by tradition. We believe it is the catechesis you can trust with your children's faith.

# Introduction

## What Is Faith?

What does it mean to have faith in God? What is faith? There are many ways we talk about faith. Faith is a theological virtue, a gift we receive at Baptism. Faith is also an act of the intellect assenting to truth through the grace of God. Such an act is born from a profound relationship with God. Faith is also spoken of as a body of belief, as when we speak of "our Catholic faith, or "our Holy faith." Here, "faith" means belief in the truths handed down to us by Jesus Christ and the Church.

Faith is one of God's most important gifts. As St. Paul said, "Faith is the substance of things hoped for, the evidence of things not seen" (Heb. 11:1). Faith in God is the necessary soil for the Christian life. It is from faith that we first come to know who God is and what He desires for us. We must make acts of faith often and desire that God increase faith within us.

To believe in the truths of the Catholic Church is part of what it means to have faith in Jesus Christ. We can lose our faith in what the Church teaches if we do not appreciate its value and neglect it. We can protect our faith if we learn about it so that we will realize what it tells us and what it means to us. Let us resolve here at the beginning of the year to study our religion better than any other subject. And let us stop here for a moment to ask the Holy Spirit to help us.

## Faith—God's Great Gift

Faith is often called the beacon light on our journey to eternity. We know that beacon lights guide planes on their course. We know too that the shining beam from a lighthouse leads ships safely to harbor. In much the same way, faith sheds a light over our path through life, showing us the errors we must avoid and the truths we are to believe.

God gave us this great gift of faith freely without any merit whatever on our part. Let us see if we can increase our appreciation for this great gift, calling to mind the words of St. Paul: "For by grace you have been saved through faith, and that not of yourselves, for it is the gift of God" (Eph. 2:8). Did you ever thank God for your faith?

The conversion of St. Paul, depicted in this painting by Caravaggio, gave him a strong appreciation for the gift of faith.

## Faith Is Necessary for Salvation

Our Lord preached and worked miracles to strengthen the faith of the people. If He did not consider faith necessary, would He have done so many things to increase their faith?

St. Paul, in his Epistle to the Hebrews, explained the necessity of faith. He said, "Without faith it is impossible to please God"(Heb. 11:6). We know that only those who are pleasing to God can enter heaven.

## Man Must Use the Gift of Faith

Everyone knows that athletes strengthen their muscles by using them in vigorous exercise. Champion runners and ball players spend many hours a day during their training period exercising, so that their muscles will become stronger and help them to victory. So it is, in a spiritual way, with faith. In order to make our faith stronger we must exercise it throughout the training period of this life.

Having a football and knowing the rules of the game does not make a football player. Can you explain why? Knowing and believing what the right thing is, is quite different from doing what is right. Just as we prove our love for our parents by obeying them, so we prove our faith by doing the things faith teaches us to do. What are some of the teachings of faith? What are some of the things we will do if we really believe them? God has told us.

You believe Christ's words, "Unless you eat the flesh of the Son of Man, and drink His blood, you shall not have life in you" (Jn. 6:54–57). To live up to this belief must you not receive Holy Communion often and devoutly?

Again, it is important to be able to list the Ten Commandments, and to know all the ways in which we can keep or break the Ten Commandments. But knowing the Ten Commandments is valuable to us only if it leads us to action. We must live according to our faith. We must observe the commandments in our lives. In other words we must do that which we believe. The great missionary St. Francis Xavier, after instructing his students in the truths of their religion, often said, "Now let us say a Hail Mary that we may believe these truths, and live according to them." Should we do the same thing this year? During our whole life?

## Man Must Protect the Gift of Faith

Anything precious must be protected. The Declaration of Independence is carefully guarded. The nation's supply of gold is kept under close watch. Valuable gems are stored in safe places. Children are shielded by their parents. So also the teachings of our faith, a gift of great value to us, must be protected.

One good way to protect what our faith teaches is to know it. We can learn to know our faith by studying the catechism, reading the Bible reverently and carefully, and reading other good books.

## Prayer as a Safeguard

We can guard our faith by making frequent acts of faith, including reciting the Apostles' Creed. In our morning and night prayers, in our preparation for confession, and before receiving Holy Communion we can say, "Sacred Heart of Jesus, I believe in Thy love for me." We should pray for a strong faith. In little troubles and trials we can pray, "Lord, increase our faith."

## Other Safeguards of Faith

Do you know how the life of St. Ignatius became charged with a strong living faith? This great man was inspired by good reading. Other saints, like Francis Xavier, were influenced by good companionship.

We Catholics must do certain things and avoid others in order to safeguard our faith.

What are the things we should do? *A Catholic can best safeguard his faith by making frequent acts of faith, by praying for a strong faith, by studying his religion very earnestly, by living a good life, by good reading, by refusing to associate with the enemies of the Church, and by not reading books and papers opposed to the Church and her teaching.* Let us do all these things. But this year especially let us study, on a higher level, the chief truths of our holy Catholic faith as found in the Apostles' Creed. Let us resolve to work hard, studying our Catholic faith so that we may appreciate how much it means to us and how good God has been to give us the great gift of faith.

## FOR ME TO REMEMBER

1. God gives us the gift of faith.
2. Faith is necessary for salvation.
3. We must use the gift of faith.
4. We must protect our faith.
5. We prove our faith by actually doing the things we say we believe in the Apostles' Creed.

## FOR ME TO DO

1. Prepare a two-minute talk on "What My Faith Means to Me," or "What Life Would Be Like Without Faith."
2. Discuss whether knowing and believing the truths of our faith is sufficient to save us.
3. Tell how the Apostles' Creed is important to you as a Catholic.
4. In your own words tell what you need to do to keep your faith strong.

### *TERMS TO KNOW*

- strengthen
- accordance
- associate
- opposed

UNIT

# 1 God, the Father Almighty, One in Three

## CHAPTER 1
# God and God's Perfections

*I believe in God, the Father Almighty, Creator of heaven and of earth . . .*

*This year in three successive sections we shall study about God: Father, Son, and Holy Spirit, as the Apostles' Creed and the Baltimore Catechism present the doctrines to us. Then in the fourth and final section we shall study about some of the most important duties we owe to God, as they are contained in the first three commandments.*

*In this first section we shall learn about God and especially about those works of God which are usually connected with the first person, God the Father.*

*In chapter 1, we shall study God and God's perfections. In chapter 2, we shall turn to God the Father as the Creator of all things, especially man. And in chapter 3, we shall learn many more important details about the Fall and its effects on us.*

LESSON 1

# God Is Our Father and Creator

Let us now turn to the Apostles' Creed and study our Faith.

## God Made Us

The first thing that our holy faith teaches us is that there is a God who made us.

Most men at some time or other have watched the countless creatures of the earth and have asked this question, "Where did they all come from?" A beautiful bird on the limb of a tree might have aroused their curiosity; an odd-looking giraffe at the zoo might have brought the question to mind; or again, it could have been a strange bug or pesky mosquito that caused them to wonder.

The many varied creatures, mighty mountains, little rivers—all such things fill man with awe. Even we who know that all creatures came from God can continue to wonder at this awesome and important question: "Where did everything come from?" What we learned as little children is true, God made all things. *God made us.* In gratitude then, we should learn as much as we can about our great and good God.

## God Is the Supreme Being

God revealed to Adam and Eve who He is. As the number of people on the earth increased, they began to spread out. The truths which God had made known to Adam and Eve were confused or forgotten in the new settlements. The people, however, reasoning from the wonderful objects and order in the world, from the way in which day followed night, and season followed season, and from their own understanding of good and bad, knew—even if in a confused manner—that there is a Supreme Being. They tried to find Him in the universe in order to worship Him. Some thought that the Supreme Being was water; others identified Him with animals or other creatures of the earth.

To keep the idea of the true God alive in men's minds God revealed to the Hebrews who He was. He helped them to remember that *God is the Supreme Being, infinitely perfect, who made all things and keeps them in existence.*

We can recall the story of creation and remember that God created other things before He made man. What are some of these creatures? Heavenly bodies? Plants? What else? All these creatures provided for man's needs. The sun, moon, and stars give him light; plants and animals furnish him food, clothing, shelter, medicine, and service. Deep in the ground as in a basement, are stores of coal, oil, and gas for fuel; of gold, silver, and other minerals and elements for man to use. Because God took care to provide for all our needs we say He is our loving Father.

When Christ came to earth He wanted to make us realize this important truth that God is our Father. The Gospels give us many examples of this teaching. Let us read over and discuss some of these references from the New Testament.

"... your Father knows what you need before you ask Him. In this manner therefore shall you pray: 'Our Father who art in heaven' " (Mt. 6:8–9).

"But when thou prayest, go into thy room, and closing thy

door, pray to thy Father in secret; and thy Father, who sees in secret, will reward thee" (Mt. 6:6).

"Therefore I say to you, do not be anxious for your life, what you shall eat; nor yet for your body, what you shall put on. Is not the life a greater thing than the food, and the body than the clothing? Look at the birds of the air; they do not sow, or reap, or gather into barns; yet your heavenly Father feeds them. Are not you of much more value than they?" (Mt. 6:25–27.)

## God Made Us to Share His Happiness

Since God has taken such care of us, we must realize that we are here on this earth because of His goodness and love. God is goodness itself. He did not need us to make Him happier. He made us so that we might share his everlasting happiness in heaven. Each one of us shows the goodness of God by the very fact of being alive.

> *"My soul, have you found what you are looking for? You were looking for God, and you have discovered that he is the supreme being, and that you could not possibly imagine anything more perfect. You have discovered that this supreme being is life itself, light, wisdom, goodness, eternal blessedness and blessed eternity. He is everywhere, and he is timeless."*
>
> *—St. Anselm of Canterbury*

Each one of us then, should always remember that God made us so that we could be happy with Him in heaven forever.

Why do some Catholics forget about the next life? Perhaps they have forgotten what they learned from their study of the catechism: *God made us to show forth His goodness and to share with us His everlasting happiness in heaven.*

## God Gave Us the Means to Serve Him

God gave to man two great powers or faculties: intellect and will. No other creature on earth possesses these two precious gifts. The intellect helps man to understand, or know; the will gives man the power to do what he knows is right. When we use these two faculties or powers, in the right way, we are giving honor and glory to God.

God wants us to keep Him foremost in our minds so that we can become holy as He is holy. This does not mean that we may never think of anything else. It does mean that we should see and reverence God in everything. God allows us to take pleasure in the good things He has created. In fact He has given us many opportunities for enjoyment here on earth. Still, God wants us to realize that no earthly joy can equal the eternal happiness of heaven for which we are striving.

Above all, God gave us His divine Son, who became man to show us the way to serve His almighty Father and, by His death on the cross, to win for us supernatural life. God's Son, our Lord Jesus Christ, established a Church and the seven sacraments, so that men for all ages would be able to share in this supernatural life and grow "strong in grace and in truth." By becoming man, He gave us the example of His own life, showing us what we should be and do in order to be pleasing to God. He is with us daily in the Blessed Sacrament, inviting us to come and tell Him our joys and our sorrows and gain from Him wisdom to know what we must do and courage to do

> *"Let us begin in earnest to work out our salvation, for no one will do it for us, since even He Himself, Who made us without ourselves, will not save us without ourselves."*
>
> *—St. Margaret Mary Alacoque*

it. By living in Christ and allowing Him to live in us, we will glorify God in all that we do.

## Our Purpose: Union with God on Earth and in Heaven

"Thy will be done on earth as it is in heaven." Our Lord tells us to pray these words in the Our Father. Eternal enjoyment with God can begin to become a reality for us on earth as we strive to grow closer to God in prayer and through all the virtues each day. Our lives here on earth must be governed by God's will if we hope to be happy with Him in heaven. In short, *to gain the happiness of heaven we must know, love, and serve God in this world.*

Can you see now that your life is a journey to the complete knowledge of God? The Church, through the articles of the Apostles' Creed points out the chief truths that are to be known about Him. By prayer and by receiving the sacraments we gain the grace to know and serve Him, and to increase our love for Him; and the commandments are the guides which show the way.

## The Church Shows Us How

We can say it briefly and clearly in these words: *We learn to know, love, and serve God from Jesus Christ, the Son of God, who teaches us through the Catholic Church.*

*I believe in God, the Father Almighty,*
*Creator of heaven and earth;*

*and in Jesus Christ, His only Son, our Lord;*

*who was conceived by the Holy Spirit,*
*born of the Virgin Mary,*

*suffered under Pontius Pilate, was crucified,*
*died and was buried.*

*He descended into hell; on the third day*
*He arose again from the dead;*

*He ascended into heaven, and is seated at*
*the right hand of God, the Father Almighty;*

*from there He shall come to judge the living*
*and the dead.*

*I believe in the Holy Spirit,*

*the Holy Catholic Church,*

*the communion of saints,*

*the forgiveness of sins,*

*the resurrection of the body,*

*and life everlasting. Amen.*

From the earliest days of the Church, the teachings of Christ have been handed down by the Apostles and their successors. The chief of these teachings have been gathered together in a prayer known as the Apostles' Creed.

As the Church grew and spread, men studied the doctrines which Christ taught. The teaching of the Church developed. In all this the Catholic Church was not adding new truths, but unfolding, or explaining the truths which God has revealed so that men might understand them more easily and more fully.

*We find the chief truths taught by Jesus Christ through the Catholic Church in the Apostles' Creed.* Do you know the Apostles' Creed so well that you can write it without making a single mistake? You must know and be able to explain each of the twelve parts. They are listed here for you.

### TERMS TO KNOW

- creature
- gratitude
- infinitely
- existence
- creed
- visible
- will
- supreme
- intellect
- doctrines

## FOR ME TO REVIEW

*Catechism Lesson*

1. **Q. Who made the world?**
   A. God made the world.

2. **Q. Who is God?**
   A. God is the Creator of heaven and earth, and of all things.

3. **Q. What is man?**
   A. Man is a creature composed of body and soul, and made in the image and likeness of God.

6. **Q. Why did God make you?**
   A. God made me to know Him, to love Him, and to serve Him in this world, and to be happy with Him forever in the next.

9. **Q. What must we do to be saved?**
   A. To save our souls we must worship God by faith, hope, and charity; that is, we must believe in Him, hope in Him, and love Him with all our heart.

11. **Q. Where shall we find the chief truths which the Church teaches?**
   A. We shall find the chief truths which the Church teaches in the Apostles' Creed.

12. **Q. Say the Apostles' Creed.**
   A. I believe in God, the Father Almighty, Creator of heaven and earth; and in Jesus Christ, His only Son, our Lord; who was conceived by the Holy , born of the Virgin Mary, suffered under Pontius Pilate, was crucified; died, and was buried. He descended into Hell; the third day He arose again from the dead; He ascended into Heaven, and sitteth at the right hand of God, the Father Almighty; from thence He shall come to judge the living and the dead. I believe in the Holy, the Holy Catholic Church, the communion of Saints, the forgiveness of sins, the resurrection of the body, and the life everlasting. Amen.

**Questions and Exercises**

*Write your answers on a separate sheet of paper*

1. How can you increase the glory of God by giving a good example?
2. What will our home in heaven be like?
3. How does the Church map out our way through life?
4. Why is the Apostles' Creed an important prayer?
5. Can we prove there is a God?

6. What is revelation?
7. How can your faith become stronger?
8. How can you use the gift of faith in everyday life?
9. Must the honor we give to God be greater than that given to any creature?
10. How can you learn to know God?
11. What can you do to prove your love for God?
12. What is the best way to serve God?
13. Name some things that God keeps in existence and explain how He does it.
14. What can you do today to prove to God that you realize how truly great He is?
15. What could you say in prayer to God as you use one of His gifts today?
16. What did Jesus Christ do to help us learn to know, love, and serve God?
17. How does sharing God's gifts with others prove our love for God?
18. Why should we love the Catholic Church?
19. How can boys and girls your age prove they believe in God?
20. What does the word *Creed* mean?

## FOR ME TO REMEMBER

1. God made us.
2. God is the Supreme Being.
3. God made us to show us His goodness and to share with us His happiness.
4. We will share God's happiness if we love and serve Him.
5. The Church teaches us how to serve God.

## FOR ME TO DO

1. Discuss what we have studied in this part and tell how it should influence the way we live.
2. Try to make the Sign of the Cross more fervently, as a profession of faith.
3. Visit our Lord in the Blessed Sacrament. Ask Him to help you to believe the truths of Catholicism which you have studied.
4. How can you help all men to know, love, and serve God?
5. What part of the answer to catechism question number two might you think of when you sit down to an excellent meal prepared by your mother?
6. Speak from your heart to God, praising Him for His greatness.
7. Make a visit to the church and ask God to help you grow each day in the grace He gave you at baptism.
8. Each time you obey someone in authority, try to remember that you are really obeying God, your Father and Creator.
9. List the truths you find in the Apostles' Creed—put them in your own words.

## Act of Faith

*O my God, I firmly believe that you are one God in three divine persons, Father, Son, and Holy Spirit. I believe that your divine Son became man and died for our sins and that he will come to judge the living and the dead. I believe these and all the truths which the Holy Catholic Church teaches because you have revealed them who are eternal truth and wisdom, who can neither deceive nor be deceived.*

*In this faith I intend to live and die. Amen.*

LESSON 2

# God Has Many Perfections

God's perfections help us know Him better. They show us how great and how good He is.

As we have already learned, God is the Supreme Being, above all creatures. This means that He is the highest power, the greatest authority that can exist. It also means that all creatures come under His power, that He has the right to rule them. Here is a definition of Supreme Being which should help us understand this better: *When we say that God is the Supreme Being we mean that He is above all creatures, the self-existing and infinitely perfect Spirit.*

## God Is a Spirit

One of the most important things we know about God is that He is a spirit. *A spirit is a being that has understanding and free will, but no body, and will never die.* Because a spirit has no body, it has no parts and will live forever.

Angels also are spirits. So are our souls spirits. They also have an intellect for knowing and understanding, and a will for choosing. But these spirits do not exist from themselves. God made them. They are not perfect. But God is a spirit who is self-existing and who is also infinitely perfect. Let us examine these two ideas.

## God Is Self-Existing

The idea of anything being self-existing is hard for us to understand. When we look around our room and see the things in it we realize they were all made from something. Some other being brought them into existence. So too we know there must have been some other person who first gave life to human beings. Indeed every created thing can be traced to some beginning from some other being. God alone had no beginning. He did not need help from any other being to exist. He is self-existing. *When we say that God is self-existing we mean that He does not owe His existence to any other being.*

## God Is Infinitely Perfect

The word *infinite* means "cannot be measured" or "having no end." Nothing could make God any greater or more wonderful than He is, for there is no end to His perfections.

Sometimes we use the word *perfect* to describe the things we do or see. When we see a rainbow in the sky we marvel at its

Although angels are spirits and have no body, they are often depicted in art in order for us to grasp their reality.

beauty. We say it is a perfect rainbow, and yet we know it is never quite perfect. At least when the rain stops the rainbow will vanish. We look forward to each birthday, and when the day comes, and we are having a happy time we say, "This is a perfect day." But even the best day has a few clouds, and just as the candles on the birthday cake burn down, so too must the day come to an end.

No matter how good the happenings of our lives may seem to be, they are not absolutely perfect, for they must all come to an end. We say they are finite, that is, limited, or having an end. But the perfections of God are infinite, without limit. *When we say that God is infinitely perfect we mean that He has all perfections without limit.*

God is so wonderful that on earth we do not fully appreciate Him. Only in heaven will we know how truly great God is. God has all perfections, that is, all good qualities found in persons or things. *Some of the perfections of God are: God is eternal, all-good, all-knowing, all-present, and almighty.* Let us examine more carefully the meaning of these perfections.

God is eternal, all-good, all-knowing, all-present, and almighty.

## God Is Eternal

Have you ever stopped to wonder where you will be fifty years from now? Certainly you will not be here two hundred years from now. Life on earth comes to an end. It was correct in 1910 to say, "Pius X *is* our present pope." Now he is spoken of in the past tense; "Pius X *was* the Holy Father." Only God can be spoken of in the present at all times. Only He is eternal. *When we say that God is eternal we mean that He always was and always will be, and that He always remains the same.* He is older than the centuries but younger than tomorrow.

## God Is All-Good

Sometimes we say we have read a good book, meaning that the book satisfied our need for recreation and gave us the information or entertainment we desired. Again we say we had a good dinner because it consisted of food we like, prepared in a way we enjoy. We often speak of someone as a good friend of ours, one who shares our pleasures and is interested in everything we are doing. Occasionally we describe a person as good, because he is kind and thoughtful, obedient and prayerful, and willing to make sacrifices for others. We say the saints led good lives.

These examples give us some idea of what goodness is. How can we apply this same quality of goodness to God? His goodness is limitless. He is Goodness itself. Everything about Him is absolutely lovable. He gives good things to everyone. He inspires us to keep trying, each in our own way, to become like Him in goodness. God loves all His creatures and bestows many blessings on them. *When we say that God is all-good we mean that He is infinitely lovable in Himself, and that from His fatherly love every good comes to us.*

God has loved every single one of His human creatures from the time of our first parents down to the present day,

*I am the Alpha and the Omega, the first and the last, the beginning and the end.*

**REVELATION 22:13**

despite all the sins that they have committed through the years. He wants us to imitate His goodness. He wants us to work and sacrifice and pray so that others may know and love Him. He wants all men to belong to His kingdom. He is good. Completely good. All-good. He wants us to be good. He wants us to be good to others, as He is good to us and to them.

> *"God loves each of us as if there were only one of us."*
>
> —*St. Augustine of Hippo*

## God Is All-Knowing

How many stars are there in the sky? A million? How many grains of sand are there in a handful? Is there anyone on earth who knows the answers to these questions? Hardly. The human mind is able to learn many things, but no human being will ever be able to know all the mysteries of life.

Try to imagine, if you can, a being capable of knowing, not only the exact answer to the mysteries of life around us now, but also the events and mysteries of life thousands of years ago, and all the happenings of the future. To our little minds this seems impossible, but nothing is impossible with God. God is all-knowing. *When we say that God is all-knowing we mean that He knows all things, past, present, and future, even our most secret thoughts, words, and actions.*

## God Is All-Present

Did you ever stop to think that you are never all alone? Even when you are completely by yourself God is with you, because God is all-present. *When we say that God is all-present we mean that He is everywhere.*

When we are in the state of grace God is present in us in another and a special way. Then He is in our souls, reigning there as a king on a throne. St. Paul, wishing to teach the people of Corinth this fact, said: "Do you not know that you are the temple of God, and that the spirit of God dwells within you?" (1 Cor. 3:16.)

Did you ever see a thought or a desire? No, because they are acts of our soul, which is a spirit. What is spiritual cannot be seen with bodily eyes. So, *although God is everywhere, we do not see Him because He is a spirit and cannot be seen with our eyes.*

Our eyes usually let us know who is in the room or in the house with us. There are times, however, when we know our father is upstairs although we do not see him for several hours. We have a feeling of security just knowing that he is near. We should always have this same feeling about God. We cannot see Him, and yet we know He is present in all things wherever we go.

We cannot ever run away from God. He sees us at work, at play. He sees our honesty in our games, and our helpfulness at home. God is pleased when we do good, and is sad when we do evil.

"Keep me, O Lord, as the apple of thine eye; beneath the shadow of Thy wings protect me."

## God Watches Over Us—Divine Providence

When Abraham was a very old man God chose him to be the Father of the Hebrews. God spoke to him, telling Abraham to leave his own country and relatives and settle in the land of Canaan. Abraham set out obediently in search of the Promised Land. He reached Canaan and settled there, and became the Father of the Hebrew nation. During the following years God's protecting care guided the Hebrews. They realized then, as we do now, that *God sees us and watches over us with loving care.*

From the history of the Hebrews we can learn much about God's loving care for His

***TERMS TO KNOW***

- creature
- gratitude
- infinitely
- existence
- creed
- visible
- will
- supreme
- intellect
- doctrines

children. For a time they would be faithful to God, and then they would begin to worship strange gods. Over and over again God sent prophets to bring the Hebrews back to Him. Just as God watched over the Hebrews and protected them, so also He watches over every action of our lives. *God's loving care for us is called Divine Providence.*

Sometimes things happen to us which cause us great sorrow or trouble and make us wonder whether God is really watching over us. God often lets things happen to test our faith and love. It is not what happens to us that counts; it is what these joys and sorrows do to us that matters, and what we do with them. If we use all the happenings of everyday life, whether glad or sad, to make us love God more, then we are His true children, deserving of His care. Do you remember the story of Job?

## Other Perfections of God

### God Is Almighty

As we said, God has all perfections. In addition to the perfections we have just studied, we could mention many others. An important one is that God is almighty. Do you understand what is meant by "almighty"? *When we say that God is almighty we mean that He can do all things.*

If a friend who does not share your religious beliefs were to question whether there are other perfections of God, could you answer, *God is all-wise, all-holy, all-merciful, and all-just?*

### God Is All-Wise

We cannot always understand why things happen as they do, but we must believe that God knows best. His wisdom will guide us through life, for He sees and knows all things, whereas we see and know only in part.

Do you remember the story of the Samaritan woman at the well? In order to bring her to eternal life, Christ showed this woman His power of seeing her secret thoughts. He told her the sins of her life. Another time Christ scolded a group of the Jews for complaining against a woman who had been discovered as a sinner. They wanted to stone her. Our Lord said that the one among them who was without sin should cast the first stone. You may recall how they slipped away one by one. God knows all our secret thoughts, words, and deeds. This sounds frightening but it should give us courage rather than fear.

### God Is All-Holy

God is infinitely and absolutely holy. God's holiness is so much greater than the holiness of any creature that we cannot even make a comparison. Whenever we think of the Blessed Virgin Mary a happy feeling enters our hearts. We realize how holy she was, since she was chosen by God to be the Mother of His Son. We respect and love her because of this great holiness. But even her holiness is as nothing compared to the infinite holiness of God. She is a creature.

### God Is All-Merciful

The great mercy of God is seen throughout the Gospels. Do you remember the story of Mary Magdalen, the sinful woman who lived during the time of Christ? Do you remember how Christ forgave her? Do you know the story of St. Peter? This beloved saint, whom Christ chose as the head of His Church, was a blustery man who loved to brag about his courage and loyalty. When Christ foretold that one of His Apostles would betray Him, Peter shook his head and declared boldly that he at least was ready to give his life for Christ. In spite of his proud boasting Peter denied our Lord; yet, his sins were forgiven.

It is the same with us. No matter how badly or how often we sin, God forgives us and

## Remember: God is...

- A Spirit
- Self-Existing
- Infinitely Perfect
- Eternal
- All-Good
- All-Powerful
- All-Present
- Almighty
- All-Wise
- All-Holy
- All-Knowing
- All-Merciful
- All-Just

Can you explain what each of these mean?

receives us back into His love if we are sorry and ask His forgiveness. Every time we receive the sacrament of Penance and Reconciliation worthily, that is, with the intention of showing God we are sorry for our sins and of leading better lives, God shows His mercy to us, as He did to Mary Magdalen and Peter.

### God Is All-Just

Some people do not believe in hell because they think that God's forgiveness extends even to those who are not sorry for their sins. God respects man's freedom. Hell exists because man has the freedom to love God or to reject God. Heaven and hell are realities that remind us of God's perfect justice.

## FOR ME TO REVIEW

*Catechism Lesson*

**184. Q. What does "supreme" mean?**

A. "Supreme" means the highest in authority; also the most excellent or greatest possible in anything. When we say that God is the Supreme Being we mean that He is above all creatures, the self-existing and infinitely perfect Spirit.

**169. Q. Why do we call God a "pure spirit"?**

A. We call God a pure spirit because He has no body. Our soul is a spirit, but not a "pure" spirit, because it was created for union with our body.

**164. Q. What do we mean when we say God is "infinitely perfect"?**

A. When we say God is "infinitely perfect" we mean there is no limit or bounds to His perfection; for He possesses all good qualities in the highest possible degree and He alone is "infinitely perfect."

165. Q. **Did God have a beginning?**
A. God had no beginning; He always was and He always will be. This is what we mean when we call God "eternal."

173. Q. **Does God know all things?**
A. God knows all things, even our most secret thoughts, words, and actions.

167. Q. **How is God everywhere?**
A. God is everywhere whole and entire as He is in any one place. This is true and we must believe it, though we cannot understand it.

168. Q. **If God is everywhere, why do we not see Him?**
A. We do not see God, because He is a pure spirit and cannot be seen with bodily eyes.

171. Q. **Does God see us?**
A. God sees us and watches over us.

212. Q. **What do we call the care by which God preserves and governs the world and all it contains?**
A. We call the care by which God preserves and governs the world and all it contains His Providence.

1388. Q. **What is meant by "the Providence of God"?**
A. By "the Providence of God" is meant the manner in which He preserves, provides for, rules and governs the world and directs all things by His infinite Will.

174. Q. **Can God do all things?**
A. God can do all things, and nothing is hard or impossible to Him. This is what we mean when we call God "almighty."

176. Q. **Is God just, holy, and merciful?**
A. God is all just, all holy, all merciful, as He is infinitely perfect.

## Questions and Exercises

*Write your answers on a separate sheet of paper*

1. Explain in your own words what infinitely perfect means.
2. What is meant by "being in a state of grace"?
3. How can we thank God for watching over us?
4. How does God show His mercy to us?
5. Write 1 to 10 on a piece of paper. Then match the following:

A. God is all-knowing.
B. God is all-merciful.
C. God is eternal.
D. God is all-present.
E. God is almighty.
F. God is infinitely perfect.
G. God is all-good.
H. Divine Providence.
I. God is all-holy.
J. God is all-just.

1. God watches over us with loving care.
2. God knows our most secret thoughts, words, actions.
3. God rewards good and punishes evil.
4. God is infinitely lovable in Himself, and from His fatherly care every good comes to us.
5. God hates what is evil and loves only what is good.
6. God can do all things.
7. God is the same, yesterday, today, forever.
8. God's perfections are without limit.
9. God forgives our sins when we are sorry for them.
10. God is everywhere.

## FOR ME TO REMEMBER

1. God has all perfections in fullest measure.
2. God loves all His creatures.
3. God cares for all men throughout their entire lives.

## FOR ME TO DO

1. When we think of God's goodness to us, we surely want to do something in return. What should we do?
2. God is all-merciful. How can we practice this virtue?
3. God knows all things. With this in mind, how should we live?
4. Prove from what you know about the universe that God is almighty.
5. How do trees, flowers, and animals give glory to God?
6. Can you tell how the human eye shows the wisdom of God?
7. Meditate on the Providence of God. Think of:

    What it means.
    How it is shown to us.
    What it should teach us to do.

8. When you eat your dinner, think of God's gifts of food and water. Thank and praise God for having given them to us.
9. Prepare an explanation you could give a non-Catholic friend who does not believe that God knows all things.
10. Give some instances of how Divine Providence is seen in the Old Testament, the New Testament, and in the world today.
11. Write a paragraph explaining why it is possible for God to guide the whole world.
12. In a drawing try to illustrate God's perfections.

## Prayer of St. Agatha

*Jesus Christ, Lord of all things! You see my heart, you know my desires. Possess all that I am—you alone. I am your sheep; make me worthy to overcome the devil.*

LESSON 3

# Reason and Revelation Prove the Existence of God

## Reason Can Prove There Is a God

God has given to men's minds the power to know Him. All men can know there is a God just by using their reason. We Catholics know it by faith. Yet we too should *know by our natural reason that there is a God, for natural reason tells us that the world we see about us could have been made only by a self-existing Being, all-wise and almighty.*

We can prove that there is such a Supreme Being to persons who do not have faith. We will learn many formal proofs in high school or college. Here we will examine just two of those that depend on reason. The first one comes from consideration of the great wide world in which we live; the second, from a consideration of the heart of man.

This wonderful world of ours could not have come into existence by itself; nor could it continue except by the power of a self-existing being. The sun must have been given its power by someone very mighty. The stars and the planets must be held in place by a master power and intellect. To think that such marvelous order could be kept up without the ceaseless watchfulness of an almighty Being is foolish indeed. The first spark of life, of beauty, or of power

present in the world must have had its beginning in some first form of life.

Man himself gives proof that there is a God. In fact, man is the best proof. His body proves it. But his intellect and desires will prove it better. Deep in the heart of every person is a longing for something infinite. When we are hungry, only food can satisfy us. When we are tired, only rest can restore our bodies. What do our hearts long for? What do our intellects long for? No amount of pleasure on earth satisfies our desires. We have longings that point only to one true satisfaction that is found in God.

## Revelation Also Proves There Is a God

Our natural reason is not the only means we have of knowing God, nor the best. As we learned in the introduction on Faith, God has revealed, or made known, many things about Himself. These truths, which God has revealed to us in Holy Scripture and Tradition, are called supernatural revelation.

God drew aside the curtain that hid Him from the eyes of men by speaking directly to the prophets of the Old Testament. As if this were not proof enough, God sent His Son, Jesus Christ, who established a Church to teach us about the nature of God. Consequently, *besides*

## The Book of Nature

We can learn many things about God by looking at the world around us. It helps to think of the world as a book—the book of Nature—and God is its author. Just as we can learn about a human author by reading a book he wrote, we can learn about God by "reading" the book of Nature. For example, we know God is beautiful because a sunset is beautiful. We know God is mighty because a rushing river is mighty. Go out and find something in the world of nature today and discover what it can teach you about God.

*knowing God by our natural reason, we can also know Him from supernatural revelation, that is, from the truths found in Sacred Scripture and in Tradition, which God Himself has revealed to us.*

We have learned much about God. It is good to know these things. But it is far better to appreciate what they mean. For then we will love and serve our great God as we should. Often those who are not so bright appreciate God far better than those who are much brighter. They think about God often and praise Him for His greatness. God loves such persons and often does marvelous things through them.

Think about God's many perfections when you pray. And praise Him for being so great, so holy, and so good. Sing "Holy God" to express your sentiments.

**TERMS TO KNOW**

- ceaseless
- revelation
- natural reason

Juan Vicente Macip's *The Last Supper* was painted in the 16th century.

## FOR ME TO REVIEW

*Catechism Lesson*

**142. Q. What does our "understanding" or "intellect" mean?**

A. Our "understanding" or "intellect" means the "gift of reason," by which man is distinguished from all other animals, and by which he is enabled to think and thus acquire knowledge and regulate his actions. Through our natural reason we can know that God exists.

**143. Q. Can we learn all truths by our reason alone?**

A. We cannot learn all truths by our reason alone, for some truths are beyond the power of our reason and must be taught to us by God.

**144. Q. What do we call the truths God teaches us?**

A. Taken together, we call the truths God teaches us Revelation, and we call the manner by which He teaches them also revelation.

### Questions and Exercises

*Write your answers on a separate sheet of paper*

1. Tell two ways in which reason proves there is a God.
2. Where do we find the clearest proof that there is a God?
3. Why must we believe all that God has revealed to us?
4. How did God make known His truths in the Old Testament?
5. How do our deepest desires tell us there is a God?
6. What reason could you give for some people not believing there is a God?
7. Is faith in God's revealed truth necessary?

8. Is reason a greater proof of the existence of God than revelation?
9. What is supernatural revelation?
10. Should our daily conduct prove to our friends that we believe in God?

## FOR ME TO REMEMBER

1. We can know by reason that there is a God.
2. Revelation is a better way to know God.
3. Revelation means the truths which God has made known to us.

## FOR ME TO DO

1. Explain why it ought to be impossible for an intelligent person to deny the existence of God.
2. Write a letter to a non-Catholic friend explaining how man himself proves there is a God.
3. Explain what is meant by supernatural revelation.

LESSON 4

# The Unity and Trinity of God

## There Is But One God in Three Divine Persons

What does God tell us about Himself? From the very beginning God made it clear that there is only one Creator, only one Lawgiver, and only one Judge. "I am the first, and I am the last, and besides me there is no God" (Isa. 44:6). In the New Testament the same truth is revealed to us: "That they may know Thee, the only true God" (Jn. 17:3). Reason also tells us there is only one Supreme Being. *Yes, there is only one God.*

Since God is supreme, He cannot have an equal. Our natural reason confirms or strengthens some of the truths God has revealed to us. It can prove there is but one God. However, *in God there are three divine Persons—the Father, the Son, and the Holy Spirit.* To the ancient Hebrews God said nothing directly about the three divine Persons in one God. There are hints of this truth in the Old Testament, however, showing that God was preparing the people for it.

After He had made the beasts of the earth, God said, "Let us make man to our image and likeness" (Gen. 1:26). Scripture used

### Understanding the Trinity with St. Patrick

It is said St. Patrick used the three leaved Shamrock (or clover) to explain the concept of the Holy Trinity to the pagan Irish during the fifth century. Just as the clover appears to be three leaves in one plant, so the one, true God is three Divine Persons: the Father, Son, and Holy Spirit.

Fridolin Leiber's depiction of The Holy Trinity. Text of "Our Father" prayer with Trinity in central column (God the Father, dove of the Holy Spirit, Jesus) and Biblical and symbolic scenes in left and right columns.

the word "us" and "our." Was it to hint that, while there is but one God, there are three Persons in God? Other references in the Old Testament lead our minds toward the Trinity, but they are not too clear.

It was God the Son who revealed fully the idea of one God in three divine Persons.

On many occasions during His public life our Lord claimed to

The third Person of the Trinity, the Holy Spirit, is depicted as a dove. The gospels recount the Holy Spirit descending on Jesus at His baptism in the form of a dove.

be true God, equal to His heavenly Father. We shall discuss those claims of our Lord later on, when we consider His divine nature. The New Testament also has a number of passages which show that there are three divine persons in one God. Since the New Testament is God's inspired word, those passages are true and must be believed.

At the very beginning of his gospel account, St. Luke tells us about the Angel Gabriel's visit to Mary to tell her that she was to be the mother of the Redeemer. The greeting of the angel to Mary mentioned three separate Persons. The angel told her: "The Holy Spirit shall come upon thee and the power of the Most High shall overshadow thee; and therefore the Holy One to be born shall be called the Son of God" (Lk. 1:35). So we see that the angel names: "The Holy Spirit," who is the third Person of the Trinity; the "most High," who is God the Father and the first Person of the Trinity; and "the Holy One," who is God the Son and second Person of the Trinity.

At our Lord's baptism by St. John the Baptist in the Jordan three Persons are also mentioned. When Jesus had been baptized, He immediately came up from the water. The heavens were opened and He saw the spirit of God descending as a dove and coming upon Him. "And behold, a voice from the heaven said, 'This is my beloved Son, in whom I am well pleased' " (Mt. 3:17). It is not hard to point out the three Persons in this incident. While God the Son, Jesus Christ, is being baptized, God the Father speaks from heaven, and God the Holy Spirit appears in the form of a dove.

Just before His Ascension into heaven, our Lord emphatically mentions the three Persons in one God. Our Lord told His Apostles to baptize in the name of the three divine Persons, saying: "Go, therefore, and make disciples of all nations, baptizing them in the name of the Father, and of the Son, and of the Holy Spirit" (Mt. 28:19–20).

Jesus commanded the Apostles to baptize "in the name of." He did not say "in the names of." St. Augustine said that where you hear one name, there is one God. The Apostles were to baptize by the power and authority of the Father, the Son, and the Holy Spirit. They were to baptize in the name of one and the same God in whom there are three Persons, the Father, the Son, and the Holy Spirit.

The Church has always taught that there are three Persons in one God. This is a mystery of faith. We cannot understand it, but we believe that it is true because God Himself has told us that it is true. We should be happy to say again and again: *The Father is God and the first Person of the Blessed Trinity. The Son is God and the second Person of the Blessed Trinity. The Holy Spirit is God and the third Person of the Blessed Trinity.*

### TERMS TO KNOW

- divine
- person
- mystery
- confirms
- existence
- attribute
- spirit
- idolatry
- Trinity
- advocate
- enlighten
- nature
- unity

## The Three Divine Persons Are One and the Same God

In the previous lesson we mentioned the Blessed Trinity. We spoke of the Father, the Son, and the Holy Spirit, as Persons of the Blessed Trinity, who are one God. *By the Blessed Trinity we mean one and the same God in three divine Persons.* We should often call on the Blessed Trinity to help us, saying: "Holy Trinity, one God, have mercy on us."

## The Three Divine Persons Are Equal but Distinct

Though they are but one God, *the three divine Persons are really distinct from one another.* The Father is not the Son, the Son is not the Holy Spirit, the Holy Spirit is not the Father or the Son. We can pray to one divine Person at one time, and to another divine Person at another time. When we address our prayers to one divine Person we are addressing them to God.

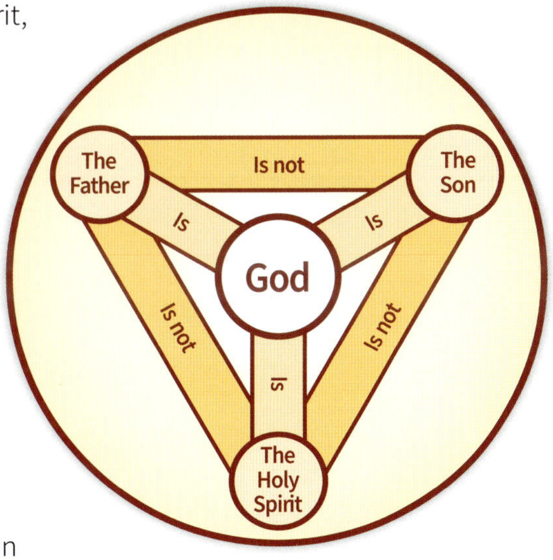

Shield of the Trinity or Scutum Fidei, used throughout history to illustrate the Blessed Trinity

Now, although we speak of the Blessed Trinity as Father, Son, and Holy Spirit this does not mean that the Father is greater than the Son, or the Son greater than the Holy Spirit. *The three divine Persons are perfectly equal to one another, because all are one and the same God.*

Holy Scripture speaks of creation as the work of the Father. To the Son we owe the reopening of the gates of heaven, that is our redemption. And the Holy Spirit shows Himself within

Though they are but one God, the three divine Persons are really distinct from one another.

us by keeping us holy. Even though we ordinarily say that the Father created us, the Son redeemed us, and the Holy Spirit sanctifies us, these works are common to all three Persons. The three divine Persons cannot be separated, for they are one and the same God. And so, when the Father created us, the Son and the Holy Spirit were also present and shared in that wonderful work. When the Son redeemed us, the Father and the Holy

Spirit also had a part in that work, although only the divine Son became man. When the Holy Spirit made us children of God at Baptism, the Father and Son also sanctified us. So we see that all three divine Persons together, create, redeem, and sanctify. The nature, the perfections, the works of God belong equally to the three divine Persons because they are one God. *The three divine Persons, though really distinct from one another, are one and the same God because all have one and the same divine nature.*

## This Supernatural Mystery Cannot Be Understood

There are many things in nature that we do not understand. How much less should we expect to understand what belongs to God. Above all *we cannot fully understand how the three divine Persons, though really distinct from one another, are one and the same God because this is a supernatural mystery.* We are unable to understand how there can be three Persons, but only one God.

If we look at the noonday sun, our eyes would be blinded by its brightness. So it is with the Blessed Trinity. If we inquire into it, we are blinded with wonder. Yet if we refuse to believe in this mystery simply because we do not understand it, we are like a blind man who will not believe that there is a sun because he cannot see it.

### This Supernatural Mystery Must Be Believed on the Word of God

No one fully understands the Trinity except God Himself. We can, however, get some idea of the nature of the Blessed Trinity by comparing it with certain facts of nature. The flames of three candles placed together form but one flame; a white light can be divided into red, yellow, and blue rays, but together these colors form but one light. No matter how we try, our reason, which is human, can never of itself understand the mystery of the Blessed Trinity, because this truth is above our power to reason.

God has made the Trinity known to us, but our little minds

cannot understand it. It is a supernatural mystery. *A supernatural mystery is a truth which we cannot fully understand, but which we firmly believe because we have God's word for it.* God asks only that we believe in this mystery; He asks only that we believe in this mystery because it has been revealed to us by Him who can neither deceive nor be deceived. God will reward our faith.

Whenever we make the Sign of the Cross, let us make it slowly and reverently, as an act of faith, in honor of the Blessed Trinity.

*Glory be to the Father, and to the Son, and to the Holy Spirit. As it was in the beginning, is now, and ever shall be, world without end. Amen.*

> *"The Father, the Son and the Holy Spirit are one because God is love and love is an absolute life-giving force; the unity created by love is a unity greater than a purely physical unity. The Father gives everything to the Son; the Son receives everything from the Father with gratitude; and the Holy Spirit is the fruit of this mutual love of the Father and the Son."*
>
> *—Pope Benedict XVI*

## FOR ME TO REVIEW

*Catechism Lesson*

**182. Q. Is there but one God?**

A. Yes; there is but one God.

**186. Q. How many Persons are there in God?**

A. In God there are three divine Persons, really distinct, and equal in all things—the Father, the Son, and the Holy Spirit.

**188. Q. Is the Father God?**

A. The Father is God and the first Person of the Blessed Trinity.

**189. Q. Is the Son God?**

A. The Son is God and the second Person of the Blessed Trinity.

**190. Q. Is the Holy God?**

A. The Holy Spirit is God and the third Person of the Blessed Trinity.

**192. Q. What do you mean by the Blessed Trinity?**

A. By the Blessed Trinity I mean one God in three divine Persons.

**187. Q. What do "divine" and "distinct" mean?**

A. "Divine" means pertaining to God, and "distinct" means separate; that is, not confounded or mixed with any other thing.

**193. Q. Are the three divine Persons equal in all things?**

A. The three divine Persons are equal in all things.

**196. Q. Can we fully understand how the three divine Persons are one and the same God?**

A. We cannot fully understand how the three divine Persons, though really distinct from one another, are one and the same God because all have one and the same divine nature.

**197. Q. What is a mystery?**

A. A mystery is a truth which we cannot fully understand.

**198. Q. Is every truth which we cannot understand a mystery?**

A. Every truth which we cannot understand is not a mystery; but every revealed truth which no one can understand is a mystery.

### Questions and Exercises

*Write your answers on a separate sheet of paper*

1. God has (*a*) one nature; (*b*) two natures; (*c*) three natures.
2. We call the three divine Persons in one and the same God (*a*) the Blessed Trinity; (*b*) the divine nature; (*c*) the Incarnation.
3. We say that the three divine Persons are really distinct from one another because: (*a*) they are different persons; (*b*) they have the same divine nature; (*c*) they are the Blessed Trinity.
4. We cannot understand how the three divine Persons are one and the same God because it is (*a*) a supernatural mystery; (*b*) an important truth; (*c*) Divine Providence.
5. We believe that the three divine Persons are one and the same God because (*a*) we can find examples in nature; (*b*) no one understands it; (*c*) we have God's word for it.
6. I profess my faith in the Blessed Trinity when I say the (*a*) Our Father; (*b*) Confiteor; (*c*) Sign of the Cross; (*d*) Morning Offering.

7. By the Blessed Trinity we mean: (*a*) three Gods in one divine Person; (*b*) three divine Persons and three Gods; (*c*) one God in three divine Persons.
8. The word which shows that the three divine Persons are really different is (*a*) equal; (*b*) distinct; (*c*) supernatural.
9. When we say one and the same God we mean: (*a*) one and the same divine nature; (*b*) equal to each other; (*c*) distinct from one another.
10. The Sign of the Cross is (*a*) an act of faith in the unity and trinity of God; (*b*) a supernatural mystery; (*c*) a prayer honoring the Blessed Sacrament.

## FOR ME TO REMEMBER

1. There is only one God.
2. In God there are three Persons; the Father, our Creator; the Son, our Redeemer; the Holy Spirit, our Sanctifier.
3. The word trinity means three in one.
4. The Blessed Trinity is a supernatural mystery; that is, it is beyond natural human understanding.
5. Although God the Father is usually mentioned first, the three divine Persons are equal.

## FOR ME TO DO

1. Write the Act of Faith. Underline the words that express ideas about the Blessed Trinity.
2. Draw as many symbols as you can that might express the mystery of the Blessed Trinity. Be able to explain them.
3. List the time throughout the day when you think of or express your belief in the Blessed Trinity.
4. Find some places in the Bible revealing the mystery of the Blessed Trinity.

## The Minor Doxology

*Glory be to the Father, and to the Son, and to the Holy Spirit. As it was in the beginning, is now, and ever shall be, world without end. Amen.*

**CHAPTER 2**

# God, Creator of All Things

LESSON 5

## God Created the Angelic World

### God Created the Angelic World

In the lesson on the perfections of God we learned that God is almighty. This almighty power explains the act of creation. We know this from the Apostles' Creed which says that God is the Creator of heaven and earth. *When we say that God is the Creator of heaven and earth we mean that He made all things from nothing by His almighty power.*

*The chief creatures of God are angels and men.* Angels are by nature superior to men. *Angels are created without bodies, having understanding and free will.* The angels are pure spirits, that is, they have and need no bodies. They are greater than man, and yet, not equal to God. Man can think, and use his will. But God made the angels above any of His other creatures and they can know and will much better than man.

Since the angels have no bodies, we cannot see them with our bodily eyes. Neither can our human reason alone prove that angels exist. But Sacred Scripture and Tradition teach that they do exist, and that they were created by God.

*When God created the angels He bestowed on them great wisdom, power, and holiness.* The angels did not have to learn from experience. They were given knowledge and wisdom superior to that of any human being. Moreover they were given sanctifying grace and great holiness.

The angels were created to love and serve God. God created them for the same reason He created men. He created them to find eternal happiness in heaven.

The angels were created to love and serve God.

How grateful we should be to our guardian angels. We owe them reverence, that is, honor and respect. As creatures closer to God than we are, they deserve our confidence and our obedience. Every Catholic child should dedicate himself to his guardian angel each morning by saying the following prayer:

Angel of God, my guardian dear,
To whom God's love commits me here
Ever this day be at my side,
To light and guard, to rule and guide. Amen.

## Some Angels Obeyed God

The angels were holy as God created them. Like man, they were given the supernatural gift of sanctifying grace. But before God admitted the angels into His eternal presence He tested their willingness to obey and serve Him. Some obeyed; others did not.

*The angels who remained faithful to God entered into the eternal happiness of heaven, and these are called good angels. They received the reward God promised them.* They fulfill the purpose God had in creating them. *In heaven the good angels see, love, and adore God.*

Besides their duties in heaven, the angels have certain duties toward man. *The good angels help us by praying for us, by acting as messengers from God to us, and by serving as our guardian angels.* Since we are made for heaven, and heaven is the home of the angels, they are greatly interested in our salvation. They pray for us in order to help us gain heaven, where we can join them in praising God. We, in our turn should pray to them: All ye holy angels, pray for us; that we may be made worthy of the promises of Christ.

## Guardian Angels

The most familiar part which angels play in our lives is that of being our guardians. When you were small you probably pictured your guardian angel in human form as you thought of your special guide beside you. Now that you are older and know that your angel does not have a body, you are likely to forget your angel's presence. Yet your angel never leaves you, in spite of your forgetfulness.

How precious each human soul must be that God would so provide for its protection. How great must God's love be to give each of us our own particular angel. St. Jerome says: "How great is the dignity of souls that each one should have from the first moment of his birth an angel delegated to guard him." Our guardian angels know better than we do just what we need. They pray not only for our bodily needs, but also for the needs of our soul. They present our prayers and good works to God, and ask favors for us. They seem to whisper in our ear to warn us of danger. Thus we see that *our guardian angels help us by praying for us, by protecting us from harm, and by inspiring us to do good.*

## Some Angels Disobeyed God

Speaking of the good angels has been pleasant, but we must also consider the fallen angels, or the angels who disobeyed God, for we know that *not all the angels remained faithful to God; some of them sinned.* We learned long ago that *the angels who did not remain faithful to God were cast into hell, and these are called bad angels, or devils.* The bad angels, after their sin, turned completely against God, the Supreme Good, and determined to keep as many souls as possible from Him.

The fallen angels work against us in many ways.

### How many angels rebelled against God?

We may wonder how many of the angels sided with Lucifer during his rebellion. We have no way of knowing for sure, but we are given a hint in Scripture. In Revelation 12, we read about a great battle that seems to allude to the angelic battle of heaven. The great dragon, representing the devil, sweeps down "a third of the stars from heaven." Some biblical scholars saw this as a clue that a third of the angels were cast from heaven with him after his rebellion since there are other instances where angels are symbolically represented by stars.

The bad angels try to harm us. *The chief way in which the bad angels try to harm us is by tempting us to sin.* They are like hunters tracking us down, laying traps to destroy us. We must remember the devils are fallen angels with the same superior intellect they possessed before the fall. They are clever; no one escapes their hatred, but everyone can fight them with the most powerful of weapons, prayer and good works.

Christ broke the power of Satan and his followers when He died on the cross. He permits the bad angels to tempt us for our own perfection, and no temptation is too strong for us if we ask for help. God is always ready to aid us with His divine grace. We should often pray to St. Michael, the leader of the good angels, in the powerful prayer: "Saint Michael the Archangel, defend us in battle, be our protection against the wickedness and snares of the devil."

Some angels obeyed God; others did not.

## Other Sources of Temptation

The bad angels however are not the only source of our temptations. *Some temptations come from the bad angels; but other temptations come from ourselves and from the persons and things about us.* Within the nature of each of us there are certain weaknesses or inclinations to evil. These attractions toward doing wrong are the result of original sin. We must be especially careful always to guard our five senses, for it is through them that temptation enters our minds and attracts our wills.

### Concupiscence

**Concupiscence is a word used to describe our inclination toward evil or immoral things. Overcoming our concupiscence is a key to our salvation, and we cannot do it without God's grace.**

Still other sources of temptations are the persons and things around us. There are always persons in the world who enjoy doing the devil's work. Sadly enough there are even children, Catholic children, who tempt other children to do wrong. Pictures, magazines, comic books, movies, the internet, and television shows are sometimes sources of temptations.

If the evil caused by sin and temptation were all we knew about, we would be discouraged and say it is too hard to be good. But we also know this: *We can always resist temptations, because no temptation can force us into sin, and because God will always help us if we ask Him.* This means that with grace, we have in us a power to say "no" which is stronger than the power of temptation. This power is our free will. We must use this power, and call on God often to help us keep away from sin. We might picture the devil as a fierce dog that is chained securely. He might snap and snarl but he cannot harm us unless we get too close. He cannot force us into sin against our free will.

At times, when temptations come to us again and again, we may become discouraged about being good and pleasing God. We should remember at such times that temptation is not a sin unless our will freely consents to it. In other words, we must really want to commit a sin before we actually commit sin.

How can we resist the attacks of the devil? We can fight the devil and all his helpers by prayer and the sacraments. "Watch and pray lest ye enter into temptation" should be our motto. We can fight the devil by acts of mortification and by avoiding idleness. We must remember that we are not fighting alone. God is there, as are the Blessed Mother, our patron saints, our guardian angels, and many others. In the divine plan temptations are permitted by God so as to test us and to give us opportunities to gain merit. With the help of God we can resist all temptation. He says to us as He said to St. Paul, "My grace is sufficient for thee" (2 Cor. 12:9).

## FOR ME TO REVIEW

*Catechism Lesson*

208. Q. **Who created heaven and earth, and all things?**
A. God created heaven and earth, and all things.

206. Q. **What is the difference between making and creating?**
A. "Making" means bringing forth or forming out of some material already existing, as workmen do. "Creating" means bringing forth out of nothing, as God alone can do.

209. Q. **From what do we learn that God created heaven and earth and all things?**
A. We learn that God created heaven and earth and all things from the Bible or Holy Scripture, in which the account of the Creation is given.

214. Q. **Which are the chief creatures of God?**
A. The chief creatures of God are angels and men.

216. Q. **What are angels?**
A. Angels are pure spirits without a body, created to adore and enjoy God in heaven.

227. **Q. Did all the angels remain good and happy?**
A. All the angels did not remain good and happy; many of them sinned and were cast into hell, and these are called devils or bad angels.

219. **Q. Were the angels created for any other purpose?**
A. The angels were also created to assist before the throne of God and to minister unto Him; they have often been sent as messengers from God to man; and are also appointed our guardians.

223. **Q. What do our guardian angels do for us?**
A. Our guardian angels pray for us, protect and guide us, and offer our prayers, good works and desires to God.

230. **Q. How do the bad angels act toward us?**
A. The bad angels try by every means to lead us into sin. The efforts they make are called temptations of the devil.

22. **Q. From what do our temptations come?**
A. Our temptations come either from the devil, our spiritual enemy, or from the world; that is, the wicked persons, places, or things in the world; or from the flesh; that is, our body with its strong passions and evil inclinations.

21. **Q. Is it a sin to be tempted?**
A. It is not a sin to be tempted, because we cannot prevent it. It is sinful only to consent or yield to the temptation or needlessly expose ourselves to it.

20. **Q. Can we always resist temptation?**
A. We can always resist temptation if we wish, for God always gives us sufficient grace and never permits us to be tempted above our strength.

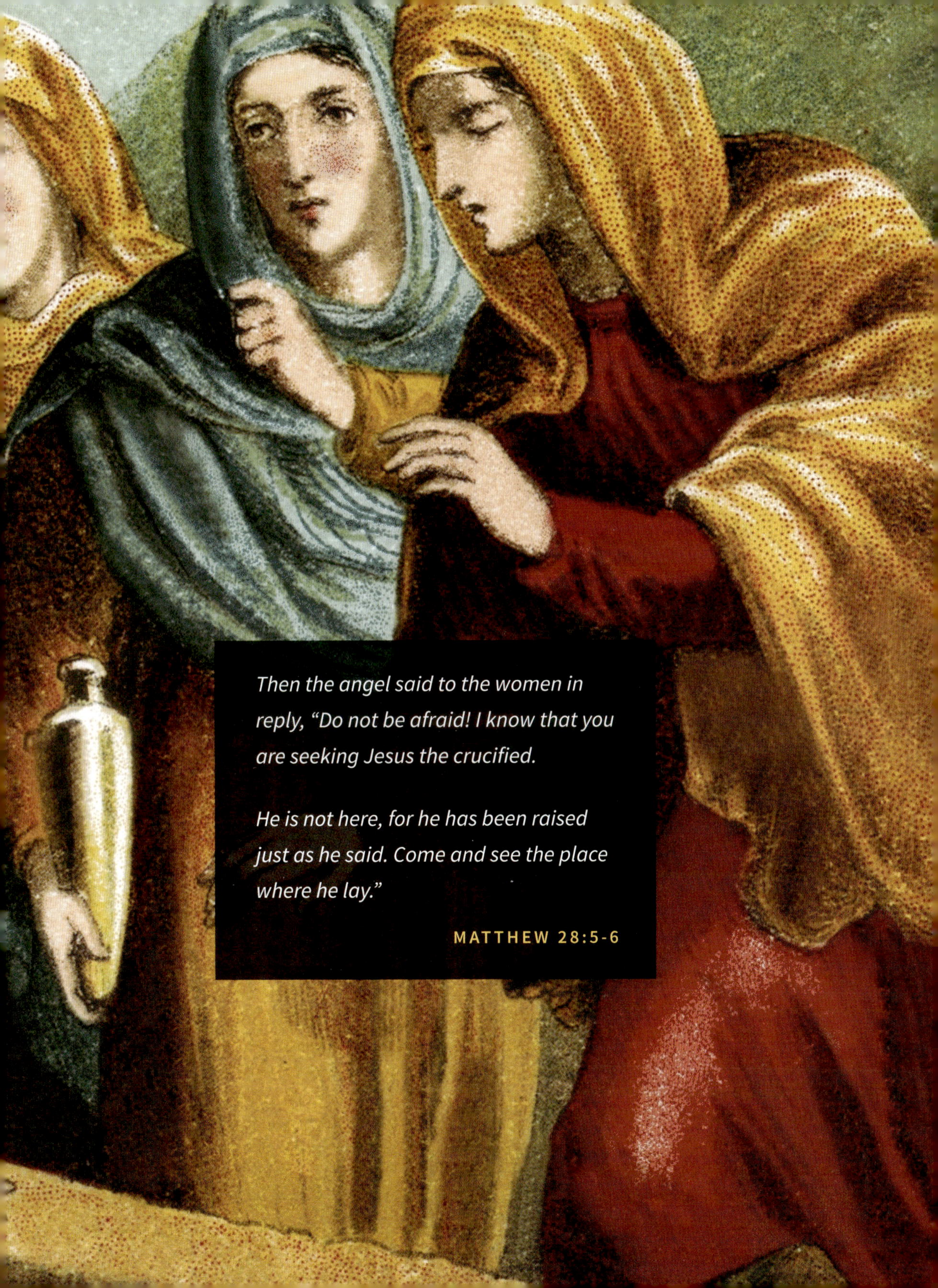

*Then the angel said to the women in reply, "Do not be afraid! I know that you are seeking Jesus the crucified.*

*He is not here, for he has been raised just as he said. Come and see the place where he lay."*

MATTHEW 28:5-6

### Questions and Exercises

*Write your answers on a separate sheet of paper*

1. In what way are the angels like God?
2. How are the angels like man and how are they different from man?
3. What three great gifts did God give the angels?
4. Why are the angels especially happy?
5. How can we be faithful to our guardian angels?
6. Is temptation a sin?
7. Explain in your own words what is meant by an occasion of sin.
8. Where can we get the help to resist temptation?
9. Number a page from 1 to 34. Write after each number the missing word for each blank from the sentences below.

   The chief creatures of God are (1) and (2).

   Angels are (3) spirits, without (4) having understanding and (5).

   When God created the angels He bestowed on the great (6), (7), (8).

   Not all the angels remained (9) to God, some of them (10) .

   The angels who remained (11) to God entered the (12) happiness of (13).

   In heaven the good angels (14), (15), and (16) God.

   The good angels help us by (17) for us, by acting as (18) from God to us, and by serving as our (19) angels.

Our guardian angels help us by (20) for us, by (21) us from harm, and by (22) us to do good.

The angels who did not remain (23) to God were cast into (24) and these are called (25) angels, or (26).

The chief way the bad angels try to harm us is by (27) us to sin.

Some temptations come from the (28) angels, but other temptations come from (29) and from the (30) and (31) around us.

We can always (32) temptation, because no temptation can force us into (33) and God will always help us if we (34) Him.

### TERMS TO KNOW

- messengers
- creation
- inspiring
- resist
- dignity
- creature
- inspiration
- bestowed
- malice
- free will
- fortified
- mortification
- inclination
- intellect
- temptation

## FOR ME TO REMEMBER

1. God made all things from nothing.
2. Angels and men are the chief creatures of God.
3. Angels are pure spirits having intellect and free will.
4. God created the angels to increase His own glory and to add to their happiness.
5. Our guardian angels help us enter heaven; bad angels or devils try to bring us to hell.
6. Temptation is not a sin so long as our will does not consent to it.
7. Prayer and the sacraments are the chief weapons against the devil.

## FOR ME TO DO

1. On Christmas night the shepherds saw the angels and heard their song, yet the angels are pure spirits. Can you explain this?
2. Do you know the prayer we say to St. Michael the Archangel? Say it; if you cannot, memorize it, and say it often.
3. Can we blame all temptations on the devil? Give some examples of times when we ourselves may be responsible for our temptations.
4. Name three ways in which the good angels help us.
5. Do you know the name of the angel who was the leader of the battle in heaven? The angel who brought the message to the Blessed Virgin Mary? The angel who guided Tobias on a journey? Look up the stories in the Bible and read them.
6. Mention other names often given to the leader of the bad angels.
7. Name as many instances as possible where angels appeared as messengers to men.
8. How many choirs of angels are there. How many can you name?
9. If one of your companions told you that stories of angels are fairy tales, how would you answer them?
10. Say a special prayer of thanksgiving to God every day for His gift of a guardian angel.

LESSON 6

# God Created the Universe

## God Created the Universe by a Mere Command

God created all things by a command or an act of His almighty will. "He spoke and they were made, He commanded and they were created." God made all things without effort and without help. God does not actually speak as we do, for He has no body. He merely willed and all things were made.

*And God saw all the things that he had made, and they were very good.*

## God Created the Universe to Help Us Reach Heaven

Have you ever wondered why God made the world and the creatures in it? To answer this question we need only consider for a moment who God is. We know from our study of God's perfections that He is all-perfect and that nothing outside of Himself can add to His perfections. Creatures therefore, do not add to God's perfections, but they do show forth His glory. By doing this they fulfill the purpose for which they were made.

While this increase of God's glory is the main purpose of creation, the world was also created for the good of God's creatures. Man, the chief creature of the visible world was to make use of all other creatures in serving God. Everything on earth that God has created for man reminds us of His goodness, and brings man closer to heaven, if properly used.

Think of the countless things in the world as stepping-stones in a brook. Each stone brings us nearer the opposite bank. If we stay on the one stone too long, we delay our journey. If we remain satisfied with standing on a stone instead of continuing on, we shall never reach our goal. For example, wealth, worldly possessions and pleasures are creatures of God. If a person devotes himself to them without taking an interest in anything else, even in God, he is using them as the goal of his life and not as steppingstones to heaven. We must remember that we can enjoy the gifts of the earth, but that they are all only means to help us reach heaven, our final goal.

## God Keeps the Universe in Existence

Have you ever heard of a baby being left on a stranger's doorstep? If so, you were probably shocked that a mother and father could do such a thing. A tiny baby is helpless. The parents should care for it by feeding, clothing, and protecting it so that the baby will become strong and healthy. The beginning of a family is important, but to keep on providing for that family is just as important.

***TERMS TO KNOW***

- universe
- constant
- material
- dependent
- providing
- dominion
- governs

Imagine a farmer plowing the ground on his farm, planting seeds in it, and then forgetting all about it. Imagine also, his going out of town on a two-month vacation. Such a man could not expect to find worth-while crops when he returned. A garden needs continual care.

The saying "Things well begun are half-done" is true. But a start such as planting seeds or beginning a family is only half the task. Constant care is also necessary. The act of creation was not only well begun by God but is also continued by His present care.

God not only created the universe but He also continually keeps it in existence. In addition, He cares for and watches over everything He has made, especially man. According to His divine plan the planets follow a regular course; the sun continues to give fight and heat; the stars remain in their proper places in the heavens; the oceans, seas, rivers, and lakes do not ordinarily spread over the dry land. God keeps watch over the universe. He protects the things He made. He governs the world so that everything follows His plan. We recall that this care in governing the world is called God's Providence. Because God's protecting hand takes care of us and of the world, we need not fear. Let us give ourselves over completely to His care. Let us follow His plans for us with full confidence. He will always protect us.

## FOR ME TO REVIEW

**Questions and Exercises**

*Write your answers on a separate sheet of paper*

1. Did God create the universe for the use of man?
2. Does God want us to use the things of this earth to honor Him?

3. Can television help us to honor God?
4. Does God stop watching over us after we sin?
5. Is the story of creation told in the book of Genesis?
6. Are all men dependent on God for all their needs?
7. Do creatures add to God's perfections?
8. Did God create the world without any help?
9. Does God actually speak to man?
10. Can we use all the things of the earth to help us to reach heaven?

> *"It is one of the most firmly established and most consoling of the truths that have been revealed to us that (apart from sin) nothing happens to us in life unless God wills it so."*
>
> *—St. Claude de la Colombiere*

## FOR ME TO REMEMBER

1. God created the universe to help us reach heaven.
2. God keeps the universe in existence.
3. God watches over every one of us with infinite love.
4. God wants us to trust in Him in all our material and spiritual needs.

## FOR ME TO DO

1. Read aloud the account of the creation of the universe as given in the Bible. Compare the works of the first three days with those of the second three days.
2. Name some of God's creatures that can bring you closer to Him. Choose two or three and tell how they can do this.
3. Be prepared to explain to a friend how God preserves the world He made; or better, how wonderfully God has planned everything to serve man.
4. Mother and Dad enjoy a trip to the country where they can be out in the open and enjoy themselves. Explain how they can be drawn closer to God because of this trip.
5. Do the words "create" and "make" mean different things? Explain.

LESSON 7

# God Created Man

## Adam and Eve Were Special Creations of God

When all the rest of creation had been completed, God fashioned man as the lord and master of His wondrous earth. In the first book of the Bible the inspired writer says that God formed man's body and breathed into it a soul. God used matter already in existence to form the body of the first man.

### God Created Man's Soul Directly

Man is a masterpiece in God's visible world of creatures. Man is the greatest of all the beings on this earth. Second only to the angels he is God's most wonderful creation. Man must, however, remember that he is but dust, and that one day his body will return to dust. This truth is especially brought home to us on Ash Wednesday. The ashes placed on our foreheads that day are to remind us not to be so concerned about our body, for it will perish, or die—although it will rise again.

And God created man to his own image

Our soul, however, will live forever. Into the body of Adam, formed from existing matter, God breathed an immortal soul.

With this spirit man became a living creature. Now that man's material body had been joined with a life-giving spirit, he had the power to move, speak, think, will, and love. It is this spirit, or soul, that makes man different from all other creatures on earth. A plant or an animal has a life-principle or 'soul,' but it is not spiritual and it is not immortal as man's soul is.

All creatures have some likeness to God, but man resembles his creator in a special way. He is made to God's image and likeness. *Man is a creature composed of body and soul, and made to the image and likeness of God.* We can read in the book of Genesis that before God made man He said: "Let us make mankind in our own image and likeness." It is this likeness to God that makes the soul so great in value. We might rightly ask: "How can man resemble God who is a spirit?" Man cannot resemble God with regard to his body, for God is a spirit and has no body. The body, however, does show forth the perfection of God. But the resemblance to God is chiefly in the spirit or soul. And this is exactly what the catechism says: *This likeness to God is chiefly in the soul.*

## God's Image and Likeness

One of the most important lines in all of Scripture is when God said in Genesis, "Let us make mankind in our own image and likeness." Being made in God's image and likeness gives us our dignity. This verse also gives us a proof for the Holy Trinity, since He says, "made in our image and likeness."

The soul has certain powers that make man able to think or reason, and to choose freely as God does. These powers we call the intellect and free will. It is clear from what we have just said about the soul that *the soul is like God because it is a spirit having intellect and free will, and is destined to live forever.*

Holy Scripture also tells us that God created the first woman. After breathing life into her body, God presented Eve to Adam. God did this to teach the human race that man is the head of the family. Although Adam is first in position and dignity in the human race, Eve is equal to man in that she has the same human nature and destiny. Finally, God wanted to show us that Eve was Adam's wife and helpmate. God united this first couple in holy matrimony, thereby teaching all human beings the importance of marriage and family life. All of us are members of the same great family and all come from the same first parents. *The first man and woman were Adam and Eve, the first parents of the whole human race.*

**TERMS TO KNOW**

- immortal
- masterpiece
- privilege
- undeserved
- image
- destiny
- control
- unruly
- nature
- inherit
- loyalty
- upright
- dependent
- resemblance
- material

## Adam and Eve Received Special Gifts

The human nature of our first parents reflected God's perfections. These chosen friends of God were by nature far above all other creatures on earth. But God decided to give them even greater gifts.

Can you imagine a flower moving from one place to another, or a bird telling you the things it had done? It is not within the nature of a bird or flower to do these things. These powers belong to the nature of man. Lower beings do not have the power to do certain things man can do. Man also can only act according to the powers of his nature. However, when God created Adam and Eve He intended that they and their descendants should receive powers far above their natural powers. These powers would enable them to live a life far above their nature as human beings. They would share in God's life and powers.

### Sanctifying Grace

God willed Adam and Eve to share in His divine life through the wonderful gift of sanctifying grace. Adam was given the free and undeserved privilege of taking part in God's life in addition to possessing the human life which was natural to him. This raising

And the Lord God took man, and put him into the paradise of pleasure, to dress it, and to keep it.

of the nature of man to a sharing in the life of God gave Adam and Eve the unbelievable privilege of becoming God's children by adoption. They could now act as sons of God—what dignity! What power!

You can understand how close this brought them to God. Think of the close bond between an adopted child and his new parents. Being adopted children of God, Adam and Eve had the right to inherit the kingdom of their heavenly Father. Sanctifying grace was a marvelous gift. Indeed *chief gift bestowed on Adam and Eve by God was sanctifying grace, which made them children of God and gave them the right to heaven.* With sanctifying grace came all the great supernatural virtues.

### Other Gifts

To prepare His children to rule over His kingdom, God gave Adam and Eve other great though lesser gifts. They were given a gift of special happiness and a special gift of knowledge. Another gift was control of their animal nature, so that no passion, such as anger, revenge, lust, or greediness, would trouble them. Their

Through the gift of freedom which God had bestowed upon Adam and Eve, the choice was theirs to make: either to obey and love God or to reject His goodness.

### The Necessity of Free Will

It may be fair for you to wonder why God even gave Adam and Eve a chance to disobey. Why even give them that choice? The answer is love. God could have programmed humans to obey him so that we had no other choice. But he did not want creatures programmed to love him the way we might program computers to carry out a task. God wanted our pure love, and love is only possible through choice, through free will. Only if we make the willful choice to obey and love God is our love true and real. This was why God gave us free will, but as we saw with Adam and Eve, we can use this free will for ill against God and neighbor.

wills were strong and upright, and their bodies were under easy control of their intellects and wills. They were not troubled with temptations of gluttony, anger, and impurity as we are now.

These gifts would seem enough, but God planned even more for man's happiness here on earth. Man was given perfect health, with no bodily discomforts, wants, or fears. His body as well as his soul was to live forever. After a long life in the Garden of Paradise, man was to be taken to heaven, bodily without dying, to share God's everlasting happiness. The catechism summarizes all this when it says: *The other gifts bestowed on Adam and Eve by God were happiness in the Garden of Paradise, great knowledge, control of the passions by reason, and freedom from suffering and death.*

## Adam and Eve Were Given the Choice To Obey God

According to God's plan, our first parents, like the angels, were given the choice to obey God. Through the gift of freedom which God had bestowed upon Adam and Eve, the choice was theirs to make: either to obey and love God or to reject His goodness. The Bible tells of this trial with the story that *God gave Adam and Eve the commandment not to eat of the fruit of a certain tree that grew in the Garden of Paradise.*

Read about Adam and Eve in the book of Genesis.

## FOR ME TO REVIEW

*Catechism Lesson*

**133. Q. What is man?**

A. Man is a creature composed of body and soul, and made in the image and likeness of God.

**136. Q. Is this likeness in the body or in the soul?**

A. This likeness is chiefly in the soul.

**137. Q. How is the soul like God?**

A. The soul is like God because it is a spirit that will never die, and has intellect and free will.

**233. Q. Who were the first man and woman?**

A. The first man and woman were Adam and Eve.

**248. Q. Which were the chief blessings intended for Adam and Eve had they remained faithful to God?**

A. The chief blessings intended for Adam and Eve, had they remained faithful to God, were a constant state of happiness in this life and everlasting glory in the next.

**249. Q. Did Adam and Eve remain faithful to God?**

A. Adam and Eve did not remain faithful to God, but broke His command by eating the forbidden fruit.

### Questions and Exercises

*Write your answers on a separate sheet of paper*

1. Is man's soul spiritual? Is it immortal? Explain.
2. Mention the many gifts God has given man.
3. Which of God's gifts were natural gifts? Which were supernatural to man?
4. Why did God command Adam and Eve not to eat the fruit of a certain tree? Does He ever give us commands similar to that?

5. What does it mean to be an adopted child of God?
6. How did God make Adam and Eve like Himself?
7. Why did God do so much for Adam and Eve? Why does He do so much for us?
8. What do we prove when we obey God's laws?

## FOR ME TO REMEMBER

1. Man is the greatest of the creatures of the earth.
2. The soul of man makes him resemble God.
3. The soul has two important powers: intellect and free will.
4. Sanctifying grace gives us a sharing in the life of God and a supernatural resemblance to Him.
5. God shows us the importance of obedience by His command to our first parents.

## FOR ME TO DO

1. Discuss how man is superior to all other creatures on earth, in his body, his imagination, his creative powers, his mind, his will.
2. Explain why your parents or superiors sometimes forbid you to do certain things.
3. Explain how you can thank God for creating you.
4. Compose a thank-you prayer to God in which you thank Him for the two special powers of intellect and free will.
5. Try to thank God for the gift of sanctifying grace received at baptism, especially after you have received Holy Communion or Penance and Reconciliation.

**CHAPTER 3**

# The Fall

LESSON 8

## Original Sin Comes Down to Us From Adam

Everything that God gave Adam and Eve was a gift, including (most especially) their free will. From the very beginning of their creation, Adam and Eve face the choice of either obeying God or rejecting Him. It was only fair that God should test them to prove their loyalty and appreciation. We already know the command He gave them. We also know that *Adam and Eve did not obey the commandment of God, but ate of the forbidden fruit.* As a fallen angel in disgrace, Satan hated God and tried to spoil His plans. We remember how Satan plotted our first parents' downfall because of his hatred and his jealousy over their happiness. The devil deceived Eve, who in turn enticed Adam to sin.

### Adam and Eve Were Punished for Their Sin

The sin of our first parents was a sin of pride and disobedience. Too late did Adam and Eve realize their serious mistake in listening to Satan who said, "No, you will not die, you will be like God knowing good and evil." With this act of disobedience came the loss of sanctifying grace. As we said before, grace was God's presence in their souls. To lose grace was man's greatest punishment and misfortune. Innocence and holiness were also lost; moreover, because of their sin, the ordinary tasks which Adam and Eve were given to do became hard for them, and at times, even

unpleasant and monotonous. They were subject to suffering and sickness until death claimed them. Their wills were weakened, and the attraction to sin was stronger.

*You know the ending of the story.* The rulers of Paradise were driven from their kingdom and the gates of heaven were also closed against them. *The matter can be summed up in these words: On account of their sin Adam and Eve lost sanctifying grace, the right to heaven, and their special gifts; they became subject to death, to suffering, and to a strong inclination to evil, and they were driven from the Garden of Paradise.*

***TERMS TO KNOW***

- descendants
- original
- origin
- deprived
- inherited
- passions

We recall from our religion lessons of other years that *this sin in us is called original sin.* We recall too that the results of our first parents' sin are very serious for us, as well as for them. Not only were Adam and Eve punished, but all their descendants until the end of time were to suffer from the results of the sin committed by their first parents. In fact *this sin is called original sin because it comes down to us through our origin, or descent, from Adam.*

## We Suffer Because of Adam and Eve's Sin

Since we came into the world with original sin on our souls we, too, are deprived of sanctifying grace. Since this was the greatest gift God gave Adam and Eve, its loss is our greatest punishment, as it was theirs.

Other punishments followed this great loss of grace. In us, as in Adam after the fall, our passions are hard to control; our intellects are less successful in attaining knowledge. We must study hard to learn the simplest things. Our wills find it difficult to keep good resolutions. You have probably often made such resolutions as "I will do my homework faithfully," or "I will help at home today." Is it easy to be faithful to these resolutions? Why not?

Besides all these punishments, man inherited another which would make life difficult. God told Adam there would often be unpleasantness, or inconvenience attached to the tasks he and his descendants would have to do to work out their salvation. You know that often when there is a difficult task to be performed, you are at first delighted at the challenge it presents. But when the difficulties are great, and the task becomes disagreeable or unpleasant, you grow weary and lose interest. This feeling of annoyance or unpleasantness or inconvenience in the work we have to do is one of the punishments which came to us as a result of Adam's sin.

If this were the end of the story, man might feel hopeless and discouraged. God, however, showed His love and mercy to Adam despite his sin. He promised to send a Redeemer. The one ray of hope for all people was faith in the Redeemer to come. The Redeemer would open the gates of heaven again for Adam and Eve and all their children. After Christ had suffered and died, God's justice would be satisfied, and man would once more enjoy the friendship of God.

On what day in your life did God make you His adopted child? On that occasion of your birthday into God's family, the supernatural gifts that were lost through Adam's sin were restored to you. With His supernatural aid, holiness is increased and the effects of original sin are decreased. To review what we have just learned, two important catechism answers should be memorized:

*On account of the sin of Adam, we, his descendants, come into the world deprived of sanctifying grace and inherit his punishment, as we would have inherited his gifts had he been obedient to God.*

*The chief punishments of Adam and Eve which we inherit through original sin are: death, suffering, ignorance, and a strong inclination to sin.*

## God's Punishment Was Just

You may at times wonder about God's justice in punishing all men for Adam's sin. Because God's justice is perfect, we should not doubt whether his punishment is just, even if we do inevitably wonder how this is the case.

Adam's sin was a grievous sin, committed with full consent of the will and complete knowledge. God measured out a just punishment. He had given special free gifts not necessary to man's nature. These special gifts would have been ours too, had Adam and Eve remained loyal to God. Adam held them in trust for us. When our first parents gave up the right to possess these gifts, God took His special, free gifts away from them and their descendants. He took away only the special gifts; not the gifts which were natural to man. However, God provides us with ways and means to regain the special, supernatural gifts. Can you mention some of these ways and means?

As we think over the sin of our first parents and its serious results we realize that *God is not unjust in punishing us on account of the sin of Adam, because original sin does not take away from us*

### The Fruit that Kills . . . The Fruit that Saves

We all know Adam and Eve ate the forbidden fruit, and that this brought death into the world. But have you ever considered how we are saved through a "fruit" as well? Think of the line from the Hail Mary prayer: "Blessed is the fruit of thy womb." This of course refers to Jesus, Mary's son. Just as Adam and Eve stood at a tree and ate the fruit that brought death to them and their children, many years later, Mary (the New Eve) would stand at the foot of a different tree, the tree of the cross, and her children would be brought back to life through the fruit of that tree, the fruit of her womb, Christ's body.

*anything to which we have a strict right as human beings, but only the free gifts which God in His goodness would have bestowed on us if Adam had not sinned.*

In the struggle for holiness God has given us the spotless example of a perfect creature. This beautiful creature was destined for more than giving us an example of perfect Godlike living. She was to be God's mother. In view of the great honor intended for Mary, as Mother of His Son, God preserved her from that blight on the human race, original sin. This privilege was earned for her by the suffering and death, or, as we say, by the merits of Christ. According to God's plan the Mother of His Son was not to be under the power of the devil for a single instant.

*The Blessed Virgin Mary was preserved from original sin in view of the merits of her divine Son; and this privilege is called her Immaculate Conception.*

**So we pray:**

*O Mary, thou didst enter the world without stain; do thou obtain for me from God that I may leave it without sin.*

## FOR ME TO REVIEW

*Catechism Lesson*

**249. Q. Did Adam and Eve remain faithful to God?**

A. Adam and Eve did not remain faithful to God, but broke His command by eating the forbidden fruit.

**253. Q. What befell Adam and Eve on account sin?**

A. Adam and Eve, on account of their sin, lost innocence and holiness, and were doomed to sickness and death.

254. Q. **What other evils befell Adam and Eve on account of their sin?**

A. Many other evils befell Adam and Eve on account of their sin. They were driven out of Paradise and condemned to toil. God also ordained that henceforth the earth should yield no crops without cultivation, and that the beasts, man's former friends, should become his savage enemies.

265. Q. **What is the sin called which we inherit from our first parents?**

A. The sin which we inherit from our first parents is called original sin.

266. Q. **Why is this sin called original?**

A. This sin is called original because it comes down to us from our first parents, and we are brought into the world with its guilt on our soul.

259. Q. **What effects followed from the sin of our first parents?**

A. Our nature was corrupted by the sin of our first parents, which darkened our understanding, weakened our will, and left in us a strong inclination to evil.

257. Q. **Is it not unjust to punish us for the sin of our first parents?**

A. It is not unjust to punish us for the sin of our first parents, because their punishment consisted in being deprived of a free gift of God; that is, of the gift of original justice to which they had no strict right and which they willfully forfeited by their act of disobedience.

268. Q. **Was anyone ever preserved from original sin?**

A. The Blessed Virgin Mary, through the merits of her Divine Son, was preserved free from the guilt of original sin, and this privilege is called her Immaculate Conception.

*The LORD God therefore banished him from the garden of Eden, to till the ground from which he had been taken.*

GENESIS 3:23

### Questions and Exercises

*Write your answers on a separate sheet of paper*

1. Did God love Adam and Eve after their sin? Does He love us after we have sinned?
2. Why do we share in Adam's punishment?
3. What promise made at baptism should we think of when tempted to sin?
4. Which punishment of Adam do we suffer every day?
5. What should we think of, from this lesson, when our daily tasks seem hard to do?
6. How would you answer someone who said God is not just in punishing us for Adam's sin?
7. How would you explain to a non-Catholic friend what is meant by the Immaculate Conception?
8. When was the Immaculate Conception proclaimed a dogma of the Church?
9. If Adam and Eve had practiced two important virtues they might not have sinned. What are these virtues?

## FOR ME TO REMEMBER

1. Through disobedience to God's law our first parents lost God's special gifts.
2. We inherit original sin because of the fall of Adam and Eve.
3. God did not take away any gifts natural to man, only the free gifts which were above the natural.
4. The Blessed Virgin Mary was preserved from original sin.

## FOR ME TO DO

1. Find and classify the things Adam and Eve lost and did not lose because of their sin of disobedience. Discuss the list and its classifications.
2. Name some things we must suffer as a result of our first parents' sin. Tell why this is so.
3. Prepare a paragraph entitled: The Blessed Virgin Mary and Original Sin. Read it to the class.
4. Find and report to your class the story of the Blessed Virgin Mary appearing to St. Bernadette. Be able to tell what the story has to do with the dogma of the Immaculate Conception.
5. What do we inherit because of the sin of Adam and Eve? Why?
6. It is often easier for you to do evil rather than good. Explain this.
7. Has original sin anything to do with the fact that you must study and work? Why?
8. There is a certain day of the year on which we are reminded of one penalty we are to pay for original sin. What is the day and how are we reminded?
9. Ask God to help you realize the sorrow and suffering that is caused by sin.
10. Make a visit to the church and ask our Lord to help you choose good friends and to be a good friend, always.
11. When you prepare for confession tell God you realize all the sufferings and sorrow that sin has caused, and ask Him sincerely to help you to keep from sin.
12. Say the Act of Contrition thoughtfully, especially the last part: "I firmly resolve, with the help of thy grace, to sin no more and to avoid the near occasions of sin."

LESSON 9

# Actual Sin

## Actual Sin Is Sin We Commit Ourselves

*Original sin,* as we just studied, is inherited from our first parents. *Original sin is not the only kind of sin; there is another kind, called actual sin, which we ourselves commit.* There are various kinds of actual sins for *actual sin is any willful thought, desire, word, action, or omission forbidden by the law of God.*

Planning to do some evil, or thinking how we can perform an evil deed, or rejoicing over an evil deed we have done, is a sin of thought. Some people think there is no such thing as a mortal sin of thought. They think that in order to commit a sin we must perform some action. This is not true; a willful, or intentional thought contrary to the law of God is an actual sin, and can be a mortal sin.

Desires, or wishes, can be sins when we wish some evil to take place, or desire to do some wrong. For instance, Jim has money in his wallet for groceries. Dan is interested in buying a catcher's glove and he knows that Jim has just the right amount of money. Carefully he plans to take the wallet and eagerly awaits his chance. However, he gets no chance to carry out his plan. Even though Dan was unable to steal the wallet, he has committed a sin of stealing in desire, and he must confess it as such.

Being careless of the use of God's name, making others unhappy by our uncharitable talk, or telling lies because we are afraid to face the truth, are examples of sinful words.

Willfully bringing harm to others, stealing, and killing are sinful deeds. These sins are usually the result of the sins of desire, but they take us one step further, to the actual doing of the sin we planned to commit.

We can also sin by neglecting to do something which God commands. Such sins are called sins of omission, as missing Mass on Sunday or holy days through our own fault, or omitting our prayers for a long time.

## Mortal Sin: The Most Serious Kind of Actual Sin

*There are two kinds of actual sin: mortal sin and venial sin.* When we sin mortally we refuse to serve God in a serious matter. *Mortal sin is a grievous offense against the law of God.* The word "mortal" means deadly, and mortal sin cuts us off from sanctifying grace, which is the supernatural life of the soul. That is why *this sin is called mortal, or deadly, because it deprives the sinner of sanctifying grace, the supernatural life of the soul.*

> *When Christ was hanging on the cross He forgave the Good Thief because he had shown he was sorry.*

God loves all of His creatures and wants to stay close to them. When man sins mortally, he chooses to become God's enemy. *Besides depriving the sinner of sanctifying grace, mortal sin makes the soul an enemy of God, takes away the merit of all one's good actions, deprives one of the right to everlasting happiness in heaven, and makes one deserving of everlasting punishment in hell.* The fact that God punishes the sinner does not mean that He hates the sinner. It is true that He hates sin, but the sinner will always be His loved child.

Did you ever carry a heavy package for an older person? Surely you may have given a seat to an older person on the bus? Such good acts are sometimes rewarded by a pat on the head, or even by a gift. These same acts done for the glory of God by persons in the state of grace, not only may receive an earthly reward, but also increase our store of treasures in heaven. Thus we receive merit for our good works.

But a person with mortal sin on his soul loses the merit of his good works. This is not restored to him until his mortal sins are forgiven.

Mortal sin also takes away the right to heaven. Through all the years of our lives we have been spurred on by the thought that one day we would see God. Yet, the sight of God in this earthly life becomes obscured when we sin mortally. In hell we can never see God, and this alone is so terrible a thought that it solemnly reminds to always flee mortal sin.

In order to commit a mortal sin, certain conditions must be present. The sin must be seriously evil; the sinner must realize the seriousness of the wrong he is doing, and he must give full consent to it.

Giving full consent to a sin means realizing that an act is sinful and still giving in to it. Sometimes we make up our minds to do something seriously wrong, but for some reason or other we are prevented from doing it. In such cases we are actually guilty of mortal sin because our wills have chosen to commit sin.

Let us summarize: *To make a sin mortal these three things are necessary: first, the thought, desire, word, action, or omission must be seriously wrong or considered seriously wrong; second, the sinner must be mindful of the serious wrong; third, the sinner must fully consent to it.*

When Christ was hanging on the cross He forgave the Good Thief because he had shown he was sorry. We should acquire the habit of going to confession often so that we may go through life with a clear conscience and keep in God's grace. "Hail, O Cross, our only hope."

### The Consequences of Venial Sin

It can be tempting to think that venial sins are not a big deal. While they are less serious than mortal sins, we should not take venial sins lightly. Venial sins that go unconfessed and which we have little or no contrition for can wound and weaken our soul, making us more vulnerable to temptation and committing mortal sin. Think of it in terms of someone's physical health. A certain sickness or injury is not as serious as death, but if someone faces enough sickness or injury, their body can still be weakened and their life threatened. The best way to avoid mortal sin is to first avoid venial sin, or confess our venial sins as soon and as often as we can.

## Venial Sin Is a Less Serious Actual Sin

Venial sin is a less serious offense against the law of God, which does not deprive the soul of sanctifying grace, and which can be pardoned even without sacramental confession.

Yet, when we commit venial sins, we are doing something so bad that there is only one worse evil—mortal sin. No matter how slight the offense, we have no excuse for offending God. Venial sin does not destroy our friendship with God, although it does lessen the warmth of our love for Him.

If we do something wrong thinking it is only a venial sin, it is usually only a venial sin. But, if we do not know our sin is of grave matter because we are lazy or careless we may be more guilty than we realize. We must listen to the instructions given, and try to realize the seriousness of the circumstances so that we may form a correct conscience in regard to the sins we commit.

*Briefly then, a sin can be venial in two ways: first, when the evil done is not gravely wrong; second, when the evil done is a grave matter, but the sinner sincerely believes it is not grave, and/or does not give full consent to the action in question.*

Venial sin makes us think less often of the things of God and of the ways of serving Him. It also keeps us from gaining the actual graces we need in order to overcome temptation. *Venial sin harms us by making us less fervent in the service of God, by weakening our power to resist mortal sin, and by making us deserving of God's punishments in this life or in purgatory.*

Since venial sins do not destroy our friendship with God we may be tempted to think that it does not matter whether we commit them. This would not be correct. Unless we are faithful in smaller things, we may soon sin in greater ways. Besides, we know that at times God has punished venial sin severely. He must, therefore, consider it a great evil.

Although we are not bound to confess our venial sins, it is well to do so. By going to confession regularly every two or three weeks, we keep ourselves very close to God. However, venial sin can be forgiven in many ways. One way is by an Act of Contrition. Expressing our sorrow for even our venial sins proves to God that we do not wish to stray from Him in even the slightest manner. Venial sin is also removed by Holy Communion, by an act of love, by works of mercy, and in other ways.

## God Has Provided the Means Which Will Keep Us From Sin

We have said that this life is a journey to heaven. What are the things we need to do on this journey so that we may avoid sin and safely reach heaven, our goal? *We can keep from committing sin by praying and by receiving the sacraments; by remembering that God is always with us; by recalling that our bodies are temples of the Holy Spirit; by keeping occupied with work or play; by promptly resisting the sources of sin within us; by avoiding the near occasions of sin.*

What is meant by that phrase, "the near occasions of sin"? *The near occasions of sin are all persons, places, or things that may easily lead us into sin.*

Prayer is a very important means of reaching our goal. Even as small children we were taught to lift our minds and hearts to God often through the day. The graces obtained in this way keep us close to God. Through the sacraments we may receive more graces. Some travelers on the road of life do not know how to use the means God offers; others neglect to use them and thus have difficulty reaching heaven.

In serving God we should always have His interests in mind. That does not mean we have to be kneeling in prayer all the time. It simply means remembering that we are always in God's presence, and that no matter where we are or what we are doing He can see us, and we can praise Him. It means remembering we are temples of the Holy Spirit through the presence of sanctifying grace received at baptism.

## The Chief Sources of Sin

In connection with the near occasions of sin we should know the chief sources of actual sin, called the capital sins. *The chief sources of actual sin are: pride, covetousness, lust, anger, gluttony, envy, and sloth, and these are commonly called capital sins. They are called capital sins, not because they, in themselves, are the greatest sins, but because they are the chief reasons why men commit sin.* The best way to overcome these bad habits, or vices, is to practice the virtue which is the opposite of each vice.

*Pride,* the first of these evils, may be said to be at the bottom of all sin. It means serving ourselves in preference to God. It was pride that tempted Eve in the Garden of Paradise for she could not bear to think anyone else was greater than she was. We can overcome pride by the practice of humility. This virtue helps us to see ourselves as we really are, and to realize that without God's help we can do nothing. Any success we have comes from God, and not from any power of our own.

The chief sources of actual sin are: pride, covetousness, lust, anger, gluttony, envy, and sloth, and these are commonly called capital sins. They are called capital sins, not because they, in themselves, are the greatest sins, but because they are the chief reasons why men commit sin.

*Covetousness* is an ugly vice. It means too great a desire for material things. The virtue of generosity, or giving, will help us to overcome a too-great desire for the things of this world.

*Lust* is a vice or bad habit of sinful acts or desires for forbidden pleasures of the body. We commit this sin when we give in to thoughts, desires, words, or actions, contrary to purity. Keeping ourselves pure and modest, and refusing to look at, read, listen to, desire, think, or do things which will be sources of temptation, help to overcome lust.

*Anger* can be a sin when it causes a person to wish great evil on another or to punish someone more than he deserves. Sometimes when a friend does things to us which we do not like, we become angry and wish for revenge. In other words we wish to "pay him back" or "get even." We should be careful, for anger is sometimes a sin. The practice of the virtue of meekness helps us to hold back our desire for revenge as well as our feelings of anger and displeasure. We should be encouraged in the practice of the virtue of meekness by our Lord's words, "Learn from me, for I am meek and humble of heart" (Mt. 11:29).

God has made His creatures in such a way that food and drink are necessary for our bodies if we are to grow, and to keep well and strong. But sometimes people get into the habit of eating and drinking too much. This excessive indulgence in eating and drinking is called *gluttony.* We can control this vice by the virtue of temperance, which means taking only a moderate amount of the things we like. If we deny ourselves some of the things we are permitted to have, it will not be so hard to keep from those which are forbidden.

*Envy* is the sin committed when we are jealous at the good fortune of others. Do you remember the story of David and Saul? David, a shepherd boy, killed the giant, Goliath, but King Saul, instead of being glad that David had killed an enemy, was jealous of the praise David received. This vice can be overcome by loving our neighbor, wishing him good, and rejoicing with him in his happiness.

*Sloth,* the last of the seven capital sins, is committed when we neglect the care of our souls through laziness (or being lazy about our soul because we busy ourselves with worldly things). We can overcome this bad habit by doing our appointed tasks carefully and conscientiously, and by showing an interest in the things of God.

We mentioned before that the seven capital sins are not more serious than other sins, but that they are the chief reasons why men commit sin. Every person will find that he can trace most of his sins to one or the other of these seven capital sins. Find out your weak spot and set to work strengthening your defenses at this point.

**TERMS TO KNOW**

- omission
- jealous
- covetous
- violated
- sufficient
- actual
- sacramental
- sloth

## FOR ME TO REVIEW

*Catechism Lesson*

**277. Q. Is original sin the only kind of sin?**

A. Original sin is not the only kind of sin; there is another kind of sin, which we commit ourselves, called actual sin.

**278. Q. What is actual sin?**

A. Actual sin is any willful thought, word, deed, or omission contrary to the law of God.

**279. Q. How many kinds of actual sin are there?**

A. There are two kinds of actual sin—mortal and venial.

**280. Q. What is mortal sin?**

A. Mortal sin is a grievous offense against the law of God.

**281. Q. Why is this sin called mortal?**

A. This sin is called mortal because it deprives us of spiritual life, which is sanctifying grace, and brings everlasting death and damnation on the soul.

**282. Q. How many things are necessary to make a sin mortal?**

A. To make a sin mortal, three things are necessary: a grievous matter, sufficient reflection, and full consent of the will.

**290. Q. What is venial sin?**

A. Venial sin is a slight offense against the law of God in matters of less importance, or in matters of great importance it is an offense committed without sufficient reflection or full consent of the will.

**293. Q. Which are the effects of venial sin?**

A. The effects of venial sin are the lessening of the love of God in our heart, the making us less worthy of His help, and the weakening of the power to resist mortal sin.

**295. Q. Which are the chief sources of sin?**

A. The chief sources of sin are seven: pride, covetousness, lust, anger, gluttony, envy, and sloth, and they are commonly called capital sins.

**313. Q. Why are the seven sources of sin called capital sins?**

A. The seven sources of sin are called capital sins because they rule over our other sins and are the causes of them.

**317. Q. What virtues are opposed to the seven capital sins?**

A. Humility is opposed to pride; generosity to covetousness; chastity to lust; meekness to anger; temperance to gluttony; brotherly love to envy, and diligence to sloth.

**771. Q. What do you mean by the near occasions of sin?**

A. By the near occasions of sin I mean all the persons, places and things that may easily lead us into sin.

### Questions and Exercises

*Write your answers on a separate sheet of paper*

1. Why should we try to receive as many graces as possible?
2. What should we do as soon as we realize we have committed a sin?
3. Where can we receive the strength to obey God's laws?
4. Will we receive a punishment for venial sins?
5. How can we atone for venial sins?
6. Why should we confess our venial sins?
7. Should we be just as sorry for our venial sins as for our mortal sins?

8. What is the worst thing that can happen to a person on this earth?
9. Why should we try to remain in the state of grace?
10. Why should we be faithful to our morning and night prayers?
11. What does the word mortal mean? Why is this a good name for this sin?
12. How many kinds of actual sin are there?
13. What is the supernatural life of the soul called?
14. Can venial sin be pardoned without sacramental confession?
15. What do we call persons, places, and things which may easily lead us to sin?
16. When any one of the three conditions for a mortal sin is not present, do we commit a mortal sin?
17. How can we protect ourselves against mortal sin?
18. Which of the chief sources of sin make us neglect our religious duties?
19. What source of sin makes us dislike people who have some things we would like to have?
20. Why is anger so dangerous?
21. Write your answers on a separate sheet of paper.

**Fill in the Blank**

Actual sin is any willful 1 , 2 , 3 , 4 , or 5 .

There are two kinds of actual sins: 6 , and 7 sin.

Mortal sin is a 8 offense against the law of God.

Venial sin is 9 serious offense against the law of God. It does not 10 the soul of 11 grace, and it can be 12 without sacramental 13.

This sin is called mortal, or deadly, because it 14 the sinner of 15 grace, the 16 life of the soul.

Venial sin harms us by making us 17 fervent in the service of God, by weakening our power to resist 18 , and by making us deserving of 19 punishments in this life or in 20.

**Matching**

1. a chief source of sin
2. actual sin
3. mortal sin
4. near occasion of sin
5. original sin
6. venial sin

(A) any willful thought, desire, word, action, or omission forbidden by the law of God
(B) a very great offense against the law of God
(C) pride
(D) a bad comic book or movie
(E) weakens our power to resist mortal sin
(F) deprives the soul of sanctifying grace
(G) makes us less fervent in God's service
(H) anger
(I) a playmate who uses sinful words
(J) takes away the merit of all good actions
(K) must be pardoned through sacramental confession

## FOR ME TO REMEMBER

1. Actual sin is a sin we commit ourselves.
2. The greatest evil in the world is mortal sin.
3. Venial sin makes our friendship with God less warm.
4. We must avoid the near occasions of sin, that is, the persons, places, and things which lead us to sin.

## FOR ME TO DO

1. Name four things mortal sin does to the soul besides depriving it of sanctifying grace.
2. Discuss the three things necessary to make a sin mortal.
3. A sin can be venial in two ways. Name them.
4. Name as many ways as you can by which we can keep from committing sin.
5. Make a list of five near occasions of sin for boys and girls of your age. Discuss them with your classmates.
6. It is good for us to think about hell occasionally. Why?
7. After studying this lesson on sin, what prayer should you remember to say every evening before going to bed. Why?
8. Does every sin deserve punishment? Explain.
9. Discuss each of the capital sins. Ask practical questions about them. For example: Do I look down on other boys and girls? Do I want everything I see? Do I go to bad movies?
10. What virtue is the direct opposite of each capital sin?

## For Avoiding Sin

*Hear, Lord, the prayers we offer from contrite hearts.*

*Have pity on us as we acknowledge our sins.*

*Lead us back to the way of holiness.*

*Protect us now and always from the wounds of sin.*

*May we ever keep safe in all its fullness the gift your love once gave us and your mercy now restores. Amen.*

# UNIT 2

# God the Son, Our Redeemer

# CHAPTER 4
# The Birth and Public Life of Christ

*I believe…*

*in Jesus Christ, His only Son, our Lord, who was conceived by the Holy Spirit, born of the Virgin Mary, suffered under Pontius Pilate, was crucified, died and was buried. He descended into hell, the third day He arose again from the dead. He ascended into heaven, and sits at the right hand of God, the Father Almighty, from thence He shall come to judge the living and the dead.*

*In unit 1 we learned many things about God and His perfections and about the work of the first person of the Blessed Trinity, God the Father. Now in this unit, we shall turn our minds to God the Son, how He became man, how He lived on earth, how He suffered and died for us and rose from the dead that we might gain eternal life.*

LESSON 10

# God Prepared the World for the Coming of the Redeemer

## God Promised a Redeemer

After the disobedience of Adam and Eve, man lost sanctifying grace, that is, friendship with God. As a result our first parents and all their descendants lost the right to everlasting happiness.

It would have been fair and just, if God had closed the gates of heaven forever, as He had done to the disobedient angels. He knew, however, man's weakness and the power of the devil. In His deep love and mercy, God promised to send a Redeemer whose blood would wash away the guilt of man's sin.

God's justice demanded that satisfaction for sin come from a human being because a human being had offended Him. The sin was a serious offense against the infinite God, and, so, in a certain sense, infinite. Therefore divine justice required infinite satisfaction. No created being could make such satisfaction because all creatures are finite. So God sent His only-begotten Son to be our Redeemer, God-made-man. As the Son of God He could offer infinite satisfaction; and as a human being He could offer the sacrifice for the human race.

God did not abandon man after Adam fell into sin, but promised to send into the world a Saviour to free man from his sins and to reopen to him the gates of heaven.

## God Made the World Wait for the Redeemer

We know that God has a reason for everything He does. He had reasons for making the world wait for the Redeemer. He permitted His creatures to suffer from the misery of sin because this suffering would help them to understand how much they needed a Redeemer. God also wished to show man how helpless he was without divine aid. In addition, man was to realize the great dignity of God who has been offended. Besides this, God planned to prepare the world for the great event that was to come.

The people of the Old Testament awaited the Promised Redeemer; some, like the Chosen People, waited eagerly; others with more or less indifference. God repeatedly renewed the promise made to our first parents after their fall. He sent His prophets to the Hebrews, to remind them of the promise. During this time, many who believed in God's promises and followed their conscience in the love and service of the one true God were saved. Since the work of redemption was still to be accomplished, these souls remained in limbo, a place of waiting, where the souls of the just remained until Christ ascended into heaven.

## God Used Certain Means in Preparing the World for the Promised Redeemer

All through history the Hebrews were made to feel, more or less strongly, the need of a Redeemer. To keep them mindful of this need, God frequently repeated His promise to send a Redeemer. He gave Adam this promise in the Garden of Eden. After God had tested Abraham's faith He renewed the promise. Again God repeated His promise to David. The repetition of this promise to His Chosen People was one way in which God prepared the world for the coming of His Son.

God also prepared the world for the Redeemer by raising up many prophets who continually reminded the people of these promises. They also foretold many things about Christ.

As the time approached for the coming of the Saviour, the air seemed to be filled with expectancy.

Have you ever gone with your father on an early morning fishing trip? Perhaps it was still dark as you settled in your boat hoping for a good catch of fish. While you waited for the first nibble on your line you probably noticed that the night sky seemed to fade away as if in preparation for the first faint streaks of light. Little by little these rays broadened until suddenly before your eyes the sun burst forth, a golden ball, shedding its bright rays over the awakening earth.

We can compare the darkness of the night sky to the misery and sin brought into the world by our first parents. Just as the first streaks of dawn announce the light of day, so the promises contained in the prophecies about the Redeemer prepared for His actual coming. We can trace these promises in the Old Testament through the history of the Chosen People.

## Biblical Typology

In addition to prophecies, God used types and figures to foreshadow the coming of Christ. A type or a figure of Christ was any person or thing which helped the people to understand what the Redeemer would be like. For example, Adam, the father of the human race, is a figure of Christ, the Father of the Redeemed race. Noah's building of the Ark to save the members of his family from the deluge is a type of Christ's founding the Church to save all men. The Paschal Lamb, the victim of sacrifice in the Old Law, is a figure of Christ, the Lamb of God who is the victim of sacrifice in the New Law. The manna, provided by God as food for the Chosen People while they were wandering in the desert, prefigured Christ in the Holy Eucharist in which He supplies us spiritual food for the journey through life.

### *TERMS TO KNOW*

- begotten
- Redeemer
- foretold
- dignity
- satisfaction
- Redemption
- type
- prefigured
- excluded
- fulfillment
- prediction
- expectancy
- figure
- renewed
- redeem
- anticipation

God used the prophecies to keep alive the faith and hope of His people and to render them ever mindful of His love. He enlightened the leaders of the Chosen Race so that they could better explain the meaning of these prophecies. Their instructions were a source of great comfort to the people who awaited the Saviour. The promise of a Redeemer encouraged men to keep faithful to the one true God. Thus we see that *God did not abandon man after Adam fell into sin, but promised to send into the world a Saviour to free man from his sins and to reopen to him the gates of heaven.*

## FOR ME TO REVIEW

*Catechism Lesson*

**319. Q. Did God abandon man after he fell into sin?**

A. God did not abandon man after he fell into sin, but promised him a Redeemer, who was to satisfy for man's sin and reopen to him the gates of heaven.

### Questions and Exercises

*Write your answers on a separate sheet of paper*

1. Tell in your own words why God did not punish man's disobedience as He punished that of the angels.
2. Why was it possible for Jesus Christ to offer satisfaction to God and at the same time offer it for the human race?
3. Why did God wait so long before sending the Redeemer?
4. What did the people of the Old Testament have to do in order to be saved?
5. Why did God remind the people often of the promise of a Redeemer?

## FOR ME TO REMEMBER

1. Original sin destroyed the friendship between God and man.
2. This infinite injury caused by original sin demanded infinite satisfaction.
3. The long wait between the fall of man and the Redemption taught man the wickedness of sin, the dignity of God, and the need of a Redeemer.

4. God prepared the world for the coming of the Redeemer by means of prophetic words and signs concerning the birth, public life, death, resurrection, and ascension of Christ.
5. God made use of persons and things to prefigure the Redeemer.

## FOR ME TO DO

1. Prepare a talk on one of the following Old Testament characters showing how he reminds us of the Redeemer: Adam, Noah, Abraham, Moses, Jonah.
2. Pretend that you were one of the Israelites. Write a letter to a Gentile friend, telling him about the manna in the desert.
3. Explain the statement: "The greater the dignity of the person offended, the greater becomes the injury."
4. Prepare a skit to express your idea of how our first parents felt when they were expelled from Paradise.
5. To whom was the Redeemer first promised?
6. To whom was the promise of the Redeemer repeated?
7. Explain how it was just for God to send the good people of the Old Testament to Limbo.
8. Why could not Noah or Abraham have offered themselves in satisfaction for the sin of Adam?
9. How could the people who lived before the Redeemer be saved?

LESSON 11

# God Sent His Divine Son as the Promised Redeemer

Did anyone ever promise you a special present several months before your birthday? You were probably so anxious to get it that the period of waiting seemed endless. The closer the day, the more excited you became.

This anxious waiting resembles the expectancy of the Jewish people before the birth of Christ. God had promised Adam and Eve a Redeemer. The exact time the promise was to be fulfilled was left uncertain. God waited thousands of years before sending His beloved Son because He wanted to prepare the world to receive its Redeemer. The prophecies indicated that the time was finally at hand.

## The Incarnation Was the Beginning of the Fulfillment of God's Promise

At last God the Father decided that the world was ready. He sent the Redeemer, the Saviour of the human race. Who was this Saviour of all men? *The Saviour of all men is Jesus Christ.* Who is Jesus Christ? He is the divine Son, made man, that is the second Person of the Blessed Trinity in human flesh. He is the God-man: God-made-man. Indeed, *the chief teaching of the Catholic Church about Jesus Christ is that He is God*

The Church commemorates the visit of the angel to Mary on a special day, the Feast of the Annunciation. The word "annunciation" comes from the verb "announce," which means "tell" or "make known." While we celebrate the birthday of Christ on Christmas Day, let us not forget that Son of God was conceived and made man on the Feast of the Annunciation, the day on which the Angel Gabriel announced to the Blessed Virgin Mary that she was to be the Mother of God. The Feast of the Annunciation is March 25. This is a feast we should celebrate with gratitude and deep devotion.

*made man.* The Son of God was always God. But *the Son of God was not always man, but became man at the time of the Incarnation.* Let us make an act of faith in Him: "Jesus, Son of the living God, have mercy on us."

God chose Mary, a spotless, humble girl of Nazareth, for the great privilege of being the Mother of Christ, that is, the Mother of the God made man. How did God bring this about? By the power of the Holy Spirit the Son of God began His earthly life as man beneath the most pure heart of Mary.

Another way of expressing this truth is as follows: *The Son of God was conceived and made man by the power of the Holy Spirit in the womb of the Blessed Virgin Mary. We call this the Incarnation. By the Incarnation is meant that the Son of God, retaining His divine nature, took to Himself a human nature, that is, a body and soul like ours.*

Let us never forget what St. Louis-Marie de Montfort said: "It was through Mary that Jesus Christ came to us and it is through her that we must go to Him."

## The Visit of the Angel

Let us recall the story of the visit of the Archangel Gabriel to Mary. It was during this visit that the Incarnation took place.

If you had been in Mary's place how surprised you would have been at the sight of the heavenly visitor. However, as soon as she learned the reason for this unusual visit, Mary's fear disappeared, and she was willing to do whatever God asked of her. We know that this was so from her answer to the Archangel Gabriel: "Behold, the handmaid of the Lord; be it done unto me according to Thy word." At these words the Son of God became man.

### Titles of the Redeemer

Our Blessed Redeemer, who began to live in this world at the moment of the Incarnation is known by several names. We call Him "Jesus" which means Saviour. We also call Him "Christ," which means "anointed one." The Hebrew word for "anointed one" is "Messiah."

Another title given to Jesus is "our Lord." We call Him our Lord because He is our ruler, both as God and as man. When we think of the human nature of Christ, that is, His birth in Bethlehem and His early life with Mary and Joseph, it is easier to ask God for favors, and to beg His forgiveness. The fact that Jesus Christ is man as well as God helps to bring us closer to Him.

## Waiting on the Messiah

At the time of Christ, the Jewish people were waiting on a messiah, but not the kind of messiah Jesus would ultimately be. They were waiting in hopeful anticipation for a political or military leader who would overthrow the Roman Empire and restore the Kingdom of David on earth. This was not what Jesus came to do. He came to help them defeat the empire of sin in their hearts and establish a heavenly kingdom, both of which he would accomplish through His Church.

### Two Natures in Christ—One Person

*Jesus Christ has two natures: the nature of God and the nature of man.* That is, He is divine and also human. He has a divine nature and a human nature. This mystery, like that of the Blessed Trinity, we accept by faith. Each nature is perfect. Our Lord is both God and man.

Although our Lord has two natures is He two persons? *No. Jesus Christ is only one Person; and that Person is the second Person of the Blessed Trinity.*

*Jesus Christ is God because He is the only Son of God, having the same divine nature as His Father.* As God, Jesus has the greatest and highest nature possible. He has every perfection in an infinite degree. Mention some of the perfections of God. Sometimes we think of these divine perfections as belonging only to the Father, but they belong equally to God the Son and to the Holy Spirit. The miracles of Christ show His divinity because He performed them by His divine nature. He showed His divine power when He said to the daughter of Jairus, "Girl, I say to thee arise" (Mk. 5:41). The miracles are a proof that Christ is the Son of God, because only God can work a miracle.

> *God became man so that man might become a god."*
>
> *—St. Athanasius*

But Jesus Christ is also man. *Jesus Christ is man because He is the Son of the Blessed Virgin Mary and has a body and soul like ours.* As man, Christ is like us in everything except sin. He had a human body which needed food and rest. He also had a human soul, with an intellect and a human will. The Son of God made man did all the things we read about in the Gospels. These records of Christ's birth, of His manner of living, His conversations, and the human sympathy He so often showed, give proofs of His humanity.

So again we can say that *Jesus Christ has two natures: the nature of God and the nature of man.* Each of these natures is whole and entire. The nature of God, or the divine nature, Christ has from His heavenly Father from eternity. Through this divine nature He forgave sins and brought the dead to life. The Son of God was not always incarnate, but became man at the time of the Incarnation when He received His human nature through Mary, His earthly mother.

Christ did not lose His divine nature when He took up a human nature, but He did hide His divine nature. His childhood actions did not appear much different from those of any other Jewish boy of the time.

Christ knew that many of the people would doubt that He was God. They might agree that He was a very unusual child and man, but not have faith in Him as God. Christ also knew that He could win many more souls for His Father's kingdom by coming into this world as a tiny infant whom all men could love if they would. He chose, therefore, to be born in poverty and simplicity.

## Mary and Joseph Prepared for the Coming of Christ

At the time when Christ was born, unmarried people were a disgrace to the nation. Furthermore, it was looked on as a curse to be married and not have children. Mary, although she knew that she would be criticized, had promised to remain a virgin. This promise meant that she, of her own free will, gave up the privilege of ever becoming a mother. She observed, however, one custom of the time and betrothed herself, that is, promised herself in marriage to Joseph, a descendant of the royal house of David. This ceremony bound Mary to Joseph for life. It was during the time of betrothal that the angel appeared to Mary. Mary gave her consent to become the Mother of God after the angel had explained to her how this would be done without loss of her virginity.

Jesus Christ is man because He is the Son of the Blessed Virgin Mary and has a body and soul like ours.

Sometime later, an angel informed Joseph, who also had taken a vow of virginity, that Mary was to become the Mother of God through the power of

the Holy Spirit. As the spouse and the protector of Mary, Joseph accepted the guardianship of the Christ Child thus becoming His foster father. *Jesus Christ had no human father, but St. Joseph was the spouse of the Blessed Virgin Mary and the guardian, or foster father, of Christ.*

So we pray:

"O St. Joseph, foster father of our Lord Jesus Christ and true spouse of Mary, the Virgin, pray for us."

### The Mother of St. John the Baptist and Mary

The angel, at the Annunciation, told Mary that her cousin Elizabeth was to have a son. Mary decided to visit Elizabeth and set out for the hill country of Judea. As she approached the doorway of Elizabeth's home her cousin greeted her with great happiness. Filled with the Holy Spirit, Elizabeth spoke the beautiful words, "And how have I deserved that the Mother of my Lord should come to me?" (Lk. 1:43.) At this moment John the Baptist, whom Elizabeth was carrying beneath her heart, was cleansed from original sin by Christ resting beneath Mary's Immaculate Heart.

The Eastern people chanted hymns at times of great joy or sorrow. Mary was so overjoyed by what had happened that her

### The Visitation

Have you ever heard of "the Visitation"? If you have ever prayed the Rosary with your family, you certainly have. The Visitation is the second Joyful Mystery. It commemorates the story of Mary visiting her cousin, Elizabeth, after the Annunciation. Elizabeth was pregnant with John the Baptist, who leapt in her womb at hearing Mary's voice.

heart sang out the beautiful words of the "Magnificat" (Lk. 1:46–55). Let us read it from the New Testament and try to understand the meaning of these words.

Mary, the most perfect of all creatures, was humble. She gave praise to God for honoring her. How much more should we remember that everything we have, all the graces we have received, all the good things we can do, all come from God. Of ourselves, we have nothing, of ourselves we can desire nothing, and without God's divine Providence and His loving assistance, we could not accomplish anything. In thanksgiving for all these favors, and knowing our dependence on God, let us often repeat this prayer: "My spirit rejoices in God my Savior, for He hath regarded my lowliness."

After visiting Elizabeth, Mary went back to Nazareth. She and Joseph spent their time preparing for the coming of the Promised Redeemer. Imagine Mary getting the baby clothes ready for Him, perhaps spinning and weaving things for Him to wear. Picture Joseph in the carpenter shop, perhaps making a little crib so that the divine Infant would be comfortable.

Caesar Augustus interrupted these preparations. Anxious to know the number of people over whom he ruled, Caesar Augustus ordered a census. When a census is taken today, census takers go from door to door to get their information. In the time

## What is a census?

A census is like a survey taken by a government of its people. In its most basic sense, a census counts the number of people living in a given region. But in practice it does more than this. A census might ask things like: How many people are in your family? How many boys vs. girls are in your family? How many people go to school? A governing body can use this information to better govern its people. One of the main reasons for a census, though, is to know how much taxes a government should be collecting from its people. Nowadays we participate in a census through the mail, the phone, or the internet. But they didn't have these things in the time of Christ. When the Roman leader, Caesar Augustus, ordered a census, and since Joseph's family came from Bethlehem, he and Mary had to go there to participate in it.

*When Jesus was born in Bethlehem of Judea, in the days of King Herod, behold, magi from the east arrived in Jerusalem, saying, "Where is the newborn king of the Jews? We saw his star at its rising and have come to do him homage."*

**MATTHEW 2:1-2**

of Caesar Augustus the people went to be enrolled in the cities of their ancestors. Thus Joseph had to go to Bethlehem because he was of the house of David, and Bethlehem was David's town.

The trip to Bethlehem at that time meant several days' journey on foot. Because Joseph and Mary knew that this journey was God's will for them, they did not complain about it. They accepted Caesars command and obeyed it humbly and willingly.

Many times God's will is made known to us through the commands of our superiors. Who are our superiors? Name some ways in which we can serve God by obeying our country's commands. Are you cheerful when you are asked to obey some law you consider difficult to observe?

## Events Surrounding the Birth of Christ

***TERMS TO KNOW***

- Incarnation
- human nature
- divine nature
- reparation
- infinite
- satisfaction

Mary and Joseph fulfilled many prophecies which foretold the coming of Christ when they carried out the decree of Caesar Augustus. You remember the story of the journey to Bethlehem and how they could find no shelter there.

You can picture the stable on the hillside in which the infinite, eternal, all-knowing, all-wise, Son of God came into this world in human form. The angels sang the beautiful hymn of praise and glory, "Glory to God in the highest."

The shepherds who were watching their flocks on the hillside heard these words. As the angels' message was made clear to them, the shepherds hastened to see the wonder which the angels announced. They hurried over to Bethlehem repeating in their hearts the song of the angels. This joyful song is part of the Mass and it takes us back in spirit to the little stable, on the hillside where *Christ was born of the Blessed Virgin Mary on Christmas Day, in Bethlehem, more than nineteen hundred years ago.*

## FOR ME TO REVIEW

*Catechism Lesson*

**321. Q. Who is the Redeemer?**

A. Our Blessed Lord and Saviour Jesus Christ is the Redeemer of mankind.

**330. Q. What do you believe of Jesus Christ?**

A. I believe that Jesus Christ is the Son of God, the second Person of the Blessed Trinity, true God and true man.

**332. Q. Why is Jesus Christ true God?**

A. Jesus Christ is true God because He is the true and only Son of God the Father.

**333. Q. Why is Jesus Christ true man?**

A. Jesus Christ is true man because He is the Son of the Blessed Virgin Mary and has a body and soul like ours.

**337. Q. Is Jesus Christ more than one person?**

A. No. Jesus Christ is but one divine Person.

**336. Q. How many natures are there in Jesus Christ?**

A. In Jesus Christ there are two natures, the nature of God and the nature of man.

**340. Q. Was Jesus Christ always man?**

A. Jesus Christ was not always man, but became man at the time of His Incarnation.

**341. Q. What do you mean by the Incarnation?**

A. By the Incarnation I mean that the Son of God was made man.

**342. Q. How was the Son of God made man?**

A. The Son of God was conceived and made man by the power of the Holy Spirit, in the womb of the Blessed Virgin Mary.

**355. Q. On what day was the Son of God conceived and made man?**

A. The Son of God was conceived and made man on the Feast of the Annunciation—the day on which the angel Gabriel announced to the Blessed Virgin Mary that she was to be the Mother of God.

**334. Q. Who was the foster father or guardian of our Lord while on earth?**

A. St. Joseph, the husband of the Blessed Virgin, was the foster father or guardian of our Lord while on earth.

**356. Q. On what day was Christ born?**

A. Christ was born on Christmas Day, in a stable at Bethlehem, over two thousand years ago.

### Questions and Exercises

*Write your answers on a separate sheet of paper*

1. On what day did the angel announce to Mary that she was to be the Mother of God?
2. Who is the promised Redeemer?
3. How many natures has Christ?
4. What word refers to God becoming man?
5. Was Jesus the Son of God after He became the Son of Mary?
6. In what city was Jesus born?
7. Who is the foster father of Christ?
8. What is the name of the hymn which Mary chanted when she went to visit Elizabeth?

9. Name three virtues Mary practiced when the angel gave her the message, or when Christ was born. Tell how she practiced them.
10. What is the name of the angel who told Mary that she was to be God's Mother?
11. How many Persons are there in God?
12. What is the nature of God called?
13. In what particular way is Jesus different from us?
14. From what royal family was Joseph descended?
15. How do Mary and Joseph teach us to respect our country's laws?

## FOR ME TO REMEMBER

1. Christ is the Promised Redeemer.
2. The Incarnation means God the Son was made man.
3. God retained His divine nature as Son of God when He became the Son of the Blessed Virgin Mary.
4. God intended the Blessed Virgin Mary to be the Mother of Jesus from all eternity.
5. Mary teaches us how to co-operate with God's grace.
6. The feast of the Annunciation, March 25, commemorates the message of the Archangel Gabriel to Mary.
7. Jesus is only one Person although He has two natures.
8. All those who believe and who are baptized in Christ are our brothers and sisters in Christ.
9. Mary and Joseph give us the example of respect and obedience to divine and civil authority.

## FOR ME TO DO

1. Explain how we live our Faith in the doctrines we are learning in this unit by joining with the Church during Advent and at Christmas.
2. Learn the names of the four great empires which existed before the birth of Christ. What part did they play in God's preparation of the world for the Saviour?
3. Look up the story of the birth of Christ in the New Testament. Which Evangelist tells us most about it?
4. Make an acrostic using the word Bethlehem.
5. Make a chart listing some incidents in the life of Christ. Indicate whether they reveal His human nature or His divine nature.
6. Write a conversation which might have taken place between Mary and Joseph on the way to Bethlehem.
7. Illustrate the visit of Gabriel to Mary.
8. How would you answer a non-Catholic friend who said that Mary is not the Mother of God?
9. Who were the first to adore the infant Christ?
10. Why did God so often remind the Chosen People of His promise?
11. Which of the three Persons of the Blessed Trinity became man?
12. Why do you think Christ chose to be born in Bethlehem?
13. What does the name "Jesus" mean?
14. What does the name "Christ" mean?
15. What is the second article of the Apostles' Creed?
16. As man, in what way is Christ unlike us?
17. How do the wine and the water at Mass represent the two natures of Christ?

## St. Andrew Christmas Novena

*Hail and blessed be the hour and moment in which the Son of God was born of the most pure Virgin Mary, at midnight, in Bethlehem, in the piercing cold. In that hour, vouchsafe, O my God! to hear my prayer and grant my desires, through the merits of our Savior Jesus Christ, and of His Blessed Mother. Amen.*

LESSON 12

# The Early Life of Christ

## Jesus Is Circumcised

Let us recall how Jesus received His name. Among the Jews, at the circumcision ceremony the father of the family named the child. This took place eight days after the birth of a child.

God the Father chose the name "Jesus," which means Saviour, for His Son. In this way God made known to the world that the work of His Son was to be the saving of mankind from the cruel slavery of sin.

This name of Jesus is so sacred that the Church has set aside a special day, usually in January, to honor the Holy Name. We show our deep respect and reverence for this name by calling on Jesus often to help us. Since He so faithfully lived up to His name and proved Himself a Saviour we can ask Christ to help us to live up to our name of Christian. Should we celebrate these two feasts with great devotion this year?

The Presentation of the Temple is another mystery of the Rosary. Do you know which one?

So we pray:

"Blessed be the most holy Name of Jesus without end."

## The Presentation in the Temple

The next event in the life of Christ was the Presentation. Under the Law of Moses first-born sons were consecrated to the Lord and had to be bought back at a set price. This was to be done on the fortieth day after Christ was born. On this occasion, the Law also required a ceremony of purification for the mother. She was to bring an

### TERMS TO KNOW

- Circumcision
- prophetess
- solitary
- personality
- Presentation
- Orient
- purification

offering of a lamb and a dove or, in the case of the poor, two doves.

Think about Mary and Joseph with the Child entering the Temple. They did not look any different from any other young couple bringing their baby to be presented to the Lord. But to two people in the Temple, they were different. The Holy Spirit had revealed to Simeon that he would not die before he saw the Child who was to redeem the world. The Holy Spirit directed Simeon to the Temple on this day. As Joseph and Mary approached the Temple, Simeon realized who was entering. Taking the Child in his arms and filled with deep love of God Simeon recited a beautiful prayer of thanksgiving that he had lived to see the Redeemer: "Lord, now lettest thou thy servant depart in peace, according to thy word: For mine eyes have seen thy salvation, which thou hast prepared before the face of all people: a light to lighten the Gentiles, and the glory of thy people Israel" (Luke 2:29–32).

Simeon, after he had said this wonderful prayer, turned to Mary and prophesied that a sword of sorrow would one day pierce her heart. He was trying to tell her that she would be united with Christ in saving the world, by suffering with Him.

Simeon had the privilege of holding the Christ Child in his arms. But this same Christ lives in our souls through sanctifying grace. We receive the same Christ in Holy Communion. Are we as fervent after Communion as Simeon was when he held Christ?

A prophetess, Anna, also happened to be in the Temple at the time when the Holy Family entered. She, too, realized who this Child was, and leaving the Temple, she spoke about Him to all who were awaiting the coming of the Redeemer.

Just as Anna, the prophetess, drew attention to Christ, so also our good conduct leads other people to follow Christ, our Friend and Leader. We can take Anna for our example and pray often to Christ that the entire world may accept Him. "Sacred Heart of Jesus, Thy Kingdom Come." We celebrate the Presentation and the feast of the Purification on February 2, Candlemas Day.

## The Magi Visit Jesus

The angels announced the birth of Christ to the Jews through the shepherds, but a star, as had been prophesied, announced Christ's birth to the rest of the world. The people of the Orient knew of the prophecy. When the Magi, or Wise Men, saw the star they set out to find the new King of the Jews. The star led them to Jerusalem, and here King Herod questioned them. He was afraid that this newborn King would take his throne. Herod told the Magi to go to Bethlehem and come back to tell him where they had found the newborn King of the Jews.

Since it was a king they were visiting the Magi brought gifts worthy of a king: gold, frankincense, and myrrh. After offering their gifts and adoring the Child the Magi returned to their own country, without going back to Jerusalem to see Herod. They had been warned by God that the wicked King planned to harm the Child.

### The Symbolism of the Magi's Gifts

Many people do not realize the magi's gifts of gold, frankincense, and myrrh had symbolic significance. The gold symbolizes Jesus's kingship, the frankincense his royal priesthood, and the myrrh foreshadowed his redemptive death, as it was like a balm that people anointed bodies with, in some cases to use like a perfume for those still living, but also after one died to cover up the odor of death.

## A Wicked King Is Surprised

When the Magi did not return to Jerusalem to report about the King they had visited, Herod realized they had outwitted him. He, therefore, ordered all baby boys under two years of age in Bethlehem and the surrounding country to be put to death. He thought in this way he would surely manage to kill the Child who threatened his throne. But before Herod's soldiers could harm the Holy Family, an angel appeared to Joseph and told him to flee to Egypt with Jesus and Mary. Joseph did not question the angel. Without a word of complaint he, Mary, and Jesus set out for Egypt over the desert sands.

After some time in Egypt, an angel again appeared to Joseph and told him to take the Child and His mother back to the land of Israel, because Herod was dead.

Are we jealous and afraid of rivals as Herod was? Do we obey the command of God as willingly as Joseph? Especially when we think the commands are difficult, do we still obey?

So we pray: "St. Joseph most obedient, pray for us."

## The Holy Family Is a Model of Obedience

We have seen how the parents of Jesus obeyed the Law of Moses in presenting the Child Jesus in the Temple. Twelve years later Mary and Joseph gave another example of their obedience to this law when they took Jesus to Jerusalem to celebrate the feast of the Pasch. Jesus would not have had to attend this feast until He was thirteen years old. Respect for the Law prompted the Holy Family to attend. For eight days they took part in the services. Then, when the celebration was over, they started for home. They traveled in a large caravan. At the end of the day, as they arrived at the stopping place for the night, both Mary and Joseph looked for Jesus. When they did not find Him they returned to Jerusalem to search for Him.

On the third day they found Jesus in the Temple amid a group of doctors, amazing them with His understanding and His questions. When Mary questioned Him about His delay in returning home, He answered with that question we all remember. "Did you not know that I must be about My Fathers business?" At their command, Jesus went home with His parents, and, as the Gospel says, "He continued in subjection to them" (Luke 2:51).

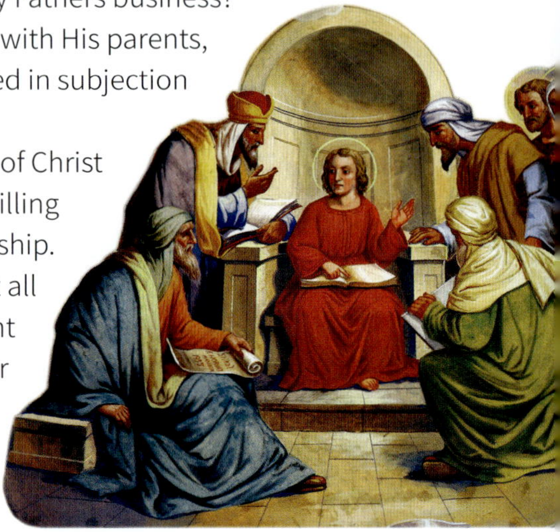

How does this incident in the life of Christ apply to us? Like Jesus we must be willing to fulfill God's laws of prayer and worship. We must be willing to do God's will at all times. Especially we must be obedient to our parents and do all in our power to make our own family life happy. Celebrating the Feast of the Holy Family properly will help us in this.

## FOR ME TO REVIEW

### Questions and Exercises

*Write your answers on a separate sheet of paper*

1. What does the name Jesus mean?
2. What do we call the ceremony at which the Hebrew fathers in the Old Testament named their sons?
3. What ceremony took place forty days after Christ's birth?
4. What other ceremony took place at the Presentation?
5. In what ways can we imitate the example of Simeon and Anna?
6. What are the three worshipers from the east called?
7. What lessons can we learn from the incident in the temple when Christ was twelve?

8. How did Jesus prepare for His great work?
9. How can we imitate Christ's example in preparing for our work in life?

## FOR ME TO REMEMBER

1. The word "Jesus" means Saviour.
2. Christ always did His Father's will.
3. The experience of Simeon and Anna on seeing the Saviour teaches us the reward of earnest prayer.
4. The Holy Family at Nazareth is the model of the Christian home.

## FOR ME TO DO

1. List ways in which the example of the Child Jesus helps us to do the will of God.
2. Write a paragraph on the Nativity story as it might be told by the shepherds, or the innkeeper.
3. Draw two pictures: (*a*) the Magi offering gold, frankincense, and myrrh; (*b*) boys and girls offering their prayers, good deeds, and sufferings to the Infant.
4. Dramatize the Presentation, with Simeon and Anna.
5. Tell how to baptize in case of necessity.
6. Explain: Christ led a hidden life at Nazareth.
7. Examine the liturgy of the Christmas season and find out how we can and should re-live the life of Christ with the Church.
8. What were the duties of each member of the Holy Family; of your family?

LESSON 13

# Christ's Public Life

The hidden life of Jesus came to an end at the marriage feast of Cana. We are now going to begin a very brief outline of the public life of Christ.

## The Preparation for the Public Life of Christ

What are some of the things we remember about St. John the Baptist, who was Jesus' cousin? During Jesus' hidden life, John lived alone in the desert. He spent much of his time in prayer and penance, making himself ready for his great work of preparing the people to receive the Redeemer.

One day a group of men from Galilee who had heard of John's work came to the Jordan to be baptized. Among them was Jesus. As John caught sight of Jesus the Holy Spirit made known to him that He was the Messiah. At first John refused to baptize Jesus, because he felt unworthy. Jesus, however, commanded

The hidden life of Jesus came to an end at the marriage feast of Cana.

him to do it. While Jesus was coming out of the water after the baptism, the heavens opened and the Holy Spirit came down upon Him in the form of a dove. The voice of the Father said, "This is my beloved Son, in whom I am well pleased" (Lk. 3:22).

### Jesus Begins to Choose His Disciples

Jesus now returned to the region around the Jordan River. The time had come for John to announce who Jesus was. John was speaking to two of his disciples when he saw Jesus coming toward him. How did he let the two disciples know that this man was Jesus? He used the words, "Behold the Lamb of God" so that these two disciples would realize that here was no ordinary man. The priest repeats these words in every Holy Mass.

The disciples were so overcome by the personality and power of Jesus that they left John and followed Christ. Andrew especially was so happy that he could not keep his joy to himself and hastened to tell his brother Simon. Simon at once went to Jesus.

Jesus returned to Galilee with His disciples. In time He attracted other men, among them Philip and Nathaniel. To answer Christ's call some, like the fishermen James and John, the sons of Zebedee, left their boats and all their possessions. As other Apostles joined the little band, it grew to be twelve. Most of them were very ordinary men. But they loved

## The Devil Tries to Tempt Jesus

After His baptism Christ went into the desert where He spent forty days and nights praying and fasting, in preparation for His public life. During this time the devil tempted Him three times but Jesus quickly and firmly resisted his attacks. The devil then left Jesus and angels came and ministered to Him.

Jesus allowed Himself to be tempted to show us that we cannot expect to go through life without temptations. Although temptations in themselves are not sinful, we must resist them as strongly as Christ did. We, therefore, should receive the sacraments often in order to obtain God's grace; they are our greatest weapons against temptations.

Christ so much that they were willing to leave everything to follow Him. With such men Christ could do much.

## The Beginning of the Public Life

The public life of Christ began at the marriage feast of Cana where He performed His first miracle. After it, He went to Jerusalem for the Passover and then returned to Galilee where most of His public life was spent, especially at Capernaum.

He preached His Gospel to the people, beginning with the famous Sermon on the Mount which opened with the Eight Beatitudes. He worked miracles, including the raising of more than one person to life, and showed divine power over all the forces of nature. He lived a life of perfect virtue.

### TERMS TO KNOW

- preparation
- Galileans
- hidden life
- solitary
- Messias
- public life
- penance
- descended
- resisted
- resist
- Passover
- ordinary
- ministry
- prophecies
- establishment
- disciples
- personality

### Mary's Powerful Intercession

As Catholics, we believe that Mary is a powerful intercessor between us and God. This means we can ask her to pray for us to God, and because God loves her so much, he will listen. This is a belief we get from Tradition, but also from Scripture. The story of Jesus's first public miracle, the changing of the water to wine at the wedding feast at Cana, gives us a clue of Mary's intercessory powers. Mary is the one who notices the couple's embarrassing situation and goes to Jesus, asking him to do something about it. This shows us that she is aware of our needs and will ask her Son to help us.

## The Envy of the Jewish Leaders

During His public life Christ traveled far and wide in the Holy Land: in Judea, in Samaria, and particularly in Galilee. He preached and did good wherever He went.

Our Lord quickly became very popular among the people, and this caused the leaders of the Jews to be envious of Him and to oppose Him. In spite of this Christ went on preaching, using many parables, to reveal, and at the same time partly to conceal His meaning. As He was preaching and performing His miracles, the prophecies concerning Him were being fulfilled in His person and in His actions.

In addition He Himself made prophecies, for instance concerning the Holy Eucharist, when He multiplied the loaves and the fishes; and about His own death, which He prophesied three times, His resurrection from the dead, and the establishment of His kingdom on earth—the Church.

The multiplication of loaves and fishes is a prophecy concerning the Holy Eucharist.

## Revealing Himself as the Promised Redeemer

In all this our Lord was revealing Himself as the Redeemer promised by God to our first parents. His preaching was such that He left room for faith in those who heard and saw Him, so that He might reward them if they freely turned to Him.

After three years of preaching, teaching, and working miracles the time had arrived for our Lord to offer to God the Father that great sacrifice of Himself for which He had come to earth. We shall study this in the next unit.

## FOR ME TO REVIEW

**Questions and Exercises**

1. How did Christ redeem us?
2. What kind of men did Jesus choose as leaders of His Church?
3. When did Christ's hidden life come to an end?
4. Who baptized Jesus? Where?
5. What happened at the baptism of Jesus?
6. How did the devil tempt Jesus?
7. Why did Jesus suffer these temptations?
8. What is our greatest help in time of temptation?
9. Where was most of Christ's public life spent?
10. What was Christ's method of teaching?
11. What are some prophecies which Christ made?
12. What virtue did Christ particularly require of men in His preaching?
13. Name some prophecies which Christ fulfilled.

## FOR ME TO REMEMBER

1. Christ was baptized by His cousin St. John in the Jordan River.
2. The three Persons of the Blessed Trinity were sensibly present at the baptism of Christ.
3. Christ set us an example in the way He overcame temptation.
4. Christ chose simple men as His helpers.
5. Christ lived all the things He preached.

## FOR ME TO DO

1. Did Jesus and John prepare for their work in the same way? Explain your answer telling what the work of each was.
2. What could you imitate in the life of St. John?
3. When the devil tempts you, do you act as our Lord did?
4. At what part of the Mass does the priest use the words of St. John? What do they mean? Why is the word "Lamb" used?
5. Does Christ call us as He called the Apostles?
6. What is the one virtue we need more than all others in order to follow Jesus?
7. Look up the Sermon on the Mount in the Bible. Tell why it could be called a lesson in good conduct.
8. The text mentions that Christ's preaching left room for faith. What does this mean?
9. Say a prayer every day that you may learn what God wants you to do and will prepare yourself for your lifework as Christ did.
10. Write a letter to a friend explaining one of Christ's parables or miracles.

**CHAPTER 5**

# Christ Redeems Us by His Passion, Death, and Resurrection

> *"Jesus Christ… suffered under Pontius Pilate, was crucified, died, and was buried."*

LESSON 14

## The Redemption

### Our Redemption by Christ Means Salvation

God the Son did not have to take our human nature and save us. Man had sinned through his own weakness and malice and not because God had neglected him. But God saw the misery sin had brought into the world and was merciful to fallen man. It was His love for us that made Christ, of His own free will, offer Himself to the eternal Father as the victim to atone, or make up, for man's sinfulness. This offering of Himself by Christ to God is the Redemption.

*By the Redemption is meant that Jesus Christ, as the Redeemer of the whole human race, offered His sufferings and death to God as a fitting sacrifice in satisfaction for the sins of men, and regained for them the right to be children of God and heirs of heaven.*

"Hail precious blood flowing from the wounds of our crucified Lord Jesus Christ and washing away the sins of the whole world."

Thus Christ's sacrifice is the cause of our salvation. The Passion of our Lord was the highest and most perfect act of His life. This voluntary offering of His sufferings and death fully paid the debt that mankind owed to God for sin. The payment of this debt meant the difference between heaven and hell for us. If Christ had not suffered, heaven could never be ours.

But did Christ need to suffer as much as He did? Even though the debt was so great, Christ could have paid it by shedding only one tear or one drop of blood. This is told very well in the beautiful hymn of St. Thomas Aquinas in honor of the Blessed Sacrament: "*Adoro Te Devote*" We ought to spend some time thinking over the words of this verse:

> O Loving Pelican! O Jesus, Lord!
> Unclean I am, but cleanse me in Thy Blood;
> Of which a single drop, for sinners spilt,
> Is ransom for a world's entire guilt.

Since every act of Christ had infinite value why did He have to suffer so much? Our Lord suffered as much as He did for several reasons. First, Christ wanted to show us what a terrible evil sin is, and how necessary it is for us to avoid it. Second, He wanted to teach us His way of living, that is, carrying on bravely in the trials of life. He is our model in every type of suffering. Third, He wanted to show us His infinite love.

As we follow our Lord step by step, the truth will become clearer to us. Christ's example not only teaches us the value of willing service of God, but also that the sorrow which we must bear from time to time can easily be made to atone for temporal punishment due to our sins. Suffering borne for Christ can have untold value.

## The Redemption by Christ Fulfills God's Promise

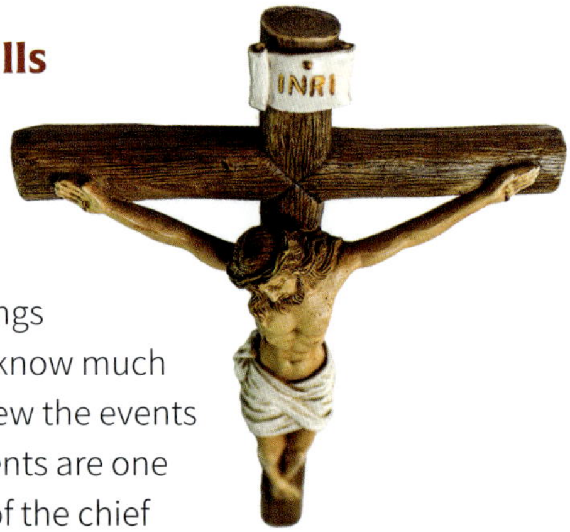


Christ, in His last days on earth, fulfilled God's promise to give mankind a chance to regain heaven. Following the story of Christ and His disciples in the Gospels brings you close to His sufferings. Although you know much of this story, it will be good for you to review the events of our Lord's last days on earth. These events are one part of the great act of Redemption, one of the chief truths mentioned in the Creed.

### The First Palm Sunday

Did you ever stop to think that the most sorrowful and solemn of all the weeks of the year, Holy Week, begins joyfully? There is a note of joy in the ceremony of the palms on Palm Sunday. "Hosanna!" the Church sings. Did this ever strike you as strange?

Christ accepted the honor paid Him by the people on Palm Sunday as a tribute to His divinity. At the same time He knew that according to the prophecy these same people would cry for His blood before the end of the week. This quick change of heart shows the influence of others on our actions. Many of these excited admirers of Jesus turned against Him because they listened to the words of His enemies. We should pray for the courage to do what is right no matter what others may urge us to do.

### Why Palms?

Have you ever wondered why the people laid palm branches on the path before Jesus as he rode into Jerusalem on a donkey? This story of course gives us the name of our feast, Palm Sunday. There are several symbolic features found in the palm. For one, in the Greco-Roman culture, people would lay palms down before a king or military leader after he has returned from battle victorious, thus, the palm became a symbol of triumph, which Jesus would soon do, triumphing over death with his resurrection. More broadly it was a custom done for people whom the people had a great respect for. The palm has also become a symbol of martyrdom, which points to Christ's sacrificial death.

### Two Gifts From the God-Man

Jesus remained near Jerusalem for the rest of the week after Palm Sunday teaching and preparing His followers for the great events to come. The time came when Jesus must make ready for the Great Supper. He told a few chosen Apostles where they were to eat the supper and how to get ready for it. No one was to spoil this last Passover with His beloved disciples. However, Christ knew one of His disciples wanted to betray Him to the Jews. Judas would do this evil deed, but not until after the Last Supper.

The feast of the Passover, as you recall, commemorated the sacrifice and eating of the Paschal Lamb just before the Hebrews escaped from the slavery of Egypt. It also foreshadowed our delivery from sin. The Passover was a very solemn feast for the Jews. The food and the special ways of preparing it had deep meaning. Christ carried out the ceremonies prescribed by the Law to the last detail.

*Above his head was placed the charge against him; it read: "This is Jesus, the King of the Jews."*

MATTHEW 27:37

I·N·R·I

When all the Apostles were reclining at the table, Jesus took a towel, poured water into a basin, and began to wash the feet of His disciples, drying them with the towel. Usually a servant did this service. Jesus did it Himself to teach an important lesson to His twelve chosen followers. The lesson was that of humility; to serve others is never a lowly task. That is why Christ washed the feet of His creatures.

### TERMS TO KNOW

- sublime
- voluntary
- Passion
- service

As the Last Supper went on, the Apostles saw that this was no ordinary feast. Toward the end of the meal, Jesus took bread, blessed and broke it and gave it to His Apostles saying, "Take, this is My body." Then He took a cup of wine and giving thanks, He gave it to them, and said, "This is My blood of the new covenant, which is being shed for many" (Mk. 14:22, 24). These words fulfilled the promise which Christ had made during His public life.

### In persona Christi

We say that the priest acts "in persona Christi", meaning "in the person of Christ."

Christ had planned for His ministry to continue on earth. Men were to take His place. They were to be other Christs, chosen from among ordinary men. They were to be priests, exercising His priesthood. The Apostles were the first priests. With the words, "Do this in remembrance of Me," Christ gave these humble fishermen the power to change bread and wine into His own body and blood. At the Last Supper the Catholic priesthood began.

The Church was to have a human leader. Christ had to prepare this supreme head of His Church. He had taught Peter many lessons during the time they spent together. He had promised that He would make Peter the head of His Church.

At the Last Supper, our Lord reminded Peter that he must trust Him completely. He predicted that before the next day, Peter would deny Him. Peter protested he would never do such a terrible thing. Then Christ told His friends that He would soon die, but promised them that the Holy Spirit would come to them. The Master knew that the Apostles had not understood much of what He had said. He told them, however, that when the Holy Spirit came upon them, they would understand everything.

Christ's Passion was now to begin. We shall review His chief sufferings.

## FOR ME TO REVIEW

*Catechism Lesson*

**451. Q. What does redemption mean?**

A. Redemption means the buying back of a thing that was given away or sold.

**453. Q. Which are the chief effects of the Redemption?**

A. The chief effects of the Redemption are two: The satisfaction of God's justice by Christ's sufferings and death, and the gaining of grace for men.

### Questions and Exercises

*Write 1 to 10 on a paper. After each number write the letter of the answer which matches it in the exercise below.*

| | |
|---|---|
| 1. Redemption | A. all men, women, and children |
| 2. Redeemer | B. the most solemn time of the year |
| 3. Human Race | C. the first pope |
| 4. Salvation | D. the regaining of heaven for all men |
| 5. Passion | E. saving our souls |
| 6. Holy Week | F. city in and near which Jesus spent His last days |
| 7. Jerusalem | G. the day Jesus triumphantly entered the Holy City |
| 8. Passover | H. our Lord Jesus Christ |
| 9. Peter | I. sufferings of Christ |
| 10. Palm Sunday | J. the feast on which the Paschal Lamb was eaten |

## FOR ME TO REMEMBER

1. Jesus Christ redeemed the entire human race.
2. Christ redeemed the world through His Passion and death.
3. Christ paid the debt for Adam's sin.
4. Christ gave us the Holy Eucharist and the priesthood at the Last Supper.

### FOR ME TO DO

1. Plan a panel discussion on: Christ's Part in My Redemption.
2. What is meant by the statement, "There is much wasted suffering in the world"?
3. What lesson about human conduct does the triumphal entry into Jerusalem teach us?
4. Learn and dramatize the ceremonies of the Jewish Passover.
5. What lesson did Jesus wish to teach the Apostles by the washing of the feet?
6. What personal fault did Peter fail to overcome?

LESSON 15

# The Passion

## The Agony in the Garden

After the Last Supper Jesus and the Apostles went to a favorite place of prayer, the Garden of Gethsemane. Here, Christ underwent the most extreme suffering of mind and body. He was taking upon His shoulders the sins of every man and woman ever born. He knew what He would have to suffer to atone for them and He broke out into a bloody sweat. The Apostles, instead of praying with Him, fell asleep. God sent an angel to comfort Christ. After receiving this comfort, Christ made an act of resignation to His Father's will.

> **"Sacred Heart of Jesus, strengthened in Thine agony by an Angel, strengthen us in our agony."**

Jesus then left the Garden and went forth to meet the soldiers who were coming to arrest Him. His heart was heavy as

He saw Judas, the betrayer, leading the approaching mob. How many times, like Judas, we prefer the things of this world to the friendship of Christ. Peter bravely drew his sword and cut off the ear of the servant, Malchus. But Christ rebuked Peter and healed the ear. The Apostles then fled like children who scatter for fear of being blamed for someone else's mischief. They were not strong enough to bear the trial with their Master.

## Insults and Accusations Against Christ

The soldiers led Christ to the high priest. We know how the entire night was spent. The rulers sent Christ from one to another. He listened to their insults and accusations mostly in silence. Pontius Pilate tried to save Jesus by letting the people choose to face either Barabbas, a criminal, or Christ, the Saviour. He was sure they would want Christ freed rather than Barabbas. But the people cried for the blood of Christ, and Pilate ordered our King to be scourged, that is, beaten with heavy whips. This punishment was usually inflicted before a prisoner was crucified. The cruel soldiers took turns in beating Christ, until His body was a mass of bleeding wounds. Then they placed a crown of thorns upon His head, struck it, and mocked Him saying, "Hail, King of the Jews." When the soldiers became tired of tormenting Jesus, Pilate sentenced Him to death because he feared to lose his position if he released Him.

## The Journey to Calvary

*Christ died on Good Friday.* They placed a heavy cross on the bleeding shoulders of our Lord, and He carried it to the place where criminals were executed. Our Lord did not complain. He was eager to bear the cross that would save mankind and give infinite glory to His heavenly Father. Do we accept unpleasant things as tiny crosses that will make us more like Jesus? We all have crosses to bear, the cross of sickness or poverty, the cross of misfortune or disappointment, or the cross of penance. We

They placed a heavy cross on the bleeding shoulders of our Lord, and He carried it to the place where criminals were executed.

only make ourselves unhappy by not accepting willingly the cross God places on our shoulders—for then we carry it alone and without merit.

## The Final Suffering of Christ

*Christ died on Golgotha, a place outside the city of Jerusalem.* Here with a crowd looking on, the soldiers stripped off His garments thereby tearing his sacred flesh. Jesus, the pure Son of

God, suffered this humiliation of nakedness to atone for our sins of impurity.

The willing Victim offered Himself meekly to the soldiers to be nailed to the cross. Hanging here between heaven and earth with outstretched arms Christ offered His final sufferings to His heavenly Father for all men.

***TERMS TO KNOW***

- centurion
- complete
- gibbet
- Golgotha
- merit
- humiliation

To say this all briefly, *the chief sufferings of Christ were His bitter agony of soul, His bloody sweat, His cruel scourging, His crowning with thorns, His crucifixion, and His death on the cross.*

Christ preached His greatest sermon from this cross. We call the brief statements uttered by Christ during His three hours' agony, "The Seven Last Words." If you are unable to list these seven important sentences, you should try to find them in the gospel stories of the Passion.

**Did You Know?**

The hill Jesus was crucified on was called Golgotha, which means, "place of the skull."

"We, therefore, pray Thee help Thy servants: whom Thou hast redeemed with Thy precious blood."

## Christ Dies for Us

The last three hours of agony were finally over. Christ had promised heaven to the good thief; He had given Mary to us as a Mother. With infinite resignation, Christ spoke His final words, "Father, into Thy hands I commend my spirit." Then He died. The great act of Redemption was over. Man was freed from the power of the devil at that awful moment. A man who was God had died to save men. Nature bore witness to this great event by covering the land with darkness, splitting the veil of the Temple in two, and by an earthquake that terrified those who saw the sad events of Calvary.

**"Be mindful, O Lord, of Thy creatures whom Thou hast redeemed by Thy precious blood."**

The silence of death remained on Calvary after Christ had breathed His last. Later the centurion opened Christ's side with a spear, and blood and water flowed from the wound. Then His lifeless body was taken down from the cross, and placed in the arms of His dear grieving Mother. What have these great sufferings meant to each of us? Every one of us can say at least that *the sufferings and death of Christ we learn God's love for man and the evil of sin, for which God, who is all-just, demands such great satisfaction.*

In the Passion we recognize the two natures in Jesus Christ. It was Christ's human nature that suffered, but it was His divine nature and Person which gave every act infinite value. Through the merits gained by Christ, our acts performed in the state of grace and especially out of love for God, are made meritorious for eternity. Our suffering Saviour not only merited God's love for us, but also taught us, how to gain this love.

You know that Christ gives all men a chance to make use of the merits He gained for them on Calvary. Sanctifying grace, which Christ merited for us, is always available to those disposed to receive it. Christ suffered for all. This is a very great truth! Why did Christ suffer and die for us? You remember that redemption means "a buying back." Through His suffering and death, Christ bought back the right to heaven for all mankind. Pause a moment and offer thanks to Jesus crucified. You were a slave and He freed you; a prisoner and He released you—by dying for you.

"Hail saving Victim offered for me and for all mankind upon the gibbet of the cross."

Resolve to be a true follower of Christ. Unite with Him in atoning for your own sins and those of others. Share His sufferings. Do not let Him suffer alone. During Holy Week especially live with Christ in the liturgy of the Church.

## FOR ME TO REVIEW

*Catechism Lesson*

**370. Q. What did Jesus Christ suffer?**

A. Jesus Christ suffered a bloody sweat, a cruel scourging, was crowned with thorns, and was crucified.

**382. Q. On what day did Christ die?**

A. Christ died on Good Friday.

**394. Q. Where did Christ die?**

A. Christ died on Mount Calvary.

**395. Q. Where was Mount Calvary, and what does the name signify?**

A. Mount Calvary was the place of execution, not far from Jerusalem; and the name signifies the "place of skulls." Also called "Golgotha."

**400. Q. What lessons do we learn from the sufferings and death of Christ?**

A. From the sufferings and death of Christ we learn the great evil of sin, the hatred God bears to it, and the necessity of satisfying for it. We also learn of God's great love for mankind.

**Questions and Exercises**

1. Did Jesus complain about His sufferings?
2. Was Jesus glad when Peter cut off the servant's ear?
3. Were the Apostles frightened when they saw the soldiers?
4. Did Pilate try to release Jesus?
5. Explain how we might sometimes act like Peter when he cut off the servant's ear, or like Pilate when he sentenced Christ to death.
6. Was Barabbas freed because he was innocent?
7. Did Christ preach a sermon from the cross?
8. Does Christ's death on the cross prove He hated sin?
9. Does Christ love us?
10. Can we share in the merits of Christ?

## FOR ME TO REMEMBER

1. Every act in the Passion and death of Christ was infinite in value.
2. The suffering and death of Christ are proof of His love for man.
3. The sorrowful mysteries of the Rosary remind us of Christ's sacrifice for us.
4. We can atone for sins by uniting ourselves with Christ in His sufferings, especially in the liturgy of Holy Week.

## FOR ME TO DO

1. Discuss how a good Catholic unites himself to Christ in His sufferings especially by celebrating the last three days of Holy Week with the Church in the sacred liturgy.
2. Write a newspaper article dated the year of our Lord's death. Suggested headline:

   | | |
   |---|---|
   | Death of a Prophet | Body Stolen? |
   | Verdict: Guilty | Emty Tomb |

3. Write a report in the form of an announcement on the Seven Last Words.
4. When did Christ speak during His trial?
5. Why was Christ silent before Herod?
6. Explain how Peter lied, denied his faith, and swore falsely, the night of Christ's arrest.
7. Mention three of Christ's sufferings.
8. On a map of Jerusalem follow Christ during His Passion.
9. Who were the people who tried to comfort Christ along His way to Calvary?
10. Describe the earth at the moment of Christ's death.
11. Who was the rich man who helped bury our Lord?
12. During what week do we especially commemorate Christ's sufferings and death?

LESSON 16

# Christ Renews the Sacrifice of Golgotha in the Mass

## The Sacrifice of the Mass and the Sacrifice of Golgotha Are the Same

The death of our loving Saviour, Jesus Christ, on Golgotha was the key act in our redemption. We remember, that only a divine Person could fully atone for the great wrong done by our first parents, and through this atonement, reopen to us the gates of heaven. God the Father willed that this atonement be made by the death of Christ.

We share in the benefits of this death through the Holy Sacrifice of the Mass. Christ is God. That is why He could tell His Apostles and their successors to do as He had done the evening before His death. They were to take bread and wine and change them into

We share in the benefits of this death through the Holy Sacrifice of the Mass.

His body and blood, the Body that had been slain, the Blood that had been spilt. They were to offer them again and again, day after day, from the rising of the sun to its going down. This is the Mass. Every Mass is the repeated offering of the crucified Christ to the heavenly Father. Thus the sacrifice of Calvary and the sacrifice of the Mass are the same sacrifice, though Calvary was bloody and the Mass is unbloody.

### The Sacrifice of the Mass Has Many Effects

You help to supply the bread and wine by your offertory gift. As the priest offers this bread and wine, put your whole self on the paten. This means your joys, prayers, works, and sufferings. Your little offering is like a drop of water compared to the boundless

> *"Let the entire man be seized with fear; let the whole world tremble; let heaven exult when Christ, the Son of the Living God, is on the altar in the hands of the priest. O admirable height and stupendous condescension! O humble sublimity! O sublime humility! that the Lord of the universe, God and the Son of God, so humbles Himself that for our salvation He hides Himself under a morsel of bread."*
>
> *—St. Francis of Assisi*

ocean of Christ's infinite gift to God. But just as your little drop is lost in the great ocean, so your little gift of self is lost in Christ's infinite gift. Yet you join yourself with Him as He produces the many effects of the Mass.

You join with Him as He gives glory, praise, and thanks to God. You join with Him as He offers satisfaction for sins. You join with Him as He asks God for the graces men need; as He prays for His Church, for sinners, for all men. Indeed you join yourself with Christ as He produces all the effects of the Mass, all the effects of the Redemption.

## We Must Take Part in the Sacrifice of the Mass

Each year we learn to know our religion better. So each year we should learn to appreciate more the chances this religion gives us to increase our store of grace. We know that the greatest prayer we can offer is the Mass, so why not assist at Mass often and devoutly?

During the Mass we should try to keep our minds on the Holy Sacrifice as the renewal of Calvary takes place before us. Using the Missal will help us to follow the Mass along with the priest, but we may also be united with Christ by thinking over

### TERMS TO KNOW

- renews
- atonement
- slain
- bloody
- unbloody
- offertory
- infinite
- boundless
- paten
- participate
- profitable
- Missal

His Passion and death, or by saying the rosary. Receiving Holy Communion with devotion during the Mass makes our sacrifice even more profitable, and increases the grace already existing in our souls.

If we realize what the Mass is, we will be deeply recollected during it. We will not be tempted to misbehave, or to talk and laugh in church. Non-Catholics are often astonished at the large number of Catholics who go to church every Sunday. On the other hand, they are often surprised that other Catholics believe all they say they do about the Mass and yet are so careless about assisting at it. Let us ask God to give us the faith and the courage to attend daily Mass whenever possible. But most of all let us ask Him for the grace of assisting at Mass as Mary assisted at the foot of the Cross, suffering every pain with Christ.

## FOR ME TO REVIEW

**Questions and Exercises**

1. How do we share in the merits of Christ's death?
2. How do we supply the bread and wine for the Mass?
3. What should we place on the paten at Mass?
4. What happens to our gift at the Consecration?
5. What is the greatest prayer we can offer?
6. Why is the Mass more powerful than any private prayer?
7. Who offers each Mass?
8. What is the best way to assist at Mass?
9. Why could Christ tell the Apostles to continue offering sacrifice?
10. How does Christ in the Mass show us He is pleased with our gift?

## FOR ME TO REMEMBER

1. The sacrifice of the Mass and the sacrifice of Golgotha are the same sacrifice.
2. A bloody sacrifice was offered on Calvary; an unbloody sacrifice is offered in the Mass.
3. The Mass is the greatest prayer we can offer.

## FOR ME TO DO

1. How can you show that you realize the value of Holy Mass?
2. Set aside one day of the week besides Sunday on which you will assist at Mass. Be there on time, and try to receive Holy Communion.
3. How do you help supply the bread and wine?
4. Name some ways in which you should assist at Mass.

LESSON 17

# The Resurrection of Christ —a Proof of His Divinity

## Christ Descends Into Limbo

As we knelt in spirit before the tomb of Christ on Good Friday, and in our minds watched the guards seal the stone, the sight should have comforted rather than grieved us. For the sealed tomb is a gateway to the most glorious proof of Christ's divinity, and instead of being sad, we should rejoice with the Son of God. We should rejoice too, with the just people who lived before the coming of Christ. They had waited long for this great day when Christ would lead them to their heavenly home. Do you recall where these just souls were waiting?

In the Apostles' Creed we say that Christ "descended into hell." Do you know what this means? *When we say that Christ descended into hell we mean that, after He died, the soul of Christ descended into a place or state of rest called limbo, where the souls of the just were waiting for Him.* This "hell" was not that of

### The Harrowing of Hell

Christ's descent into hell after his death is often called "The Harrowing of Hell." He went to liberate the just souls who had died before his redemptive resurrection. Since they died before he opened the gates of heaven, they were unable to join God in paradise until Jesus's death and resurrection. Those of us who live now, after the time of Jesus, face judgment right after our death.

the damned, but a place of natural happiness free from torments, yet without the supernatural happiness of heaven. Can you name some of the holy people who were waiting in limbo?

These souls in limbo were looking forward to the reopening of the gates of heaven. They were faithful friends of God who had heard His word and kept it. Their one hope of release from the prison of limbo was the Promised Redeemer. *Christ went to limbo to announce to the souls waiting there the joyful news that He had reopened heaven to mankind.* How happy these souls must have been at the sight of their Master!

*While His soul was in limbo, Christ's body was in the holy sepulcher.* There it remained under guard in the place where the Apostles had laid it after His death.

## Christ Rises From the Dead

Holy Scripture tells us what we know of Christ's resurrection from the dead. One of the most important reasons for the resurrection is this: it shows that Christ is divine. It was the greatest of His miracles, and the one which He foretold as proof of His divine mission. When the Jews asked for a sign from our Lord to show that He came from God, Jesus answered: " 'Destroy this temple, and in three days I will raise it up.' The Jews therefore said, 'Forty-six years

### The Firstborn of the Dead

Jesus has many names: the Christ, the Messiah, King of Kings, Alpha and Omega, the Son of God, the Son of Man. One that most people aren't as familiar with is his title of "first-born of the dead." We get this title from Colossians 1:18, and it refers to how Jesus was the first one to rise from the dead. Some theologians have compared Mary's womb to Christ's tomb; as he was born by natural means from her womb, so he would rise to new life from the tomb on Easter Sunday.

has this temple been in building, and wilt thou raise it up in three days?' But he was speaking of the temple of His body. When, accordingly, he had risen from the dead, his disciples remembered that he had said this, and they believed . . . the word that Jesus had spoken" (Jn. 2:19–22).

The Resurrection of Christ is the most important teaching of the Catholic Church. The Church has realized this from the very beginning, for the great Apostle, St. Paul, wrote to His followers: "If Christ has not risen, vain is our preaching, vain too is your faith" (1 Cor. 15:14).

The New Testament tells us what happened after Christ's resurrection. In the Gospel we read what the angel said to Mary Magdalen and the holy women who had come to the tomb on the third day after the burial of Jesus: "He is not here: He is risen." The same Man who had died on the cross arose from the tomb that first Easter morning. This we learned long ago. Our catechism tells us: *Christ rose from the dead, glorious and immortal, on Easter Sunday, the third day after His death.*

Christ rose from the dead, glorious and immortal, on Easter Sunday, the third day after His death.

***TERMS TO KNOW***

- limbo
- visible
- glorious
- profound
- torments
- immortal
- sepulcher
- hell

There is no mention of Christ's visiting His Mother, but we know that He must have paid her a visit soon after His resurrection. The Gospels, however, do tell us of Christ's appearance to Mary Magdalen. We can imagine her joy in discovering that the man she thought was the gardener was her beloved Master. The Gospels also tell us of Christ's meeting with the holy women, of His journey to Emmaus in company with His disciples, and of His meeting with Peter.

During the forty days after the Resurrection, Christ appeared many times to the Apostles, talking to them, eating and drinking with them. We like especially to recall two of these appearances: first, when Christ entered the Upper Room through closed doors (Acts 1), and second, when He performed the miracle of the fishes on the shores of the Lake of Galilee (John 21). Take a moment and revisit these stories by reading them in your Bible.

## The Resurrection Proves That Christ Is God

Christ wanted to prove that He was what He claimed to be. Coming back to life through His own power, as He predicted, after He was known certainly to be dead, was the supreme proof that He was divine. He also wanted us to understand that death is not the end of all things, but only the beginning. One day we too, if we have been faithful, shall rise from the dead, to begin a new life with Christ in heaven. Let us remember then, that *Christ rose from the dead to show that He is true God and to teach us that we, too, shall rise from the dead.*

The Church teaches us that *all men will rise from the dead, but only those who have been faithful to Christ will share in His glory.* Those who have been unfaithful, and have not repented, will be denied the special privileges reserved for the chosen friends of God. Those who have been faithful will join the company of the angels and will see God face to face forever. The hope

*His appearance was like lightning and his clothing was white as snow. The guards were shaken with fear of him and became like dead men.*

MATTHEW 28:3-4

of one day joining the heavenly hosts who continually praise God, should encourage us to persevere to the end in doing good.

## The Resurrection Is the Greatest of All Miracles

The Resurrection is the greatest of all miracles because Christ raised Himself from the dead as He had foretold He would. No other dead person has ever been able to perform such a miracle. It is true that Lazarus arose from the dead, but it was not through his own power. Lazarus arose at the command of Christ. Besides, Lazarus had to die again later. But Christ arose from the dead never to die again. The God-Man really conquered death and secured for us a share in His victory.

Lazarus arose at the command of Christ.

## The Feast of the Resurrection Ranks as the Highest of All Feasts

While your first choice of feast days may be Christmas, the feast that commemorates Christ's great victory over sin and the redemption of the human race is truly the most important. Easter Sunday gives proof beyond all doubt that Jesus Christ was divine. It assures man of his redemption. The feast of the Resurrection, therefore, holds the central position in the Church year.

The feast of the Resurrection holds the central position in the Church year.

## Christ's Reasons for Remaining on Earth After His Resurrection

Christ remained on earth forty days after His Resurrection to prove that He had truly risen from the dead, and to complete the instruction of the Apostles.

It might seem to us that Christ's resurrection was a fitting end to His life here on earth. Why then did He not return at once to heaven to His Father? Christ did not return to heaven at once for several reasons. By staying on earth after His Resurrection, and by appearing to His Apostles and disciples and even eating with them, Christ proved that He had truly risen and made the Apostles witnesses for Him. To see Him alive after His cruel death was for them a proof beyond doubt that Jesus Christ had truly risen from the dead.

Then too, Christ had some last instructions to give to His Apostles. Now that they had witnessed many of the things foretold by Christ, the Apostles were ready for more profound teachings. The divine Teacher had taught slowly during the three years the Apostles were with Him. The time had finally come to confirm and complete these teachings.

## FOR ME TO REVIEW

*Catechism Lesson*

**401. Q. Where did Christ's soul go after His death?**

A. After Christ's death His soul descended into hell.

**402. Q. Did Christ's soul descend into the hell of the damned?**

A. The hell into which Christ's soul descended was not the hell of the damned, but a place or state of rest called Limbo, where the souls of the just were waiting for Him.

**403. Q. Why did Christ descend into Limbo?**

A. Christ descended into Limbo to preach to the souls who were in prison—that is, to announce to them the joyful tidings of their redemption.

**404. Q. Where was Christ's body while His soul was in Limbo?**

A. While Christ's soul was in Limbo His body was in the holy sepulchre.

**405. Q. On what day did Christ rise from the dead?**

A. Christ rose from the dead, glorious and immortal, on Easter Sunday, the third day after His death.

**1392. Q. In what state will the bodies of the just rise?**

A. The bodies of the just will rise glorious and immortal.

**1393. Q. Will the bodies of the damned also rise?**

A. The bodies of the damned will also rise, but they will be condemned to eternal punishment.

**Questions and Exercises**

1. Where did Christ's soul go immediately after death?
2. Where was Christ's body placed after His death?
3. How have we learned of Christ's Resurrection?
4. On what day did Christ rise from the dead?
5. Who thought Christ was the gardener when she met Him?
6. What did Christ's Resurrection prove?
7. Who will share in Christ's glory?
8. How does the Resurrection rank as a miracle? Why?
9. Why did Christ remain on earth after His Resurrection?
10. How did Lazarus rise from the dead?

## FOR ME TO REMEMBER

1. "Christ descended into hell" means Christ descended into the limbo of the Patriarchs, a place where the souls of the just awaited the Redeemer.
2. The Resurrection is the great proof of Christ's divinity.
3. The Resurrection is the greatest feast of the Church year.
4. The Apostles were Christ's first missionaries.

## FOR ME TO DO

1. Talk about some Old Testament persons who were waiting in limbo for the Redeemer.
2. Why is the Resurrection the greatest of Christ's miracles?
3. Memorize the words of Christ that made the Apostles missionaries. Where are they to be found?
4. Imagine you were one of the persons to whom Christ appeared after He rose from the dead. Write a letter to a friend describing the meeting.
5. Illustrate one of the following scenes: the sealed tomb with the guards before it; the holy women on their way to the sepulcher; Christ and Mary Magdalen; Christ and Peter; Christ in limbo.
6. Report on the Easter vigil service and show how it helps us to know and to live our faith in Christ.
7. What proof do we have that Christ rose from the dead?
8. What is meant by the expression "Death is a beginning"?
9. Which Apostle at first doubted our Lord's Resurrection?
10. What must we do if we want our bodies to rise gloriously at the end of the world?

LESSON 18

# Christ Ascends Into Heaven

## Why Christ Ascended Into Heaven

After spending forty days on earth proving that He had truly risen, and giving further instructions to His Apostles, the time came for Jesus to return to heaven, body and soul, humanity and divinity. In His last talk with His Apostles, Jesus explained to them that it was necessary that He go to prepare a place for them and for us. He told them that, just as He had come from heaven to do a certain work on earth, He now must return to heaven. He also told the Apostles that He would send the Paraclete, the Holy Spirit, the third Person of the Blessed Trinity, who would sanctify them and who would be with them always.

Christ ascended, body and soul, into heaven forty days after His Resurrection.

**TERMS TO KNOW**

- sanctify
- Paraclete
- uplifted
- triumphant

After finishing His talk, Christ led the Apostles up the Mount of Olives overlooking Jerusalem. There He blessed them with uplifted hands, and the Gospel tells us that He "departed from them and was carried up into heaven" (Lk. 24:51).

What feelings must have filled the Apostles as they watched Christ ascend higher and higher until a cloud received Him out of their sight. The gates of heaven were at last opened! The angels joyously greeted their triumphant Lord, who entered, body and soul, by His own power into His heavenly home. The souls from limbo accompanied Him.

*Christ ascended, body and soul, into heaven forty days after His Resurrection.* The day on which we commemorate this event is the Feast of the Ascension, and it is a holy day of obligation.

Let us now turn to the last article of the part of the Creed we are studying. Notice that it says that Jesus Christ sits "at the right hand of God the Father" in heaven, and that "from thence He shall come to judge the living and the dead."

*When we say that Christ sits at the right hand of God, the Father Almighty, we mean that our Lord as God is equal to the Father and that as man He shares above all the saints in the glory of His Father and exercises for all eternity the supreme authority of a king over all creatures.*

## Christ Gives Us the Means to Attain Heaven

Now that we know so much of Christ's life on earth, His sufferings, death, resurrection and ascension, we have many added graces to help us reach our heavenly goal, to see Him forever. God has given us many means to come closer to Him. Prayer is one. Good works another. The best way is to receive the sacraments of Penance and Holy Eucharist frequently and devoutly. The purpose of all these means is to live in communion with God in this life and in the next. We must remember the words of our Lord, "Thy will be done on earth as it is in heaven." Our eternal joy in heaven will be in proportion to our love and union with God on earth. Each life will look unique in its own way, but if it is a life lived well in grace, and according to God's commands, it will be a life of joy and peace, even amidst suffering. The gift of heaven can be experienced in part here on earth, and then only fully after death.

## Christ Will Come Again From Heaven to Judge All Men

We read that as the Apostles watched Christ go up into heaven, two men in white garments suddenly stood by them and said, "Men of Galilee, why do you stand looking up to heaven? This Jesus who has been taken from you into heaven will come in the same way as you have seen Him going up into heaven." These words refer to Christ's coming to judge mankind at the end of the world. What does that mean? *When we say that Christ will come from thence to judge the living and the dead, we mean that on the last day our Lord will come to pronounce a sentence of eternal reward or of eternal punishment on everyone who has ever lived in this world.*

How different will be this second coming! The first time Jesus came to redeem fallen man He appeared meek and

### The Lamb and the Lion

You will hear it often said that Jesus came the first time as a lamb, as a small baby in a humble manger in Bethlehem, but that he will come the second time as a lion on the Day of Judgment. These are not just nice metaphors; they actually come from Scripture. Most of us know that Jesus was referred to as the lamb who takes away the sin of the world by John the Baptist (John 1:29), but in Revelation chapter 5, during a description of the end times, we read about the "lion of the tribe of Judah" coming to conquer. Judah was the Jewish tribe from which Jesus descended, so this quite clearly refers to him. Thinking about Jesus coming as a ferocious lion at the end of the world should not scare us if we are living the way we should, as children of his Church, receiving the sacraments and living in a state of grace. Instead, it should inspire us! We should have confidence in the face of evil knowing we have this Lion leading us into battle.

humble, a little babe in Bethlehem. In His second coming, He will appear mighty and majestic, as a King and a just Judge having power to judge all men. Everyone who has ever lived will stand before Christ on that day to receive a final sentence of reward or punishment.

No one knows exactly when this day will come. We must live each day as though it were our last, so that on the day of judgment we will hear the consoling words of our Lord, "Come, ye blessed of my Father, possess you the kingdom which is prepared for you."

## Christ Has a Purpose in Judging All Men

Let us note two definite reasons for the General Judgment. First, the honor and glory of Jesus Christ will be made known at that time; His supreme power and authority over the universe will be recognized by everyone. Second, at the General Judgment, all men will receive their just reward or punishment, both as individuals and as members of the human race.

If we expect to hear the consoling message that we are saved, we must live this present life according to the teachings of our faith. We must love and serve God and never cut ourselves off from Him by sin. We should often think of the last judgment and prepare each day to meet our just and merciful King.

### FOR ME TO REVIEW

*Catechism Lesson*

**414. Q. After Christ had remained forty days on earth, where did He go?**

A. After forty days Christ ascended into heaven, and the day on which he ascended into heaven is called Ascension Day.

**411. Q. How long did Christ stay on earth after His Resurrection?**

A. Christ stayed on earth forty days after His Resurrection to show that He was truly risen from the dead and to instruct His Apostles.

**419. Q. What do we mean by saying that Christ sits at the right hand of God?**

A. When we say that Christ sits at the right hand of God the Father we mean that Christ as God is equal to His Father in all things, and that as man He is in the highest place in heaven equal to his Father.

**1371. Q. When will Christ judge us?**

A. Christ will judge us immediately after our death, and on the last day.

### Questions and Exercises

1. Who is the Paraclete?
2. What is the name of the mount from which Christ ascended into heaven?
3. How long after the Resurrection did Christ ascend into heaven?
4. What is the day on which Christ ascended into heaven called?
5. What authority does Christ hold over all creatures?
6. How will Christ appear in His second coming?
7. Why will there be a general judgment?
8. What will be the words of reward Christ uses at the last judgment?

9. How did Christ ascend into heaven?
10. What does Christ's Ascension into heaven mean to us personally?

## FOR ME TO REMEMBER

1. Christ had His human body when He ascended to His Father.
2. The final phrase in many prayers "Through Christ our Lord" teaches us that the surest way to God the Father is through His divine Son.
3. Christ is the judge of the living and the dead.
4. "Christ sitteth at the right hand of God the Father" means He is equal to the Father and the Holy Spirit in all things.

## FOR ME TO DO

1. Explain what Christ meant when He said, "In my Father's house there are many mansions."
2. Be ready to explain the need for a second judgment: the general judgment.
3. Explain how your conscience can act as a judge.
4. Find scripture passages about the end of the world and the Last Judgment.
5. How will Christ's second coming differ from His first coming?
6. What is the best way to reach our heavenly goal?

## On the Feast of the Ascension

*Dear Lord Jesus Christ, right before your Ascension into heaven you told your apostles to be His witnesses to the ends of the earth upon receiving the Holy Spirit. May I be similarly inspired to spread your Gospel message in word and deed, according to your will for me. And may I do so prudently and joyfully, with your help, your guidance, and your grace! And remembering this glorious event, help me to seek what is above, heaven, where you are seated at the right hand of God the Father!*

# UNIT 3
# The Holy Spirit and the Church

# CHAPTER 6
# I Believe in the Holy Spirit

*I believe in the Holy Catholic Church, the communion of saints, the forgiveness of sins, the resurrection of the body, and life everlasting. Amen.*

*We now come to the third Person of the Blessed Trinity, the Holy Spirit. We shall study Him in Himself (chapter 6), in the grace He brings, and in His works (chapter 7), especially in the Church (chapter 8).*

*In connection with the power of the Holy Spirit in the Church we shall study the forgiveness of sins, the four last things, and our eternal life with God (chapter 9).*

LESSON 19

# The Holy Spirit Is God, Third Person of the Blessed Trinity

Which Persons of the Blessed Trinity have we studied thus far? Which divine Person remains to be studied? What knowledge do we have of the Holy Spirit? In which prayers have we invoked Him? In which Bible references have we met Him?

Before we begin to learn more about the Holy Spirit let us recite or sing the following hymn that we may gain His grace to help us:

> Come, Holy Spirit, Creator blest,
> And in our souls take up Thy rest,
> Come with Thy grace and heavenly aid,
> And fill the hearts which Thou hast made.

## The Holy Spirit Is God

Long ago we learned that the *Holy Spirit is God and the third Person of the Blessed Trinity.* Who is God? We remember that God is the Supreme Being. He is infinitely perfect. He made all things and keeps them in existence. The Holy Spirit is the third Person in God, the Supreme Being. He, too, is above all creatures. He, too, is the self-existing and infinitely perfect Spirit. He is eternal, all-good, all-knowing, all-present, and almighty. He is all-wise, all-holy, all-merciful, and all-just.

> *"Those whose hearts are pure are temples of the Holy Spirit."*
>
> **—St. Lucy**

Let us make the sign of the cross and thoughtfully pray these words, "In the name of the Father, and of the Son, and of the Holy Spirit. Amen."

Why do we call the Holy Spirit the third Person of the Blessed Trinity? We call the Holy Spirit the third Person of the Blessed Trinity because Christ Himself mentioned the Holy Spirit third when He told the Apostles to baptize ". . . in the name of the Father, and of the Son, and of the Holy Spirit" (Mt. 28:19). We call the Holy Spirit the third Person also because He goes out from, or proceeds from, the Father and the Son.

## The Holy Spirit Proceeds From the Father and the Son

A missionary Father explained to the natives in the Belgian Congo in Africa that in the far North water freezes and becomes like rock so that elephants can walk upon it. The natives shook their heads. They could not understand this, because they had never seen ice. It is even more difficult for us to understand the relations of the three Persons in the Blessed Trinity.

We can never fully understand how the Holy Spirit proceeds from the Father and the Son because this is a supernatural mystery, a truth which our minds can know when God reveals it, but cannot understand even after it has been revealed. Yet we believe it because the Church teaches it. We can, however, learn something about this truth.

God the Father knew that He was God from all eternity. This eternal knowledge was not like a thought of ours, by which, for example, we know a tall tree. Nor was it simply a thought in the mind of God. This eternal knowledge generated or begot a living, distinct Person, God the Son. The two Persons, God the Father and God the Son, loved each other. But this love they had for one another was not like ours, a feeling or a well-wishing. This mutual love of Father and Son is a third person, the Holy Spirit. That is what we mean when we say *the Holy Spirit proceeds from the Father and the Son.* All three Persons are equal; all three are coeternal. And what we must not forget: God is a most pure spirit. He has no body. Our human minds can never completely grasp what He is.

## The Holy Spirit Is Equal to the Father and the Son

Why is the Holy Spirit equal to the Father and the Son? *The Holy Spirit is equal to the Father and the Son, because He is God.* He has the same divine nature as they have.

## Various Names Are Used for the Holy Spirit

In Holy Scripture various names are given to the Holy Spirit. Find some of these titles in the following passages, and discuss what they mean.

"And I will ask the Father and he will give you another Advocate to dwell with you forever, the Spirit of truth whom the world cannot receive, because it neither sees Him nor knows Him. But you shall know Him, because He will dwell with you, and be in you" (Jn. 14:16–17).

### The Paraclete

Did you know this was another name for the Holy Spirit? Have you ever wondered what this funny sounding word means? It is derived from the Greek word parakletos, which means "comforter" or "counselor" or "one called to the side of another." And this is just what the Holy Spirit is. When Christ left to ascend into heaven and sit at his Father's side, the Spirit came to "be at our side" and "comfort" and "console" us. He guides us in the way of truth so that we, too, can join Jesus in heaven.

"Do you not know that you are the temple of God and that the Spirit of God dwells in you?" (1 Cor. 3:16).

***TERMS TO KNOW***

- proceeds
- supernatural
- Advocate
- Consoler
- conversions

What do the titles tell you about the Holy Spirit? As our Advocate, the Holy Spirit pleads for us, protects, assists, and defends us. We may also call the Holy Spirit a Consoler because He consoles us; and an Intercessor because He intercedes for us. As the Spirit of truth, He shows us the truth and protects us in it.

Let us make an act of faith in the Holy Spirit as we find it in the Nicene Creed of the Mass. "I believe . . . in the Holy Spirit, the Lord the giver of life; who proceeds from the Father and the Son, who with the Father and the Son is adored and glorified, who has spoken through the prophets"

## Various Symbols Represent the Holy Spirit

There are some symbols which are often used to represent the Holy Spirit. These will help us to remember Him. Among them are water, fire, wind, the dove, and oil.

Why does water remind us of the Holy Spirit? Without water living things wither and die. Water reminds us of life and freshness. The Holy Spirit brings supernatural life with the waters of baptism and renews and refreshes our souls with grace.

A second symbol is fire. Why does fire remind us of the Holy Spirit? He descended in tongues of fire on the first Pentecost. Fire gives light, warmth, and makes a great change in anything it touches. Like a flaming fire the Holy Spirit kindles fresh light in discouraged hearts, and burns away what is evil. A forest fire is irresistible. So too are Christians who have been genuinely inflamed with the spiritual fire of the Holy Spirit.

Why is wind a symbol of the Holy Spirit? On the first Pentecost there was a sound of a mighty wind as the Holy Spirit came upon the Apostles. The Holy Spirit purifies souls and like a powerful wind sometimes brings sudden conversions.

The dove symbolizes the Holy Spirit because it gives an idea of rest, joy, and gentleness. When did the Holy Spirit appear in the form of a dove?

For which sacraments does the Church use holy oils? Why? Oil softens, strengthens, cures, heals wounds, takes away stiffness, and ignites fire. The Holy Spirit gives joy and strength to souls, softens what is hard, cures, heals, and sets a fire within us.

Say a little "thank you" prayer in your heart to the Holy Spirit. Promise Him that you will remember that He is dwelling in your soul.

When did the Holy Spirit appear in the form of a dove?

## FOR ME TO REVIEW

*Catechism Lesson*

**420. Q. Who is the Holy Spirit?**
A. The Holy Spirit is the third Person of the Blessed Trinity.

**423. Q. From whom does the Holy Spirit proceed?**
A. The Holy Spirit proceeds from the Father and the Son.

**424. Q. Is the Holy Spirit equal to the Father and the Son?**
A. The Holy Spirit is equal to the Father and the Son, being the same Lord and God as they are.

### Questions and Exercises

1. Is the Holy Spirit true God?
2. How does the work of the Holy Spirit prove God's love for us?
3. Why should Catholics practice devotion to the Holy Spirit?
4. Why do we call the third Person of the Blessed Trinity the Holy Spirit?
5. How are we temples of God?
6. How does the Holy Spirit dwell in us?
7. What is the work of the Holy Spirit as our advocate?
8. How is the Holy Spirit mentioned in the Nicene Creed?
9. Why is belief in the Holy Spirit a test of our faith?
10. How could you express your thanks to the Holy Spirit in prayer?

## FOR ME TO REMEMBER

1. We call the Holy Spirit, the Spirit of Truth, the Spirit of God, the Advocate, the Consoler.
2. Water, fire, wind, oil, and the dove are symbols of the Holy Spirit.
3. The Holy Spirit is God, and is equal to the Father and the Son.

## FOR ME TO DO

1. Write a prayer to the Holy Spirit. Use as many names for Him as you understand.
2. Make a symbol of the Holy Spirit and write several sentences to explain it.
3. Write a letter to a younger friend or relative explaining just how the Holy Spirit helps him every day.
4. Make a visit to Christ in the Blessed Sacrament. Ask Him to increase your devotion to the Holy Spirit.
5. Whenever we want to make an important decision we should pray especially to the Holy Spirit. Why?
6. Say the prayer to the Holy Spirit every day.
7. Make a list of the times when you might need the help of the Holy Spirit.

LESSON 20

# The Holy Spirit Dwells in the Church and Sanctifies Souls—Grace

## The Holy Spirit—Source of Life in the Church

Ten days after Christ had ascended into heaven, He sent the Holy Spirit upon the Apostles and disciples gathered together in the Upper Room. At once the Apostles, the first bishops of the Catholic Church, began to preach and baptize. They were not afraid to carry out Christ's command because the Holy Spirit gave them courage. They and their successors have carried out the command of Christ even though they met great hardships and persecutions. The successors of the Apostles will continue to teach Christ's truths until the end of time because the Holy Spirit who came on that first Pentecost day will stay with the Church forever.

**Did You Know?**

Pentecost is considered the birth of the Church.

This is the first work of the Holy Spirit. He abides, or dwells, in the Church. He is the soul of the Church.

Christ established His Church to lead us all to heaven. None of us can get to heaven by our own human powers. None of us can enter heaven unless we are holy. Another big work of the Holy Spirit is to make each one of us holy through the gift of grace. This, then, is His twofold work: *The Holy Spirit dwells in the Church as the source of its life and sanctifies souls through the gift of grace.*

## Grace, a Supernatural Gift

We must now study carefully the important and not easy topic of grace. You have all seen butterflies. Did you ever hear one of them speak? Why can it not speak? It is beyond the nature of a butterfly to speak.

Johnny Jones is an eleven-year-old boy. He has a human nature. What are some of the things Johnny Jones can do? Johnny can think and choose just as the angels can. He can feel, see, hear, touch, and move. Johnny can grow and live like the grass that his father plants on his front lawn. Like a baseball or a stone, Johnny also exists. Johnny is a whole wonderful little world by himself.

Despite all his powers, there are some things Johnny cannot do. No matter what Johnny can do, or think, or invent, he cannot gain supernatural life by himself. Of and by himself he cannot become a child of God. He is a creature. He cannot get grace by himself. It is beyond his human nature. But God can give grace to him as a special gift if He wishes.

God has made Johnny and therefore loves him more than any one of us could even understand. He sent His only Son, Jesus Christ, into the world. Every act and word of Jesus on earth was an eternal, infinite, and divine act because Jesus is God. Every act of Jesus earned eternal, boundless merits for us. Through His death on the cross Jesus paid the full price of our redemption. These merits gained grace for men. The Holy Spirit distributes these graces, to Johnny and to all of us. We call these graces gifts because God gives them freely. Johnny and the rest of us neither deserve them nor can we ever earn them by ourselves. This should help us understand that *grace a supernatural gift of God bestowed on us through the merits of Jesus Christ for our salvation.*

Let us thank God the Father, the Son, and the Holy Spirit for the wonderful gift of grace. When we glance at the crucifix and remember what Christ suffered to earn grace, let us pray, "We adore Thee, O Christ, and we bless Thee; because by Thy holy Cross Thou hast redeemed the world."

## There Are Two Kinds of Grace

*There are two kinds of grace: sanctifying grace and actual grace.* Christ earned both for us and the Holy Spirit distributes them. First let us study carefully what sanctifying grace is and does.

### 1. Sanctifying grace is the supernatural life of the soul.

God can do all things. He can give us a supernatural, divine life by the gift of grace, while at the same time we remain true human beings. St. Thomas Aquinas says that, "By the action of the Holy Spirit we are transformed into gods." Briefly then, *sanctifying grace is that grace which confers on our souls a new life, that is, a sharing in the life of God Himself.*

Do you remember the fairy tale about King Midas who was supposed to have the power of turning into gold everything he touched? The gift of sanctifying grace which the Holy Spirit brings into a person's soul when he is baptized does a far more wonderful thing than this. To the natural life of the soul it adds a supernatural life—a sharing in the very life of God.

To help us to understand what sanctifying grace is, Jesus used a little comparison. He said, "I am the vine, you are the branches. He who abides in me, and I in him, he bears much fruit; for without me you can do nothing" (Jn. 15:5). By grace we live in Jesus, in God. We live by His divine life. Life-giving sap flows from the vine to the branches making them live and produce fruit. Sanctifying grace, like the sap in a vine, brings God's life. When Johnny Jones receives sanctifying grace, he shares in the life that God lives.

With sanctifying grace, the soul of Johnny Jones not only becomes God's dwelling place, it becomes holy and pleasing to God as well. When iron is in fire, it looks like fire, and is as hot as fire. With sanctifying grace Johnny's soul is supernaturally like to God, who is infinitely holy.

Besides, by grace God adopts Johnny into His family. This adoption into God's family is different from the adoption of an orphan child. Adopted children do not resemble their foster parents, but those whom God has adopted actually become like God. Their holiness is a share of God's holiness. They become

God's sons by grace, as Jesus is God's Son by nature. A wonderful inheritance comes with adoption into God's family. This inheritance is the right to heaven.

To put it briefly the chief effects of sanctifying grace are: *first, it makes us holy and pleasing to God; second, it makes us adopted children of God; third, it makes us temples of the Holy Spirit; fourth, it gives us the right to heaven.*

"O Holy Spirit, sweet Guest of my soul, abide in me and grant that I may ever abide in Thee."

Why is sanctifying grace necessary for salvation? Sanctifying grace is necessary because there is no natural power on earth that can help us to get to heaven. We can attain the happiness of heaven only through God's grace which Jesus Christ earned for us and which the Holy Spirit distributes. *Sanctifying grace is necessary for salvation because it is the supernatural life, which alone enables us to attain the supernatural happiness of heaven.*

Sanctifying grace is that grace which confers on our souls a new life, that is, a sharing in the life of God Himself.

### 2. Actual grace is a supernatural help to do good and avoid evil.

The supernatural life of sanctifying grace must be kept alive. Just as we must fight germs and disease if our bodies are to be healthy and live, so also we must fight temptations and sin if we are to have the supernatural life of grace in our souls. To help us to attain or keep supernatural life, the Holy Spirit offers another special supernatural gift called actual grace. The word explains itself. It is the grace that helps us see which acts are good and pleasing to God and urges our wills to choose those good acts and to keep away from evil.

Actual grace is different from sanctifying grace because we have it only for a time. It is a passing help. Sanctifying grace, on the contrary, remains as long as we do not commit mortal sin.

Some holy people, like St. Aloysius, never committed a mortal sin. They had sanctifying grace from the time of their baptism until they died, and they will have it for all eternity.

Actual graces, however, come and go. The Holy Spirit gives us many actual graces all during life. We receive actual grace, for example, when our parents give us good advice, while we are reading good books, when we see others acting kindly and properly, when we are tempted but resist sin , and at many other times. Some actual graces that we have received are a Catholic home, a Catholic education, and the continual presence of Jesus in our churches. *Actual grace is a supernatural help of God which enlightens our mind and strengthens our will to do good and to avoid evil.*

## We Can Refuse or Resist Grace

Have you seen the picture of Christ knocking at a door? When the artist painted this picture he called his friends together to ask them what they thought about it. One of his friends wondered why the door did not have a knob. The artist explained that the door which he had painted represented the human heart. The knob is only on the inside. Each person opens his heart only to the one he chooses to love.

God gives us the grace to let Him in, but He does not force His way into our hearts. God gave us a free will. He will not force His gifts upon us. We can accept them or refuse them. How did St. Peter act when Christ glanced at him as he was warming himself by the fire the night of our Lord's arrest? With what words did Christ offer actual grace to Judas in the Garden of Gethsemani? (Mt. 26:50.) The Angel Gabriel greeted Mary with the words, "Full of grace!" What do you think Mary did with every actual grace that God offered to her?

Can we resist the grace of God? *We can resist the grace of God, for our will is free, and God does not force us to accept His grace.* Do you remember Judas?

It is just as impossible for Johnny Jones to remain in sanctifying grace without the accompanying actual grace as it is for a man to stay alive without breathing. Actual grace helps us keep, develop, and increase the virtues and gifts, and thereby, protects our supernatural life and makes it strong. Therefore, *actual grace is necessary for all who have attained the use of reason, because without it we cannot long resist the power of temptation or perform other actions which merit a reward in heaven.*

A person is considered to have the use of reason when he has reached the age of seven. Some people reach it sooner and others later. The Little Flower must have reached it at the age of three years because later she wrote that from that time on she had never refused Christ a sacrifice. At the age of reason we know the difference between good and evil. It is then that we begin to need actual grace.

**TERMS TO KNOW**

- Pentecost
- inheritance
- successors
- persecutions
- abides
- human powers
- finite
- boundless
- resist
- transformed
- resemble
- original
- merits
- actual
- reason
- attain

*And the angel said to her in reply, "The holy Spirit will come upon you, and the power of the Most High will overshadow you. Therefore the child to be born will be called holy, the Son of God."*

LUKE 1:35

## FOR ME TO REVIEW

*Catechism Lesson*

**435. Q. How was the Church sanctified through the coming of the Holy Spirit?**

A. The Church was sanctified through the coming of the Holy Spirit by receiving those graces which Christ had merited for His ministers, the bishops and priests, and for the souls of all those committed to their care.

**456. Q. What do you mean by grace?**

A. By grace I mean a supernatural gift of God bestowed on us, through the merits of Jesus Christ, for our salvation.

**459. Q. How many kinds of grace are there?**

A. There are two kinds of grace, sanctifying grace and actual grace.

**461. Q. What is sanctifying grace?**

A. Sanctifying grace is that grace which makes the soul holy and pleasing to God.

**475. Q. What is actual grace?**

A. Actual grace is that help of God which enlightens our mind and moves our will to shun evil and do good.

**477. Q. Can we resist the grace of God?**

A. We can, and unfortunately often do, resist the grace of God.

### Questions and Exercises

1. Why does God give us grace?
2. Why should we pray to the Holy Spirit before confession?
3. Some say we should pray to the Holy Spirit especially before tests. Do you agree with him? Why?

4. In what two ways can we increase the supernatural life received at baptism?
5. If we really appreciate sanctifying grace, what resolution would we make?
6. Why should we accept the actual grace God offers us?
7. Name some actual graces you receive every day.
8. Do we sometimes act like the young man to whom Jesus said, "If thou wilt be perfect sell what thou hast and follow me." How did this young man refuse actual grace?
9. Does God force us to accept His grace? How could you prove this?
10. Why is actual grace so important in our daily life?

### Sanctifying Grace or Actual Grace

*Write S on your paper for each phrase that describes sanctifying grace, A for actual grace.*

1) Shares in the life of God.
2) Received first in baptism.
3) Helps one to know right from wrong.
4) Makes one a child of God.
5) Helps one to avoid evil.
6) Helps one to do good.
7) Is lost by mortal sin.
8) Passes when a good deed is performed.
9) Is offered to a person many times a day.
10) Gives a desire to do good.

11) Is the supernatural life of the soul.

12) Makes my soul God's dwelling place.

13) Makes me holy and pleasing to God.

14) Stays at all times until mortal sin is committed.

15) Makes one an heir to heaven.

16) Is given to all to help them to get to heaven.

### Matching

*Number your paper from 1 to 12. After each number write the letter in front of the words in Column One, which best match the explanation in Column Two.*

| Column I | Column II |
|---|---|
| A. Holy Spirit | 1. Not belonging to nature, but above it |
| B. Proceeds | 2. Power to choose |
| C. Grace | 3. Go against, refuse, reject |
| D. Actual Grace | 4. Sanctifier |
| E. Sanctifying Grace | 5. Goes out from |
| F. Supernatural | 6. Always was and always will be |
| G. Use of Reason | 7. Reward |
| H. Resist | 8. Third Person of the Blessed Trinity |
| I. Free Will | 9. Supernatural gift |
| J. Merit | 10. An urge or prompting to do good |
| | 11. Distributor of grace |
| | 12. Power to think |

## FOR ME TO REMEMBER

1. Sanctifying grace is the greatest treasure in the world. We must rather die, like Maria Goretti, than lose it by committing mortal sin.
2. The Holy Spirit gave the Apostles, who were the first members of the Catholic Church, the courage to preach and baptize.
3. We receive grace through the merits of Christ.
4. Sanctifying grace gives us the right to heaven.
5. The Holy Spirit gives us actual graces many times during life.

## FOR ME TO DO

1. Discuss the advantages of living in the state of sanctifying grace.
2. Tell about the descent of the Holy Spirit. Explain how He helped the Apostles and how He helps us every day.
3. Kneel before a crucifix. Look at our Lord and think how His sufferings on the cross brought the Holy Spirit to us.
4. Try to call on the Holy Spirit every day to help you out in some difficulty, however small.
5. How do you prove that you believe your body is a temple of the Holy Spirit?
6. Could you prove that one of the greatest graces is the keeping of our souls in the state of sanctifying grace?
7. Explain how the merits of Christ bring grace to our souls.

LESSON 21

# Prayer and the Sacraments, Especially the Holy Eucharist, Are the Principal Means to Obtain Grace

Since actual grace and sanctifying grace are absolutely necessary for us, how can we obtain these graces from God? *The principal ways of obtaining grace are prayer and the sacraments, especially the Holy Eucharist.*

## Prayer Brings Grace

To speak to God in prayer we need only our mind and our will. No matter where I am, or where I go, or what I am doing I can pray. I can pray anywhere and at any time. When I am in the state of grace God is in my soul. I need only to think of God with love and gratitude, begging forgiveness and asking His help. God will not let even a little prayer go unanswered. The poet Alfred Tennyson once very truthfully stated, "More things are wrought by prayer than this earth dreams of."

To help us pray better we could use some of the following hints. In church it will help to keep our eyes on the tabernacle or a statue. In a more public place, it is helpful to keep our eyes cast down. Kneeling shows our acknowledgment of God's greatness and help us to be humble. An up-right posture at prayer shows reverence, respect, and love.

Some people in the Old and New Testament have spoken so beautifully to God that their conversations have come down to us through long ages, for example, the Psalms of King David. Let us try to talk worthily to God. We need His graces, His gifts, His heavenly home. We want others to get there, too. We want to know the language of heaven even here on earth. But we should learn to talk to God in our own words, too.

## The Sacraments Bring Grace

Another way to obtain God's supernatural gifts, besides prayer, is by receiving the sacraments. Can you name the seven sacraments? Which brings the most grace? The Holy Eucharist brings the most grace because it contains Christ Himself, the source of all grace. Some sacraments give sanctifying grace while others increase it in our soul. Besides sanctifying grace each sacrament also gives sacramental grace which provides special help to achieve the purpose of that sacrament.

We must not forget that the Eucharist is both a sacrament and a sacrifice. We can receive great graces from the Holy Eucharist as a sacrifice just as the good thief did. He prayed devoutly and contritely at the bloody sacrifice on Calvary and entered Paradise that very day. We, too, can assist devoutly at Mass. We can go to Mass every day. When we go to Mass, why should we be on time? Why should we stay for the entire Mass?

Other ways of obtaining grace are by performing good works, and using sacramentals. *Sacramentals are holy things or actions of which the Church makes use to obtain for us from God, through her intercession, spiritual and temporal favors.* God gives us grace when we perform good acts for His honor and our neighbor's good.

The Holy Eucharist brings the most grace because it contains Christ Himself, the source of all grace.

## We Must Be Grateful for the Gift of Grace

### TERMS TO KNOW

- unanswered
- King David
- acknowledgment
- gratitude
- increase
- source
- reverence
- posture
- sacramental
- psalms

Do you recall the story of the five wise and the five foolish virgins? There are many foolish boys and girls who do not realize the value of keeping in the state of grace. We should feel sorry for them because they do not know what they are losing. The wise persons are those who keep in the state of grace. They are wise because even their ordinary good actions, like eating, playing, and sleeping can give them double pay. While they are growing physically they can merit eternal rewards. The greater their love of God is, the more these wise people merit for heaven. They make certain

> *"We know certainly that our God calls us to a holy life. We know that he gives us every grace, every abundant grace; and though we are so weak of ourselves, this grace is able to carry us through every obstacle and difficulty."*
>
> *—St. Elizabeth Ann Seton*

that their acts gain more supernatural merit by daily praying the Morning Offering.

The least that we can do to show our gratitude for the gift of grace is to remain in the state of grace. We should try to increase grace by prayer and by receiving the sacraments, and do everything God wants us to do. There is no limit to the holiness God wants us to strive for, because to each one our Lord has said, "You therefore are to be perfect, even as your heavenly Father is perfect" (Mt. 5:48).

*We can make our most ordinary actions merit a heavenly reward by doing them for the love of God and by keeping ourselves in the state of grace.*

## FOR ME TO REVIEW

*Catechism Lesson*

**1098. Q. Is there any other means of obtaining God's grace than the sacraments?**

A. There is another means of obtaining God's grace, and it is prayer.

**Questions and Exercises**

1. What kind of prayer is most pleasing to God?
2. What is the simplest kind of prayer?
3. Is just reminding ourselves that we are in the presence of God a prayer? How?
4. Why should we receive Holy Communion frequently?
5. How does the Holy Eucharist especially give grace?
6. Does having sanctifying grace in our souls mean the same thing as being free from mortal sin? Explain.
7. How can we receive grace from the Holy Eucharist as a sacrifice?
8. Is overcoming temptation a means of gaining grace? How?
9. What is the best way to show our gratitude for the gift of grace?

## FOR ME TO REMEMBER

1. Receiving the Holy Eucharist is the principal way of obtaining grace.
2. Sacramental grace is a special grace which accompanies each sacrament.
3. We must try to be recollected in prayer; that is, we must try to keep our minds on what we are saying when we talk to God.
4. We should thank God every day for His gift of grace.

## FOR ME TO DO

1. Explain to the class how you can keep in the state of grace.
2. How can you gain grace while you are playing?
3. Assist at Mass more devoutly in thanksgiving for the sacrifice which made grace possible to you.
4. Why do we need God's graces?
5. Compose a prayer to our Blessed Mother in which you ask her to keep you close to her Son through His gift of grace.
6. If you do not already know the prayer to the Holy Spirit, learn it, and say it at least once each day.
7. Read the story of the Wedding Garment (Mt. 22). Explain to the class how it is related to this lesson.

LESSON 22

# The Holy Spirit Also Brings or Infuses Supernatural Gifts—The Theological Virtues, the Gifts, Fruits, and Beatitudes

We have been learning about the Holy Spirit. Who is the Holy Spirit? What is His main work? When Christ told His Apostles He was going to leave them and go to the Father, they were troubled. In order to comfort them He made a promise to them. What was it? Yes, Christ told them He would send them an Advocate, a Comforter. This was the Holy Spirit. Tell the story of the coming of the Holy Spirit. Why did His coming have such a great effect on the Apostles?

## Why is Love the Greatest?

St. Paul mentions the three theological virtues of faith, hope, and love in his first letter to the Corinthians (13:13). Here, he says that "the greatest of these is love." Have you ever wondered why love (or charity) would be considered the greatest of these virtues? Think of it this way. When we get to heaven, we will no longer need faith, because we will see that which we have put our faith in, God himself. Likewise, we will no longer hope for anything; everything we long for will be ours when we are with God. But love remains, and in fact will be increased, when we reach heaven. This is why "the greatest of these is love."

## The Holy Spirit Bestows Theological Virtues on the Soul

*The three theological virtues are faith, hope, and charity.* These virtues make us able to direct our minds and hearts to God. They help us to believe in God, to hope in Him, and to love Him with all our hearts for His own sake, and our neighbor as ourselves for the love of God. These virtues are powers for doing good which are infused or poured into the soul by God. They give our minds and wills *supernatural* power. They come from God as special supernatural helps to lead us back to Him. In order to have merit before God all other virtues must spring from these three.

*These virtues are called theological virtues because they have God for their proper object.* God is the One whom we believe, trust, and love. Although all virtues are directed to God, still, they do not all deal *directly* with Him, as for example, the virtue of justice, which deals directly with what is owed to another. Because faith, hope, and love have God for their object or end they get the name, theological, which comes from the Greek word which means study of God.

We know that this first coming of the Holy Spirit took place on Pentecost. When do we first receive the Holy Spirit? The Holy Spirit comes to us for the first time in baptism. Because His chief work is to make us holy, He brings with Him sanctifying grace. This grace gives us a new life and nature. It gives us a part in the nature of God Himself. It also brings some very wonderful powers that help the soul to produce fruits. These powers are supernatural, that is, they are above our natural capacity of willing, thinking, acting. *The chief supernatural powers that are bestowed on our souls with sanctifying grace are the three theological virtues and the seven gifts of the Holy Spirit.* They help produce the fruits of the Holy Spirit and the beatitudes in our lives. First let us look at the three theological virtues.

## Faith Is the Virtue of Belief

The first supernatural power which sanctifying grace brings is the gift of faith. Faith gives our intellect or understanding the power to know, and to believe in a supernatural way.

Since faith is a gift of God, we can obtain this power to believe only through God's grace. We might say, this virtue impels the soul to believe the truths which God has revealed. Faith is very necessary in the life of every Christian for it is the foundation of all other virtues. Although we do not fully understand the mysteries in the Apostles' Creed, faith makes it possible for us to believe firmly in the Creation, Redemption, and all other doc-

The first coming of the Holy Spirit took place on Pentecost.

trines of the Church. *Faith is the virtue by which we firmly believe all the truths God has revealed, on the word of God revealing them, who can neither deceive nor be deceived.*

We say that faith is the virtue by which we "believe." This means that we do not know or understand completely. A fact, such as "one and one are two," we understand. But through the gift of faith we accept all the doctrines of the Church, all the truths that God has revealed, even though we may not understand them. God cannot deceive. Furthermore, no one can deceive Him. Why not? God is all-knowing. No one can hide anything from Him.

How can we strengthen our faith right now? We develop our muscles by using them regularly; so too, we must develop our faith by frequently making acts of faith. Let us review our Act of Faith as it is written in this text. In this prayer, let us find a definition for the virtue of faith.

We should often thank God for the gift of faith. We can show that we appreciate it by living it in our daily lives. This means that we should see God's loving Providence in everything that happens to us. In the pleasant and unpleasant happenings of the day, let us learn to say, "Thank You, God." What are some daily occurrences that may demand the exercise of our virtue of faith?

When we find it hard to see God's loving plan for us, let us pray, "Lord, increase our faith." Let us also remember, "For he who comes to God must believe that God exists and is a rewarder to those who seek him" (Hebr. 11:6).

## Hope Is the Virtue of Trust

Are we sure of getting what we hope for from human beings: our parents, teachers, friends? How does this hope differ from that which we place in God? When we place our hope in God, we practice the supernatural virtue of hope. The virtue of hope gives our will the supernatural power to put our complete trust in God. It gives us the supernatural habit of firmly trusting God, depending on Him to fulfill His promises. Why? Because He is all-powerful. There is nothing He cannot do. Furthermore, He is faithful to His promises. "Heaven and earth will pass away, but my words will not pass away" (Mt. 24:35).

For what do we hope? The most important thing of course, is our eternal salvation and the means to obtain it. We are certain that God will give us all the means and graces we need to get

Simeon, the prophet, who foretold the great sorrows of our Lady, is an excellent example of the practice of the virtue of hope. God had made a promise to him. Simeon waited many years before he saw the promised Redeemer. A legend says that he was so overjoyed at having seen Jesus that he died that very day.

to heaven. Why, then, do some people go to hell? They go there because they neglect or refuse to use the means to get to heaven, which are prayer and the sacraments.

Often we hear people say, "I have no confidence in myself." If these people practiced the virtue of hope, they would realize that with God's help they can do all things. St. Paul said, in the midst of most difficult work, "I can do all things in him who strengthens me" (Phil. 4:13). We know, too, from our own experience that if we really believe people are truthful, we are confident that they will keep the promises they make to us. Certainly God is more worthy of our trust than any human person. Therefore, we should seek God's help in everything we do. We should try to be patient and brave, for *hope is the virtue by which we firmly trust that God, who is all-powerful and faithful to His promises, will in His mercy give us eternal happiness and the means to obtain it.*

We have all heard the saying, "While there is life, there is hope." In eternity there is no need for hope. Why is there no hope in heaven? In hell?

Because we can strengthen ourselves in the practice of the virtue of hope by frequently making acts of hope, let us review, at this point, the Act of Hope so that we know it by heart.

## Charity Is the Virtue of Love

Before beginning the study of the third theological virtue, let us ask ourselves some very important questions. Why did the second Person of the Blessed Trinity live on earth for thirty-three years? It is because God loves us infinitely that He became man. Why do so many missionaries leave their native lands to live in a foreign country among people whom they do not know? Why do so many priests and religious leave everything that is dear to them? It is charity, or love of God and neighbor, that prompts these people to make such heroic sacrifices.

There are many saints whose lives are outstanding examples of the practice of the virtue of love. You remember how much St. Maria Goretti loved God. When a cruel death threatened her, she would not turn her back on Him. Again and again she repeated the prayer, "My God, I love Thee." Are we willing to suffer anything rather than commit a mortal sin? Is our charity equal to hers?

The virtue of charity gives our wills the supernatural power to love God and our neighbor in a supernatural way. The virtue of love is a supernatural gift which accompanies sanctifying grace. It has nothing to do with our feelings, which are natural. We may not like a certain individual, but by exercising this supernatural gift of love we can truly say that we love him because he is our neighbor and a child of God like ourselves. We wish him well because God made him to His own image and likeness. We must even love those who treat us unjustly because our Lord said, "Do good to those who hate you" (Mt. 5:44).

**The following definition for the virtue of charity may help us to understand it better and lead us to practice charity toward God and men. *Charity is the virtue by which we love God above all things for His own sake, and our neighbor as ourselves for the love of God.***

We can increase the virtue of charity by receiving the sacraments. How can we strengthen this virtue when we are in the state of grace? Every time we have kind thoughts, every time we speak kind words, every time we perform good deeds for someone, realizing we are doing them for the love of God, we can strengthen the virtue of charity. But we must remember that the motive is an important thing in any of our actions. What does "motive" mean? The motive of an act means the reason why we do that act. For example: two students may perform the very same kind deed; one may greatly strengthen the virtue of charity by his action and the other may not. How can this happen? The motive or reason why we perform an action is important.

### TERMS TO KNOW

- Advocate
- partake
- theological
- legend
- doctrines
- confidence
- revealing
- virtue
- deceive
- proper object
- motivate
- motive

## FOR ME TO REVIEW

*Catechism Lesson*

**468. Q. Why are faith, hope and charity called virtues?**

A. Faith, hope and charity are called virtues because they are not mere acts, but habits by which we always and in all things believe God, hope in Him, and love Him.

**469. Q. What kind of virtues are faith, hope and charity?**

A. Faith, hope and charity are called infused theological virtues to distinguish them from the four moral virtues— prudence, justice, fortitude and temperance.

**465. Q. What is faith?**

A. Faith is a divine virtue by which we firmly believe the truths which God has revealed.

**466. Q. What is Hope?**

A. Hope is a divine virtue by which we firmly trust that God will give us eternal life and the means to obtain it.

**467. Q. What is charity?**

A. Charity is a divine virtue by which we love God above all things for His own sake, and our neighbor as ourselves for the love of God.

**Questions and Exercises**

1. How do we partake of the nature of God?
2. Why is faith necessary in the life of every Christian?
3. How should we develop our faith?
4. When is hope a supernatural virtue? When is it a natural virtue?
5. How do we practice the virtue of hope in our daily lives?
6. Why is there no need for hope in heaven?
7. What do we mean when we say we must love our neighbor as ourselves for the love of God?
8. Why should we pray for our enemies?
9. What does the word "neighbor" mean?
10. What motive, or reason, should we have for all we do?

## FOR ME TO REMEMBER

1. The three theological virtues are faith, hope, and charity.
2. The Holy Spirit infuses the theological virtues into our souls at baptism.
3. We cannot truly love God unless we love our neighbor.
4. Even the most difficult task can be performed with God's help.
5. Through the gift of faith, we believe all that God has revealed even though we cannot always understand it.

## FOR ME TO DO

1. Compose an Act of Love including love of God and neighbor.
2. How is love of neighbor a proof of our love for God?
3. After receiving Holy Communion say a special prayer to our Lord, asking Him to increase your faith, hope, and love.
4. Recall the story of Jesus and St. Peter when Jesus asked Peter three times if he loved Him. Show what lesson you can take from this Gospel.
5. Find and explain the symbols of faith, hope, and charity. Draw them.
6. Why can the supernatural power to believe be given only by the grace of God?
7. What is the difference between knowing and believing?
8. What are some of the truths of our religion which we believe without understanding them fully?
9. What are some ways in which we can increase and strengthen the theological virtues?
10. Why is charity called the queen of virtues?

## Act of Love

*O Lord God, I love you above all things and I love my neighbor for your sake because you are the highest, infinite and perfect good, worthy of all my love. In this love I intend to live and die. Amen.*

LESSON 23

# The Holy Spirit Bestows His Seven Gifts

## The Seven Gifts of the Holy Spirit

Besides the three theological virtues which we receive with sanctifying grace we also receive seven other gifts. These gifts provide additional assistance which helps us to live a life of grace. Since they come with sanctifying grace, they can be lost through mortal sin. We can strengthen and increase the gifts by using them.

*The seven gifts of the Holy Spirit are: wisdom, understanding, counsel, fortitude, knowledge, piety, and fear of the Lord.* Four of these gifts, wisdom, understanding, counsel, and knowledge enlighten our minds, that is, they help us to understand God's will. The other three, fortitude, piety, and fear of the Lord, strengthen our will and help us to heal the wounds of sin in our souls.

> The seven gifts of the Holy Spirit are: wisdom, understanding, counsel, fortitude, knowledge, piety, and fear of the Lord.

In a general way, then, *the gifts of the Holy Spirit help us by making us more alert to discern and more ready to do the will of God.* "Now we have received not the spirit of the world, but the spirit that is from God, that we may know the things that have been given us by God" (1 Cor. 2:12). Let us now learn something about each gift of the Holy Spirit.

### Wisdom

We all like stories from the life of Christ. In the story of Mary and Martha, Christ said, "Martha, Martha, thou art anxious and troubled about many things; and yet only one thing is needful. Mary has chosen the better part, and it will not be taken away from her" (Lk. 10:41–12). What did our Lord mean by the better part? Had Mary shown real wisdom?

Wisdom, we know, helps us to put first things first; to think about eternal truths, to place a correct value on our salvation, and to love the things of God. Isn't this what Mary was doing? That is what our Lord meant by the best part.

People often say, "Put first things first." The gift of wisdom helps us to know that the first things, that is the most important things, are the things of God because He made us and we are His creatures. Our Christian sense of values should lead us to choose the things that will help us toward salvation rather than those which might lead us to sin.

### Understanding

Pope Pius XI once had an audience with a group of pilgrims. As he was passing among the group, his eyes fell on a blind boy. He paused before Him and raised his ring to the boy's lips. Immediately the blind boy sensed what was happening. His lips trembled and his eyes filled with tears. Sympathetically, the Pope told the boy that his blindness was only physical and that we all experience spiritual blindness when we consider the truths of religion.

Only the Holy Spirit can help us to understand the teachings of the Church. It is His gift of understanding that helps us grasp in a small way an explanation of the meaning of the mysteries of faith.

God gives us the means to increase the gift of understanding. Some of the means are: listening attentively to sermons, earnestly studying our religion, and reading good Catholic books, magazines, and pamphlets. Can you think of other ways?

The better we understand our religion, the more capable we are of helping to spread God's kingdom here on earth. St. Thomas and St. Augustine, great doctors and teachers of the

Church, used this gift of understanding to draw others to Christ and to increase the honor and glory of God.

### Counsel

Counsel is the gift by which the Holy Spirit helps us to make wise decisions and puts us on our guard against the attacks of the devil. Our Lord told many parables while He was on earth to explain how we are to use the gift of counsel. He gave us His own example on how to meet the attacks of the devil at the time He was tempted in the desert.

In one of His parables He said that the Kingdom of Heaven is like a treasure which a man found in a field. He then hid the treasure. He was so happy at finding such a treasure that he sold all he had to buy the field.

Again Christ said the Kingdom of Heaven is like a precious pearl. A merchant seeking for precious pearls found one. At once he sold everything he had to get money to buy the precious pearl.

We, too, using our gift of counsel, can ward off the deceits of the devil and the world. We can choose those things that are going to lead us on the way of eternal salvation and give greater glory to God. We can give up the things that are of little value in order to win heaven.

### Fortitude

Fortitude is the gift of firmness of soul in bearing all difficulties. It is the gift of the Holy Spirit which helps us to practice constant patience and self-denial, to withstand persecution, and to carry out good resolutions regardless of the difficulties we may meet. We might call it spiritual bravery.

There are many examples of the practice of fortitude in the lives of the saints. One story is that of St. John Nepomucene. Over 500 years ago, King Wenceslaus IV of Bohemia appointed St. John as court preacher. Recognizing St. John's holiness, Queen Johanna chose him as her confessor. The King became madly jealous of his wife. One day he summoned St. John and demanded that he repeat what the Queen had told him in confession. Without hesitation, the confessor refused the King's request. The King, thinking he could win over St. John, promised him honors and riches. Seeing that this had no effect on the Saint, he began to threaten him, and finally imprisoned and tortured him on the rack. Still the priest remained firm in his refusal. Then the King granted him freedom. St. John spent this time preparing himself for the death he was sure would follow.

Several days later the King saw St. John walking in the garden. He called him and again tried to get him to reveal the Queen's confession. Because St. John would not do so, the King condemned him to death. At the King's command, soldiers put a wooden gag into the saint's mouth, bound his hands and feet, and threw his body into the river at night. A bright light appeared and surrounded the body as it floated. By means of this light the Christians on the shore were able to find the body and give it Christian burial.

Many years later they opened the casket, and found only the tongue of the Saint. The rest of the body had decayed. God has preserved his tongue because St. John practiced great fortitude in keeping the seal of confession.

Although most of us will never have to practice fortitude in the heroic degree of St. John, we have many opportunities during the day to practice this virtue. Can you mention some? How can we be practicing fortitude right now? Are Catholics in other countries practicing fortitude in a heroic degree?

## Knowledge

The gift of knowledge helps us to recognize the things that will lead us to salvation. It assists us in using everything we meet in this world to help us to get to heaven.

The great St. Dominic, while still a youth, was a university student during a famine. In order to give a little help to the starving people, Dominic sold all of his furniture. Realizing that the people still needed help, he sold his most precious possession, his books. When a fellow student visited him he saw the empty bookshelves.

"What sort of knowledge should I get out of dead books," said Dominic, "while living men, brethren of mine, are dying of hunger?"

True knowledge is knowledge of God's will. Let us pray for true knowledge in this little prayer, "Teach me, O Lord, to do Thy will, for Thou art my God."

### Piety

St. Thérèse of Lisieux, a saint of our times, taught us much about the gift of piety. In her "little way" she always tried to please God by giving Him as much love as possible. "From the age of three, I have not refused the good God anything," she said. How many of us are able to say the same thing? Do our lives show that God and His interests are important to us? If we try to please God more and more, we are using our gift of piety. This gift helps us at all times to find joy in humble prayer and in performing our actions only to please God.

### Fear of the Lord

Fear of the Lord is a reverence for God which leads us to avoid offending our loving Father. St. Rose of Lima, the first canonized saint of the New World, was a very beautiful child. She feared that it might cause her to become vain. To prevent this, she cut off her curls. Thus she was willing to sacrifice a natural gift to prevent an offense against God.

"Fear of the Lord is the beginning of wisdom," says the scripture. The thought of God's justice in rewarding good and punishing evil is a wholesome thought. There is a saying that the thought of hell has filled heaven. Christ Himself often mentioned hell and God's eternal punishment to His listeners.

## Understanding Fear of the Lord

The gift of the Holy Spirit "fear of the Lord" is often misunderstood. It does not mean fear like when we are afraid of something. This sort of fear is more an "awe" or amazement in the awesome power and might of God. It is having such a reverence for him that we do not want to offend or disappoint him.

## The Virtues and Gifts Help To Produce the Twelve Fruits of the Holy Spirit

*Some of the effects in us of the gifts of the Holy Spirit are the fruits of the Holy Spirit and the beatitudes.* The fruits of the Holy Spirit carry a reward even here on earth, in the peace of soul which we enjoy when we practice the virtues. *The twelve fruits of the Holy Spirit are: charity, joy, peace, patience, kindness, goodness, long-suffering, mildness, faith, modesty, continency, and chastity.*

**Fruits of the holy spirit**

| | |
|---|---|
| 1. Charity | Love of God and neighbor |
| 2. Joy | Happiness of mind and heart in serving God; realization of God's goodness |
| 3. Peace | The tranquility which comes from a well ordered soul |
| 4. Patience | Calmness in trials and troubles |
| 5. Kindness | Sweetness of temper and disposition; gentleness |
| 6. Goodness | Wishing, thinking, and doing what is right |
| 7. Long-suffering | Calmness or patience in long trials |
| 8. Mildness | Meekness and forbearance |
| 9. Faith | Belief in all the truths God has revealed |
| 10. Modesty | Reverence of self; acceptance of praise in a balanced way |
| 11. Continency | Control of anger, impatience, evil desires and actions |
| 12. Chastity | Purity of soul and body |

## The Theological Virtues and the Seven Gifts Help Produce the Eight Beatitudes

Another effect of the gifts of the Holy Spirit is mentioned in Christ's Sermon on the Mount. Great crowds of people came to hear Christ. When He saw the multitude so eager to learn, He began to teach them the rules of conduct which lead to true happiness. We call them the eight beatitudes.

**The eight beatitudes are:**

1. Blessed are the poor in spirit, for theirs is the kingdom of heaven.
2. Blessed are the meek, for they shall possess the earth.
3. Blessed are they who mourn, for they shall be comforted.
4. Blessed are they who hunger and thirst for justice, for they shall be satisfied.
5. Blessed are the merciful, for they shall obtain mercy.
6. Blessed are the clean of heart, for they shall see God.
7. Blessed are the peacemakers, for they shall be called children of God.
8. Blessed are they who suffer persecution for justice' sake, for theirs is the kingdom of heaven (Mt. 5:3–10).

God expects us to co-operate with grace and to produce within ourselves the fruits of the Holy Spirit. In the Gospel He tells us, "Every tree that does not bear good fruit is cut down and thrown into the fire" (Mt. 7:19).

Besides using these gifts as a means to gain our own salvation, God wants us to use them to attract others into His fold. The power of example is great. We should use as our motto the saying, "Don't go to heaven alone." We never know when our smallest act may influence others and lead them to eternal happiness. Let us pray many times, "Sacred Heart of Jesus, let me love Thee and make Thee loved."

## FOR ME TO REVIEW

*Catechism Lesson*

**699. Q. Which are the gifts of the Holy Spirit?**
A. The gifts of the Holy Spirit are wisdom, understanding, counsel, fortitude, knowledge, piety, and fear of the Lord.

**700. Q. Why do we receive the gift of fear of the Lord?**
A. We receive the gift of fear of the Lord to fill us with a dread of sin.

**701. Q. Why do we receive the gift of piety?**
A. We receive the gift of piety to make us love God as a Father, and obey Him because we love Him.

**702. Q. Why do we receive the gift of knowledge?**
A. We receive the gift of knowledge to enable us to discover the will of God in all things.

**703. Q. Why do we receive the gift of fortitude?**
A. We receive the gift of fortitude to strengthen us to do the will of God in all things.

**704. Q. Why do we receive the gift of counsel?**
A. We receive the gift of counsel to warn us of the deceits of the devil, and of the dangers to salvation.

**706. Q. Why do we receive the gift of understanding?**
A. We receive the gift of understanding to enable us to know more clearly the mysteries of faith.

**707. Q. Why do we receive the gift of wisdom?**
A. We receive the gift of wisdom to give us a relish for the things of God, and to direct our whole life and all our actions to His honor and glory.

*Blessed are the peacemakers,*
*for they will be called children of God.*

**MATTHEW 5:9**

**719. Q. Which are the twelve fruits of the Holy Spirit?**

A. The twelve fruits of the Holy Spirit are charity, joy, peace, patience, kindness, goodness, long-suffering, mildness, faith, modesty, continency, and chastity.

**708. Q. Which are the Beatitudes?**

A. The Beatitudes are:

1. Blessed are the poor in spirit, for theirs is the kingdom of heaven.
2. Blessed are the meek, for they shall possess the land.
3. Blessed are they that mourn, for they shall be comforted.
4. Blessed are they that hunger and thirst after justice, for they shall be filled.
5. Blessed are the merciful, for they shall obtain mercy.
6. Blessed are the clean of heart, for they shall see God.
7. Blessed are the peacemakers, for they shall be called the children of God.
8. Blessed are they that suffer persecution for justice' sake, for theirs is the kingdom of heaven.

***TERMS TO KNOW***

- spiritual blindness
- eternal salvation
- natural gifts
- self-denial
- discern
- audience
- alert
- beatitudes
- physical
- pilgrims
- deceits
- enlighten

**Questions and Exercises**

1. How are the seven gifts of the Holy Spirit lost?
2. What is the best way to strengthen and increase the seven gifts?
3. Give an example from daily life showing how you use each of the seven gifts.

4. To whom especially should we pray to understand the teachings of the Church?
5. Why is there such great need for every Catholic to understand his religion?
6. How do the little acts of self-denial we practice every day help us gain the gift of fortitude?
7. What other virtues besides fortitude did St. John Nepomucene practice? What lesson does that teach us?
8. "True knowledge is knowledge of God's will." Explain in your own words what this means and tell how it applies to you.
9. How do we use the gift of piety?
10. What is meant by peace of soul? How can we obtain it?
11. How can we be poor in spirit?
12. How can we apply to ourselves the quotation from the Gospel, "Every tree that does not bear good fruit is cut down and thrown into the fire"?

### Matching

*Number your paper from one to seven. Write the letter of the word in Column One which is explained in Column Two.*

| Column I | Column II |
|---|---|
| A. Wisdom | 1. Helps me to avoid sin through fear of offending God. |
| B. Understanding | 2. Helps me to love the things of God. |
| C. Counsel | 3. Gives me strength and courage to resist temptations. |
| D. Actual Grace | 4. Sanctifier |
| E. Knowledge | 5. Shows me how to offer due worship and service to God. |

| | |
|---|---|
| F. Piety | 6. Puts me on guard against the deceits of the devil. |
| G. Fear of the Lord | 7. Helps me to distinguish rightly between what I should and should not believe, and shows me what God wants me to do. |

## FOR ME TO REMEMBER

1. The Holy Spirit infused the seven gifts into our souls at baptism. These gifts are increased at confirmation.
2. When we use the seven gifts they produce the twelve fruits of the Holy Spirit.
3. The eight beatitudes are rules of conduct which form a perfect Christian character.

## FOR ME TO DO

1. Write a letter to a friend. In it explain how the seven gifts of the Holy Spirit help us.
2. Prepare a report on the Gifts of the Holy Spirit. Show how the use of these gifts results in the fruits of the Holy Spirit and the Beatitudes.
3. Make a chart of the twelve Fruits of the Holy Spirit. Using the chart give a talk to the class showing how each of these twelve fruits can be applied to our daily life.
4. Find saints to exemplify each of the Beatitudes.
5. Explain how a person who is wealthy can be poor in spirit.
6. Explain how a person who has little material wealth might not be poor in spirit.

LESSON 24

# The Holy Spirit Also Bestows Moral Virtues

*Besides the theological virtues of faith, hope, and charity there are other virtues, called moral virtues.* The theological virtues and the moral virtues in our souls grow more intense with every increase of sanctifying grace. These virtues become easier to exercise each time we practice them.

While the theological virtues deal directly with God, the moral virtues have to do with created things. *These virtues are called moral virtues because they dispose us to lead moral, or good, lives by aiding us to treat persons and things in the right way, that is, according to the will of God.*

A moral virtue or action may be either natural or supernatural. For example, a man pities a beggar. He gives him some money because he feels sorry for him. Was this a natural or a supernatural act? On another occasion he gives help to a beggar. This time, however, the man is in the state of grace and he looks upon the beggar as his brother whom Christ has redeemed. He gives the beggar alms because he knows Christ commanded him to love his brother as himself for God's sake. In this case his act is supernatural. He practiced divine charity, Christlike charity.

In order to gain merit for heaven a good act must be supernatural. It must be performed while in the state of grace.

A natural moral virtue can have only a natural reward. However, moral virtues, when performed in a state of grace and with the intention of pleasing God, increase our union with God in this life, and enable us to enjoy Him more fully in heaven. Such actions are moral supernatural virtues.

*The chief moral virtues are prudence, justice, fortitude, and temperance; these are called cardinal virtues.*

*These virtues are called cardinal virtues because they are like hinges on which hang all the other moral virtues and our whole moral life. The word "cardinal" is derived from the Latin word "cardo" meaning hinge.*

Let us learn the nature of these four moral virtues.

*Prudence disposes us in all circumstances to form right judgments about what we must do or not do.*

*Justice disposes us to give everyone what belongs to him.*

*Fortitude disposes us to do what is good despite any difficulty.*

*Temperance disposes us to control our desires and to use rightly the things which please our senses.*

## Prudence Is Knowing What To Do or Not To Do

This virtue does two things. It helps us to see clearly what is right and what is wrong. It also helps to find the best means to do good and avoid evil.

Prudent boys and girls are those who not only "use their heads" but also pray that they may do good and avoid evil. Prudence tells us to think before we act. It urges us to seek the advice of our parents, priests, and teachers before we decide on important actions.

If we are prudent and know that certain persons, places, or things are occasions of sin for us, or cause scandal to others, we avoid them. If it is our habit to come late for Mass, prudence would lead us to set the alarm ten or fifteen minutes earlier or have someone call us.

Some good words to remember are the words of the Psalmist: "Your ways, O Lord, make known to me; teach me your paths" (Ps. 24:4).

## Justice Is the Habit of Being Fair To Everyone

First, justice is being fair to God: We must love, and serve God. We must worship Him as the Supreme Being both in private and in public. We should make every effort to keep His commandments, to pray to Him, and to do penance for having offended Him by our sins.

Second, justice is being fair to our neighbor: God gave us parents to love, reverence, and obey. He wishes us to be respectful, obedient, and loyal to our priests, teachers, civil authorities, and all others whom He has placed over us. He wants us to study well and be honest in our schoolwork. He expects us to be kind, just, and honest with our companions. He expects us to play fair and observe the rules in our games and social activities. He expects nations, like neighbors, to practice justice among themselves.

Third, justice is being fair to ourselves. We must be just to ourselves by taking care of our spiritual and physical health, by mixing play with work, and by being truthful, pure, and honorable in all our actions.

Justice demands that we respect and protect all God-given rights of man such as those that are written in our just laws.

Fortitude is the virtue which overcomes fear and directs our conduct to endure difficulties for God.

There was peace in King Solomon's kingdom because he insisted that every man be given his just due. Let us ask God to help us to be just in every way, especially to Him.

## Fortitude Is Strength in Doing Hard Things

Fortitude is another word for strength. It is the virtue which overcomes fear and directs our conduct to endure difficulties for God. We need courage in our striving toward salvation. We must pray for it. It takes strength from God to obey, to be truthful, to be patient, to suffer disappointment, sickness, and the like, and to resist temptation.

In one of his letters, St. Paul tells us about his difficulties and hardships (2 Cor. 11:22–31). He triumphed over all his troubles, however, and died a martyr. It is heroic to overcome difficulties for God. Christ said about such conduct, "Therefore, everyone who acknowledges me before men, I also will acknowledge him before my Father in heaven" (Mt. 10:32) and again, ". . . he who loses his life for my sake, will find it" (Mt. 10:39). When we need to be brave during temptation, trouble, or sickness, or when problems face us, let us ask the Holy Spirit for this gift of strength.

> *"Temperance is simply a disposition of the mind that sets bounds to the passions."*
>
> *—St. Thomas Aquinas*

## Temperance Is the Habit of Control of Self

Everything which God made is good, but sometimes men make bad use of the things He created. They overeat or overdrink and in other ways misuse His gifts, and thus break His laws. Temperance means not going too far in anything. It helps us to control our habits of eating, drinking, speaking, dressing, playing, and working.

Temperance is not easy. Yet with practice and God's grace, this moral virtue will bring much joy to our lives. Resisting excess gives rise to a more authentic happiness in our souls––the happiness of a life lived well in Christ.

Let us imitate the Blessed Virgin and good St. Joseph who practiced the supernatural moral virtues perfectly.

## Other Moral Virtues

There are also other moral virtues which the Holy Spirit gives to us. Besides the cardinal virtues, *some of the other moral virtues are: Filial piety and patriotism, which dispose us to honor, love, and respect our parents and our country.* Charity, however, commands us to think of others also. We should be able to see good in every human being and to wish for the welfare of all other nations as well as our own. Our charity should therefore be universal and exclude no one. Only then is it Catholic.

We remember Tobias, the younger, particularly for his filial piety, because he obeyed his father in all things and had a great reverence for him.

### *TERMS TO KNOW*

- moral
- interior
- civil authorities
- dispose
- patriotism
- cause of scandal
- virtue
- limitations
- welfare of other nations
- liberality
- meritorious

Under justice we consider the virtue of *obedience, which disposes us to do the will of our superiors.* By this we mean that it helps us obey those who have a right to command us or who have responsibility for us, as our parents, teachers, priests, and others. We should train ourselves to do what they command us promptly and cheerfully. Christ is the Model of obedience. It made no difference whether He was to help His mother in the house or His foster father in the carpenter shop. In doing their will He realized He was doing the will of His Father in heaven. He obeyed completely and lovingly even to the death on the cross.

Under justice also comes truthfulness or honesty, *which disposes us to tell the truth.* We need not tell everything we know. In fact there are times when we should not tell what we know. But we should always be truthful because we are children of God who is Truth itself. The boy Samuel practiced the virtue of honesty. Although greatly frightened, he told Heli, the high priest, that God was about to punish his two sons.

Justice also includes *liberality, which disposes us rightly to use worldly goods.* We should always be ready to give generously to those in need. Many American boys and girls give some of their spending money to the missions. Their parents give clothes to those who are needy. Some families share their homes with orphan children. They help the poor; make their holidays cheerful. These people know that what they give and do for the poor, they give and do to Christ.

A part of the virtue and gift of fortitude is *patience, which disposes us to bear up under trials and difficulties.* Job practiced the virtue of patience. God had blessed him with wealth, friends, a good family, and many other things which make life enjoyable on this earth. To try Job, however, God allowed the devil to take all these good things away from him and replaced them with sorrow and suffering. But despite his misfortune, Job did not complain. He continued to praise God (Job 19:25–26).

Temperance includes *humility, which disposes us to acknowledge our limitations.* Compared to God, who are we? What do we have that is our very own? Our wealth, appearance, dress, abilities, or what others think of us, these are not the most important things in life. The virtues that we practice to please God are the only treasures we can take with us when we die. Christ said, ". . . learn from me, for I am meek and humble of heart; and you will find rest for your souls" (Mt. 11:29). He also said: "Seek first the kingdom of God and His justice, and all these things shall be given you besides" (Mt. 6:33).

Temperance includes *chastity, or purity, which disposes us to be pure in soul and body.* Many martyrs died to keep the virtue of chastity. Recall the stories of the martyrdom of St. Agnes and St. Maria Goretti. Let us have a special devotion to the Blessed Virgin and ask her daily to help us to be pure. Memorize this prayer, "My Queen! my Mother! I give thee all myself, and, to show my devotion to thee, I consecrate to thee my eyes, my ears, my mouth, my heart, my entire self. Wherefore, O loving Mother, as I am thine own, keep me, defend me, as thy child and possession."

*Besides these, there are many other moral virtues.* We must remember, however, that the virtue of religion, which is a part of the virtue of justice, is the highest moral virtue. By practicing it we give God the worship that belongs to Him. We practice this virtue especially when we unite with Christ in His perfect prayer and sacrifice, the Holy Mass. "Blessing and glory and wisdom and thanksgiving, honor, might and power be unto our God for ever and ever. Amen."

## FOR ME TO REVIEW

*Catechism Lesson*

**470. Q. Why do we say the three theological virtues are infused and the four moral virtues acquired?**

A. We say the three theological virtues are infused; that is, poured into our souls, because they are strictly gifts of God and do not depend upon our efforts to obtain them, while the four moral virtues—prudence, justice, fortitude and temperance—though also gifts of God, may, as natural virtues, be acquired by our own efforts.

**Questions and Exercises**

1. Explain how the practice of the moral virtues will make you a better citizen of your country as well as a better Catholic.
2. Are the moral virtues meant only for Catholics? Explain your answer.
3. When are the moral virtues supernatural?
4. In what sense are the cardinal moral virtues hinges?
5. How do we practice justice toward God?
6. How can we practice the virtue of liberality?
7. Mention three ways in which you can practice patience.
8. Why should St. Maria Goretti have a special appeal for boys and girls your age?
9. What is meant by the virtue of religion?

## FOR ME TO REMEMBER

1. The moral virtues are of two kinds, natural and supernatural.
2. We receive the supernatural moral virtues at baptism.
3. The supernatural moral virtues increase in our souls with the increase of sanctifying grace.
4. The Blessed Virgin Mary and St. Joseph possessed the supernatural moral virtues in their entirety.
5. The practice of the moral supernatural virtues keeps us on the right road to God.
6. The cardinal virtues are called such because they are like hinges on which hang the many other moral virtues. In fact, our whole moral life hinges on these fundamental four. "Cardo" means "hinge" in Latin.

   Here's how these four cardinal virtues help us to lead a good life:

   Prudence enables us to form right judgments about what we must do or not do.

   Justice enables us to give everyone what belongs to him.

   Fortitude enables us to do what is good in spite of any difficulty.

   Temperance enables us to control our desires and to use rightly the things which please our senses.

Some of the other moral virtues include:

> Filial piety and patriotism, obedience, honesty, liberality, patience, humility, chastity, or purity.

## FOR ME TO DO

1. Write an original prayer in which you ask God to increase the moral supernatural virtues in your soul.
2. Play a guessing game on the cardinal virtues listed in this lesson.
3. Make a visit to St. Joseph and ask him to help you practice that moral virtue which you think you need most.
4. Discuss how St. Joseph practiced faith, obedience, charity, humility, courage, prudence, and other virtues.
5. Read the life of St. Martin de Porres and tell the class how he practiced the moral virtues.
6. Tell how the two kinds of moral virtues differ.
7. Name the virtues we practice when we:

    are fair to everyone,

    control ourselves,

    are strong in doing hard things,

    know what to do or not to do,

    tell the truth,

    are pure in soul and body,

    see how weak we are and how great God is,

    honor and respect our parents,

    use money for good purposes,

    do not complain when we are hurt or when we suffer.

8. On a separate paper write the numbers from one to ten and write the moral virtues which are practiced in the following acts.

    1) Promptly answering your mother when she calls.
    2) Never cheating in schoolwork.
    3) Showing respect and regard for traffic officers and patrol boys.
    4) Thinking before acting.
    5) Not doing a wrong act even when our friends think it is a clever thing to do.
    6) Letting others use your baseball glove, or ball and bat.
    7) Contributing to the support of the Church in the Sunday collection.
    8) Taking time to greet Mother and tell her about the day.
    9) Consulting your parents before making a judgment about what movie to watch with your friends.
    10) Knowing when to stop whether eating, playing, joking, or working.

# CHAPTER 7
# Christ Sends the Holy Spirit To Guide His Church

LESSON 25

## The Church Leads All Men to Salvation

In the chapter we have just completed we learned that the Holy Spirit loves us so much that He remains with us when we are in the state of sanctifying grace, and always helps us with actual grace. In gratitude we certainly have promised to show our love for Him by praying to Him before confession, before study or big undertakings, in temptation, and at many other times.

Now we shall review what we know about the Church and learn many new things about how the Holy Spirit gives us His grace through the Church. We shall then better appreciate our belonging to the Church. We will also do all we can to help others to find the true Church.

## Christ Promised To Send the Holy Spirit

Just as the Father sent His divine Son into the world to save sinful men, so Christ together with the Father sent the Holy Spirit to continue the work of salvation. Before Christ ascended into heaven He organized His Church, and promised to send the Holy Spirit, to dwell in the Church until the end of time. It is through the Holy Spirit that the Church brings all men to salvation (Jn. 16:7–15).

## The Apostles Prepared for the Coming of the Holy Spirit

Just before His Ascension, Christ told His Apostles to stay in the city, ". . . until you are clothed with power from on high" (Lk. 24:49). So they went back from the Mount of Olives to Jerusalem and hid themselves in the Upper Room. The Blessed Virgin and the other disciples were with them. Here they waited in prayer for nine days, making the first novena in the Church.

## The Church Is the Congregation of All Baptized People

The Catholic Church is Christ's society which trains men for heaven. It is a supernatural society, because its founder, Jesus Christ, was true God. It is a supernatural society, because its purpose is to give all men the supernatural life of sanctifying grace and to enable them to attain eternal happiness in union with the Triune God in heaven. It is a supernatural society, because it administers the seven sacraments or seven channels of divine grace established by Jesus Christ to allow men to share in the fruits of His redemption.

Besides this, the Church is a visible society. It is a visible society because it is made up of men and women of flesh and blood. It has a visible head, the pope, who acts as the vicar of Christ, its

invisible head. The supernatural life of sanctifying grace, which the Church brings to men through the sacraments, makes use of visible, sensible signs: water in baptism, bread and wine for the Eucharist, oil for Confirmation and Anointing of the Sick.

The members of this society must do the following: they must receive the sacrament of Baptism and believe the teachings of the Church. They must assist at the Holy Mass and receive the sacraments. They must obey the Holy Father and the bishops who are united with him.

Our Lord often spoke of the Church He was establishing. In His parables He compared it with the things the people saw about them, such as a sheepfold, a kingdom, a grain of mustard seed, a city placed on a mountain, a light on a candlestick. Christ also likened His Church to a vine. He said, "I am the vine, you are the branches" (Jn. 15:5).

In other parts of the Bible, there are other names for the Church. These are "a body" (Eph. 1:23); "the house of God" (Tim. 3:15); and "a holy city" (Apoc. 21:10). A symbol for the Church is the ark. Do you know the story of Noah and the ark? Why might the ark be a symbol of the Church?

When we say "Catholic Church" we do not mean a building of stone or wood, even though we find this comparison in Scripture (Eph. 2:21). When we speak of the Catholic Church we mean that *the Church is the congregation of all baptized persons united in the same true faith, the same sacrifice, and the same sacraments, under the authority of the pope and the bishops in communion with him.*

*Jesus Christ founded the Church. Jesus Christ founded the Church to bring all men to eternal salvation.*

The Church instructs us in our duties to God, our neighbor, and ourselves. It provides us with the sacraments which make us pure, strong, and holy.

## The Holy Spirit Dwells in the Church

*The Church is enabled to lead men to salvation by the indwelling of the Holy Spirit, who gives it life.* We mentioned before how the Holy Spirit dwells in the Church. *God the Father and God the Son sent the Holy Spirit to dwell in the Church. The dwelling of the Holy Spirit in the Church was first visibly manifested on Pentecost Sunday, when He came down upon the Apostles in the form of tongues of fire.* It will last as long as the world exists, for *the Holy Spirit will dwell in the Church until the end of time.*

As the soul in the human body helps it to grow, act, and become perfect, so the Holy Spirit dwells and works in the Church and all its members. The Holy Spirit is the soul of the Church.

*The indwelling of the Holy Spirit enables the Church to teach, to sanctify, and to rule the faithful in the name of Christ.* These are the three great works or missions of the Church. *By teaching, sanctifying, and ruling in the name of Christ is meant that the*

*Church always does the will of its divine Founder, who remains forever its invisible Head.*

### The Church Teaches Its Members

The Church has power to do Christ's work in His name. Christ said to the Apostles He had chosen: "As the Father has sent me, I also send you" (Jn. 20:22). He bade them teach the doctrine He had taught. He gave them all power saying, "He who hears you, hears me; and he who rejects you, rejects me" (Lk. 10:16). He sent them to all nations and promised to be with them until the end of the world (Mt. 28:20).

### The Church Sanctifies Its Members

The Church sanctifies its members by uniting them to Christ. It does this through the Mass, the sacraments, especially the Holy Eucharist, and by the many opportunities it offers for practicing the supernatural virtues.

### The Church Rules Its Members

Before He ascended into heaven, our divine Lord told His Apostles, who were the first bishops of the Catholic Church, "Go, therefore, and make disciples of all nations . . . teaching them to observe all that I have commanded you" (Mt. 28:18, 20). He thereby gave His Apostles and their successors, the bishops of the Catholic Church, the power to rule the members of His Church.

Any organization or society needs law if it is to carry out its work. The Church also, the supernatural society founded by Christ, has laws and rules which its members must obey. The laws of the Church are intended to help men reach heaven. They help us know what we must believe and what we must do if we are to be happy forever with God.

Since the Church can make laws, it can also punish us if we disobey them. In very serious cases, the Church can even punish us by excommunication. This means that a person is no longer a member of the Church. Because of his disobedience he has been cut off from the society founded by Jesus Christ. He has revolted against Christ and deprived himself of the full use of the means to attain salvation. Even when the Church excommunicates a person, however, she is always ready to welcome him back. Like Christ, the Church rejoices at the return of repentant sinners.

## Christ Is the Invisible Head of the Church

Christ had told His Apostles that even though He would ascend to His Father, He would be with them always: ". . . and behold, I am with you all days, even unto the consummation of the world" (Mt. 28:20). This is what we mean when we say Christ is the invisible Head of the Church.

With Christ, the Apostles became the governing members of the Church. There is no Church without them, just as there is no Church without Christ. For, *Christ gave the power to teach, to sanctify, and to rule the members of His Church to the Apostles, the first bishops of the Church.*

Christ commanded the Apostles to teach all nations, but He did not intend that the Apostles alone should have this power. *No, Christ intended that this power should be exercised also by their successors, the bishops of the Church.*

Besides giving them the power to teach and govern, Christ had also ordained His Apostles priests with the right to offer the sacrifice of the Mass. ". . . do this in remembrance of me" (1 Cor. 11:24).

The Apostles went to all the nations as Christ commanded them. As the number of Christians increased, the Apostles chose men who were outstanding in virtue and ability, and made them bishops and appointed them as rulers of the new Christian communities. These new bishops also had power to ordain and appoint others. The bishops are the successors of

### Did You Know?

The first martyr of the Church was St. Stephen, who was one of the first ordained deacons of the Church. He was stoned to death. St. Paul, then known as Saul of Tarsus, a persecutor of Christians, was there to witness it. Saul would have a vision of Jesus later and convert, taking his Christian name of Paul.

the Apostles and, as such, they have the full power to teach, govern, and sanctify. The priests do not have the fullness of these powers. The deacons have less power than the priests. Today, *the priests, especially parish priests, assist the bishops in the care of souls.*

## St. Peter Was the First Visible Head of the Church

Christ had instructed His Apostles to carry on His work in all nations. He knew that as the Church grew and spread, problems would arise. In His visible society there would have to be a visible head who would solve the problems as they came up. Whom did Christ choose for this important task? *Christ gave special power in His Church to St. Peter by making him the head of the Apostles and the chief teacher and ruler of the entire Church.* St. Peter, therefore, had the final word in all matters of faith and good conduct.

But Peter could not live on this earth forever. He lived for a short time at Antioch. Then he went to Rome, and from there ruled the Church. He was the first bishop of Rome, the vicar or representative of Christ on earth, and the visible head of the Church. Rome thus became the city of the pope. There Peter died the death of a martyr about the year 67.

Linus succeeded Peter as pope. Because he was the lawful successor of St. Peter he became the head of the Church.

Christ said to St. Peter, "And I will give thee the keys of the kingdom of heaven; and whatever thou shalt bind on earth shall be bound in heaven, and whatever thou shalt loose on earth shall be loosed in heaven" (Mt. 16:19). St. Peter, therefore, had the supreme right to rule God's Church. He had the right to forgive or not to forgive. If Peter forgives, God forgives. If Peter removes punishment due to sin, so also does God. Peter binds and looses in the name of God and by His power.

Cletus succeeded Linus. So it has continued to our own day. Pope has succeeded pope in an unbroken line to our present Holy Father. This happened because *Christ did not intend that the special power of chief teacher and ruler of the entire Church should be exercised by St. Peter alone, but intended that this power should be passed down to his successor, the pope, the bishop of Rome, who is the Vicar of Christ on earth and the visible head of the Church.*

## We Are Members of the Church

The Church is made up not only of a pope, cardinals, archbishops, bishops, and priests, but of laity as well. *The laity of the Church are all its members who do not belong to the clerical or to the religious state.*

Ordained men belong to the clerical state, as bishops and priests. Priests, brothers, and sisters who have made the vows of religion belong to the religious state.

We, the laity of the Church, have a work to do in the Church. We must try to be good members of the Church, true Christians, other Christs.

St. Thomas More is one of the great laymen of the Church.

The laity play an important part in the Church. Many saints were lay people as for example, St. Elizabeth of Hungary, St. Louis of France, St. Thomas More, and St. Dominic Savio.

The clergy cannot perform the great work of the Church alone, for as Christ says: "The harvest indeed is great, but the laborers are few" (Mt. 9:37). The clergy need the help of every member of the Church. But how can the laity help the Church in her care of souls? They can help by leading good lives that will show or reflect the holiness of the Church. ". . . let your light shine before men, in order that they may see your good works and give glory to your Father in heaven" (Mt. 5:16). The laity can engage their faith in an active way by being real apostles of Christ under the guidance of their bishops and priests. They can do this by helping the priest with parish activities, aiding the missions, performing spiritual and corporal works of mercy, attending parish functions, and in many other ways. Can you think of a few?

Briefly, *the laity can help the Church in her care of souls by leading lives that will reflect credit on the Church, and by co-operating with their bishops and priests, especially through their parish activities.*

God's ministers in the priesthood, especially the Holy Father, have a heavy burden. We should pray earnestly and often for them.

*A Prayer for the Holy Father*

"Lord Jesus, shelter our Holy Father the Pope under the protection of Thy Sacred Heart. Be Thou his light, his strength and his consolation."

## FOR ME TO REVIEW

*Catechism Lesson*

**489. Q. What is the Church?**

A. The Church is the congregation of all those who profess the faith of Christ, partake of the same sacraments, and are governed by their lawful pastors under one visible Head.

**508. Q. Why did Christ found the Church?**

A. Christ founded the Church to teach, govern, sanctify, and save all men.

**425. Q. On what day did the Holy Spirit come down upon the Apostles?**

A. The Holy Spirit came down upon the Apostles ten days after the Ascension of Our Lord; and the day on which He came down upon the Apostles is called Whitsunday, or Pentecost.

**444. Q. Will the Holy Spirit abide with the Church forever?**

A. The Holy Spirit will abide with the Church forever, and guide it in the way of holiness and truth.

***TERMS TO KNOW***

- consummation
- laity
- doctrine
- congregation
- regulations
- authority
- foundation
- prevail
- excommunication

**430. Q. Who sent the Holy Spirit upon the Apostles?**

A. Our Lord Jesus Christ sent the Holy Spirit upon the Apostles.

**434. Q. Why did Christ send the Holy Spirit?**

A. Christ sent the Holy Spirit to sanctify His Church, to enlighten and strengthen the Apostles, and to enable them to preach the Gospel.

**435. Q. How was the Church sanctified through the coming of the Holy Spirit?**

A. The Church was sanctified through the coming of the Holy Spirit by receiving those graces which Christ had merited for His ministers, the bishops and priests, and for the souls of all those committed to their care.

**437. Q. How were the Apostles strengthened through the coming of the Holy Spirit?**

A. The Apostles were strengthened through the coming of the Holy Spirit by receiving the grace to brave every danger, even death itself, in the performance of their sacred duties.

506. Q. **Who are the successors of the other Apostles?**
A. The successors of the other Apostles are the bishops of the Holy Catholic Church.

495. Q. **Who is the invisible Head of the Church?**
A. Jesus Christ is the invisible Head of the Church.

496. Q. **Who is the visible Head of the Church?**
A. Our Holy Father the pope, the bishop of Rome, is the Vicar of Christ on earth and the visible Head of the Church.

499. Q. **Why is the pope, the bishop of Rome, the visible Head of the Church?**
A. The pope, the bishop of Rome, is the visible Head of the Church because he is the successor of St. Peter, whom Christ made the chief of the Apostles and the visible Head of the Church.

979. Q. **Besides bishops and priests, who are the other ministers of the Church?**
A. Besides bishops and priests, the other ministers of the Church are deacons, who have received some of the Holy Orders, but who have not been ordained to the full powers of the priest.

116. Q. **What do you mean here by a "lay person"?**
A. By a "lay person" I mean here anyone who is not a priest. All such persons and those not dedicated to the service of the Altar, taken together, are called the "laity," as all those who have received sacred Orders or who are dedicated to the service of the Altar, taken together, are called the "clergy."

### Questions and Exercises

1. Why should we be grateful for belonging to the Catholic Church?
2. What must a person do in order to belong to this body?
3. How did Christ try to make the people He preached to understand what the Church is?
4. Why did Jesus Christ go to so much trouble to found the Church?
5. How does the Church bring us to salvation?
6. To which Person of the Blessed Trinity do we ascribe the work of sanctifying the members of the Church?
7. Who has the place of St. Peter in the Church today?
8. Why are the laity important members of the Church?
9. Mention several particular ways in which the laity can help the Church.
10. Why should we pray for priests and bishops?
11. How did the Holy Spirit appear to the Apostles on Pentecost?

### Matching

*Number one to five. Complete the sentences in Column Two by writing on your paper the letters in front of the phrases in Column One which complete them.*

| Column I | Column II |
|---|---|
| A. by the Holy Spirit | 1. The Holy Spirit proceeds |
| B. with the Church forever | 2. The Holy Spirit will abide |
| C. from the Father and the Son | 3. We should often pray to the Holy Spirit |

D. for enlightenment
E. enables the Church to teach, sanctify, and rule

4. The Church is sanctified
5. The Holy Spirit

**Fill in the Blank**

*On a separate sheet of paper, write the missing words.*

1. Our bodies are . . (1) . . of the Holy Spirit.
2. The Holy Spirit first comes to us when we receive . . (2) . . .
3. The . . (3) . . and the . . (4) . . sent the Holy Spirit upon the Apostles.
4. The Holy Spirit is equal to the . . (5). . and the . . (6) . . .
5. The Holy Spirit came upon the Apostles in the form of . . (7) . . .
6. Jesus Christ . . (8) . . the Church to bring all men to salvation.
7. The Church is enabled to lead all men to salvation by the indwelling of the Holy Spirit, who gives it . . (9) . . .
8. The laity can help the Church in her care of souls by leading lives that will reflect credit on the . . (10) . . .

## FOR ME TO REMEMBER

1. God the Father and God the Son sent God the Holy Spirit to complete the instruction of the Apostles and to bring all men to salvation.
2. The Apostles prepared for the coming of the Holy Spirit by prayer.
3. Pentecost Sunday is often referred to as the "birthday" of the Church.
4. The Church needs the Holy Spirit to make it live and to keep it alive.
5. The Holy Spirit guides the Church in the way of holiness and truth.

## FOR ME TO DO

1. Why should we have great respect for every priest?
2. Give some examples of how the laity can help the Church today.
3. Why should we love the Catholic Church?
4. Write a paragraph on the present pope, on your bishop, and on your pastor.
5. Make a visit every day and pray for God's blessing on each of the authorities in the Church. Ask some special blessing for each of them.

## Come Holy Spirit

*Come Holy Spirit, fill the hearts of your faithful and kindle in them the fire of your love. Send forth your Spirit and they shall be created. And You shall renew the face of the earth.*

*O, God, who by the light of the Holy Spirit, did instruct the hearts of the faithful, grant that by the same Holy Spirit we may be truly wise and ever enjoy His consolations, Through Christ Our Lord, Amen.*

LESSON 26

# The Catholic Church Has Certain Marks and Attributes

Has anyone ever asked you why you believed that the Catholic Church is the true Church? Were you able to convince the person who asked you that *the one true Church established by Christ is the Catholic Church?* Were you also able to explain that *we know that the Catholic Church is the one true Church established by Christ because it alone has the marks of the true Church?*

## The Marks of the Church

In an earlier grade we learned that the marks of the Church are like signposts. They point out the Catholic Church as the only true Church. Now that we are a bit older let us see how this Church can be the only true Church by considering its special characteristics, that is, its signs or marks.

Our catechism says: *By the marks of the Church we mean certain clear signs by which all men can recognize it as the true Church founded by Jesus Christ.* Each person has his own individual features by which he can be recognized. In the same way the marks of the Church set it off as the one true Church, and not as any other organization. No other Church has all these marks or signs, by which it can be recognized as the true Church. *The chief marks of the Church are four: It is one, holy, catholic or universal, and apostolic.*

### The Church Is One

To understand how the Church is one we must recall that when Christ promised to make St. Peter the head of the Church He said, ". . . upon this rock (Peter means "rock") I will build my Church" (Mt. 16:18). He clearly said "Church" not "Churches."

Since this one true Church was founded by Jesus Christ, all its members are united in three ways: first, in doctrine, that is, in truths taught and believed. No matter where we go, we will find the essential teachings of the Church are the same. This is what we mean when we say the Church is one in doctrine, or united in faith.

Second, the Church is united in worship. Everywhere in the world the Church offers the same sacrifice and administers the same seven sacraments. A Chinese baby is baptized with the same words as a child in Australia or America. The absolution of a priest takes away the sins of Catholics in any part of the world. Bread and wine are changed into the body and blood of Christ by all Catholic priests regardless of color, race, nationality, or rite.

Third, the Church is one in government. When Jesus promised to build the Catholic Church on one rock and gave special powers to St. Peter, He wanted only one chief ruler or head. He intended that Peter pass on his authority, or right to rule, to the popes who would come after him. Always and everywhere the pope is the visible head of the Church as successor of St. Peter.

Now we understand that *the Catholic Church is one because all its members, according to the will of Christ, profess the same faith, have the same sacrifice and sacraments, and are united under one and the same visible head, the pope.*

## The Church Is Holy

*The Catholic Church is holy because it was founded by Jesus Christ, who is all-holy, and because it teaches, according to the will of Christ, holy doctrines, and provides the means of leading a holy life, thereby giving holy members to every age.*

Christ founded the Church. He is Holiness itself. His Church teaches the holy doctrines which Christ taught. It offers everyone the means to lead a holy life. In this way the Church gives holy members to every age. This we can understand if we think of the saints who, at all times and places, followed Christ and became holy. Name some saints of various countries and different times. How much do you know about them?

Besides people whom the Church has declared to be saints, there are many other holy people in the Church. They use the means to become holy: the Mass, the sacraments, and good works. These are the same means the saints used. These are the means that we, too, must use to become holy.

## The Church Is Catholic

Does it seem strange that one of the marks of the Catholic Church is that it is "catholic"? Not if you know that the word "catholic" means "universal." Christ Himself explained it when He said, "Go, therefore, and make disciples of all nations . . ." (Mt. 28:19); ". . . behold, I am with you all days" (Mt. 28:20). The word "catholic," therefore, means *all* truths, to *all* nations, for *all* times.

Whenever we want to explain "catholic" we must remember three words: "time," "place," and "teaching." "Time" stands for all ages. "Place" means all nations. "Teaching" means all truths that

Christ taught. It is not hard, therefore, to explain that *the Catholic Church is catholic or universal because, destined to last for all time, it never fails to fulfill the divine commandment to teach all nations all the truths revealed by God.*

### The Church Is Apostolic

The fourth mark of the Church is that it is apostolic. We say *the Catholic Church is apostolic because it was founded by Christ on the Apostles and, according to His divine will, has always been governed by their lawful successors.* From His disciples or followers, Christ chose twelve men to whom He gave more instructions than to the others who followed Him. He commanded these twelve to teach all nations. An apostle is one who is sent. This is why we call the twelve chosen disciples of Christ who received the command to teach everywhere the twelve Apostles. Christ gave to Peter, one of the twelve, outstanding power.

All people to the very end of time were to hear Christ's teachings, so the Apostles had to appoint others to succeed them. Today the bishops of the Catholic Church are the lawful successors of the Apostles, and the Holy Father is the lawful successor of St. Peter. They teach the same doctrine which the Apostles taught. They administer the same sacraments.

The Catholic Church is apostolic because it was founded by Christ on the Apostles and, according to His divine will, has always been governed by their lawful successors.

It is important that we know and understand the marks of the Church in these days when people think one religion is as good as another. We must study our religion to be able to explain that *we know that no other church but the Catholic Church is the true Church of Christ because no other church has these four marks.*

## The Attributes of the Church

The four marks of the Church are like the rays of a lighthouse which give guidance to all those who are seeking the one true Church. Besides these marks, the Church also has three other great qualities, or attributes, which also point her out as the one true Church. *The chief attributes of the Catholic Church are authority, infallibility, and indefectibility. They are called attributes because they are qualities perfecting the nature of the Church.*

### The Four Marks of the Church

- One
- Holy
- Catholic
- Apostolic

Can you explain what each of these mean?

### The Church Has the Attribute of Authority

To understand how authority perfects the nature of the Church, let us think of the way our homes are ordered. If there is to be happiness and order in the home, someone must have the authority to set rules and expectations. This place of authority is held by the father, because by becoming a leader the father becomes perfected in love. However, just as Eve was a helpmate to Adam, the mother of the household can also share in the authority of the father. She also trains the children in all good habits so that they may grow in Christian living.

Just as the father shares his authority with the mother, so also does Christ share His with the Church. He did not intend to remain visibly on earth forever, and so He gave His authority to St. Peter, the head of His Church, who passed it on to the succeeding popes and bishops.

Thus we see that *by the authority of the Catholic Church is meant that the pope and the bishops, as the lawful successors of the Apostles, have power from Christ Himself to teach, to sanctify, and to govern the faithful in spiritual matters.*

### The Church Has the Attribute of Infallibility

When God created each one of us He planted deep down in our hearts a desire for the truth. When our older brothers and sisters or friends tell us something we find hard to believe, we immediately turn to our parents and say, "Is that true, Dad?" or "That's not right, is it, Mother?"

As we go to our natural parents to learn the truth, so we should also always go to our Mother the Church for divine truth. Sometimes our parents are not able to answer our questions or explain things clearly, but the Church never fails in her duty to guide us along the right path. She has divine help.

When Christ sent the Holy Spirit to guide the Apostles in their preaching of the truth, He promised that this Spirit of Truth would remain with the Church always. This special help of the Holy Spirit remains in the Church today through the gift of infallibility. This word means "freedom from error."

Let us name some ways in which the Church is free from error. The Holy Spirit guides the Church in all her teachings of faith and morals. In these matters the Church can never make a mistake. Faith means believing. Morals means the right or wrong in human conduct. Therefore, when the Church tells us what we are to believe or how we are to act, she is infallible.

Christ gave this infallibility to St. Peter and the other Apostles. It is found today in the pope, the successor of St. Peter, and in the bishops, who are the successors of the other Apostles. The pope, as Vicar of Christ and successor to Peter, is infallible when, as head of the Church, he teaches matters of faith or morals. The bishops, when united under the pope and called together in a General Council, or even when dispersed throughout the world are also infallible when they teach faith or morals.

**By the infallibility of the Catholic Church is meant that the Church, by the special assistance of the Holy Spirit, cannot err when it teaches or believes a doctrine of faith or morals.**

We can be certain of what the pope and bishops teach us on matters pertaining to faith or morals. We can be certain because we know that Christ promised to remain with His Church forever

*Then he summoned his twelve disciples and gave them authority over unclean spirits to drive them out and to cure every disease and every illness.*

MATTHEW 10:1

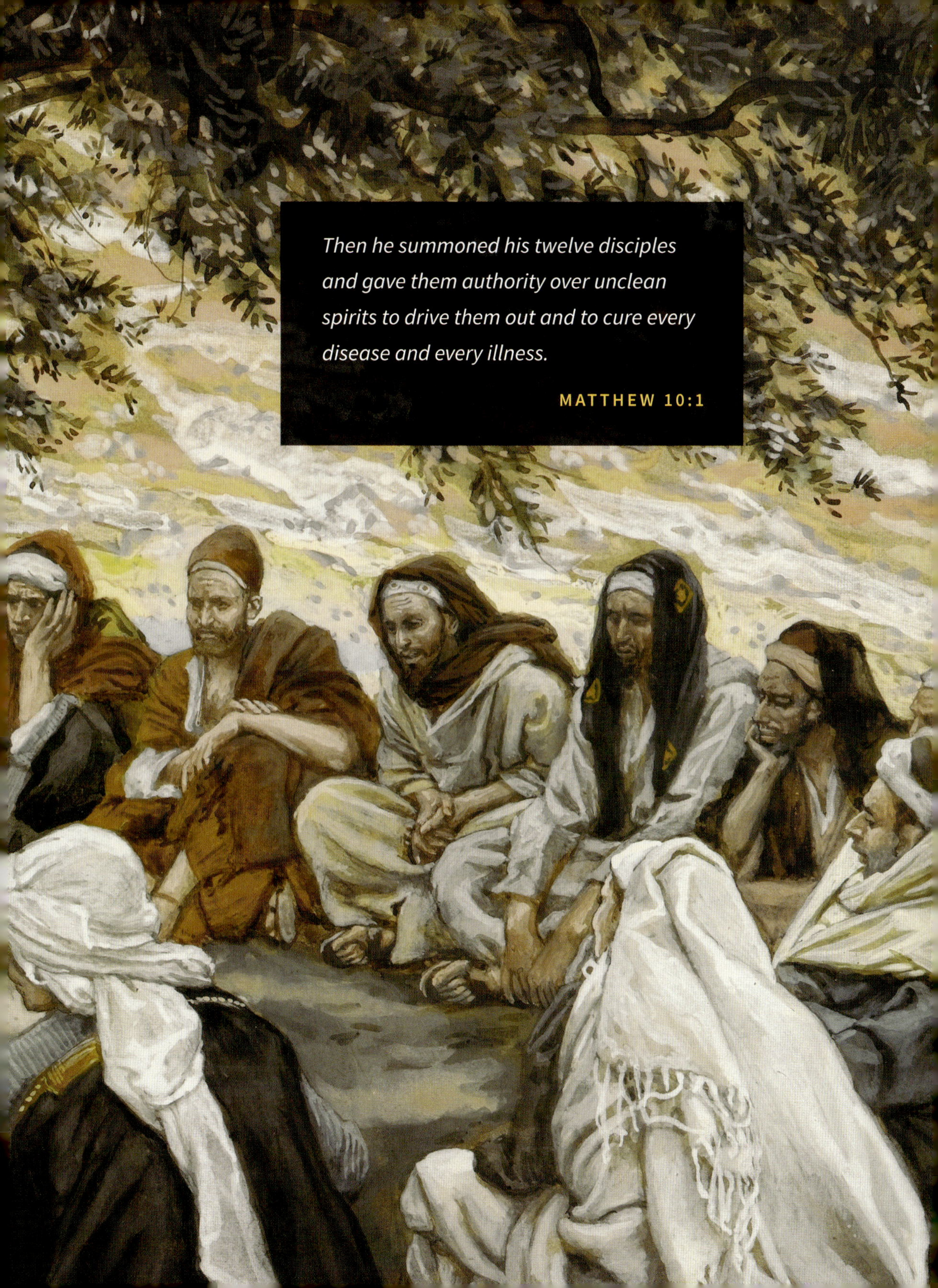

(Mt. 28:20). He also sent the Holy Spirit, the Spirit of Truth, to guide His Church and to keep it from error. Knowing this, it is easy for Catholics to accept the teachings of the pope and bishops.

Sometimes false teachings spring up, and then the pope may call together a General Council, or meeting of the bishops, in order to make clear what is true in regard to these teachings. We firmly believe that when the pope announces to the Catholic world what he and the bishops united in Council have decided, their teaching is infallible. Sometimes the pope alone, as pastor and teacher of the entire world, explains what we are to believe and to do in order to be saved. Good Catholics accept these teachings without question.

***TERMS TO KNOW***

- characteristics
- apostolic
- catholic
- err
- infallibility
- administers
- qualities
- defines
- indefectibility
- attributes
- morals
- General Council

We can summarize these thoughts in the following statement. *The Church teaches infallibly when it defines, through the pope alone, as the teacher of all Christians, or through the pope and the bishops, a doctrine of faith or morals to be held by all the faithful.*

### The Church Has the Attribute of Indefectibility

Christ is God, eternal and unchangeable. He founded the Church and said that the gates of hell will not prevail against it. This means that nothing will ever be able to destroy the Church. The Church is, therefore, indefectible. *By the indefectibility of the Catholic Church is meant that the Church, as Christ founded it, will last until the end of time.*

Is not that a consoling thought? Do not all these things make us grateful to God, especially for giving us the grace to be Catholics and members of His one true Church? Should we not resolve to help as many people as possible to find Christ's true Church?

## FOR ME TO REVIEW

*Catechism Lesson*

**489. Q. What is the Church?**

A. The Church is the congregation of all those who profess the faith of Christ, partake of the same sacraments, and are governed by their lawful pastors under one visible Head.

**519. Q. How do we know that the Church must have the four marks and three attributes usually ascribed or given to it?**

A. We know that the Church must have the four marks and three attributes usually ascribed or given to it from the words of Christ given in the Holy Scripture and in the teaching of the Church from its beginning.

**522. Q. Which are the attributes of the Church?**

A. The attributes of the Church are three: authority, infallibility, and indefectibility.

**563. Q. How is the Church Holy?**

A. The Church is Holy because its founder, Jesus Christ, is holy; because it teaches a holy doctrine; invites all to a holy life; and because of the eminent holiness of so many thousands of its children.

**564. Q. How is the Church catholic or universal?**

A. The Church is catholic or universal because it subsists in all ages, teaches all nations, and maintains all truth.

**567. Q. How is the Church Apostolic?**

A. The Church is Apostolic because it was founded by Christ on His Apostles, and is governed by their lawful successors, and because it has never ceased, and never will cease, to teach their doctrine.

570. **Q. In which Church are these attributes and marks found?**
A. These attributes and marks are found in the Holy Roman Catholic Church alone.

573. **Q. By whom is the Church made and kept one, holy, and catholic?**
A. The Church is made and kept one, holy, and catholic by the Holy Spirit, the spirit of love and holiness, who unites and sanctifies its members throughout the world.

525. **Q. What do you mean by the authority of the Church?**
A. By the authority of the Church I mean the right and power which the pope and the bishops, as the successors of the Apostles, have to teach and to govern the faithful.

526. **Q. What do you mean by the infallibility of the Church?**
A. By the infallibility of the Church I mean that the Church cannot err when it teaches a doctrine of faith or morals.

527. **Q. What do we mean by a "doctrine of faith or morals"?**
A. By a "doctrine of faith or morals" we mean the revealed teaching that refers to whatever we must believe and do in order to be saved.

543. **Q. What do you mean by the indefectibility of the Church?**
A. By the indefectibility of the Church I mean that the Church, as Christ founded it, will last till the end of time.

**Questions and Exercises**

1. Explain how the Church is one.
2. Why cannot the Lutheran Church be the one true Church?
3. In what three ways are the members of the one true Church united?

4. Who is the visible head of the Church?
5. What three means of becoming holy, mentioned in this lesson, should we use?
6. Why is "Catholic" an appropriate name for our Church?
7. What would you say to convince a friend that one religion is not as good as another?
8. Who gave St. Peter the authority to be the first head of the Church?
9. Who is it that keeps the Church from making a mistake?
10. In what matters does the Holy Spirit guide the Church?
11. Can the Catholic Church be destroyed?
12. What can you do to make yourself a more holy member of the Church?
13. What is a General Council?

**Matching**

*Choose the letter in front of the word below which is explained in the following statements.*

A. One

B. Holy

C. Catholic

D. Apostolic

E. Authority

F. Infallibility

G. Indefectibility

1) The Church is destined to last until the end of time.

2) All the members profess the same faith.
3) The Church cannot err in teaching a doctrine of faith or morals.
4) The Church gives holy members to every age.
5) All the members of the Church are united.
6) The Church will never change its doctrines.
7) The Church is governed by the lawful successors of the Apostles.
8) The Church teaches all truths to all nations.
9) The power to teach, to govern, to sanctify came from Christ.
10) All members may receive the same sacraments.

## FOR ME TO REMEMBER

1. The Catholic Church is the one true Church established by Christ.
2. The Church is united in doctrine, in worship, and in government.
3. The Church is catholic or universal in regard to time, place, and teaching.
4. The Church has given holy members to every age.
5. The Church was founded on the Apostles.
6. The pope cannot make a mistake when as head of the Church he teaches a doctrine of faith or morals.

## FOR ME TO DO

1. Look up and discuss the parables of the Mustard Seed, the Marriage Feast, and the Leaven. Show how these parables of Christ foretold the spread of the Church in the whole world.
2. Reread the story of the descent of the Holy Spirit upon the Apostles. Be able to explain how Peter began the work of teaching all nations.
3. Prove that the Lutheran Church is not apostolic.
4. Prepare a discussion of the subject, "Can the pope make a mistake?"
5. Prepare a group discussion on the following problems. Elect a spokesman to give the findings of each group. Were they correct?

a) How can you be sure you have the same teachings the Apostles had?

b) The Sovereign of the British Empire is the head of the Church of England. Why isn't this the true Church?

c) Why don't Catholics eat meat on Friday? Explain the existence of days of fast and abstinence as a means of sanctifying the members of the Church.

d) Explain the existence of convents and monasteries as a sign of the holiness of the Church.

e) How do the many persecutions suffered by the members of the Catholic Church through the ages prove its indefectibility?

6. In what three ways is the Church one?
7. Where are the chief doctrines of the Church to be found?
8. What is meant by the power to teach, to govern, and to sanctify?
9. Under what conditions does the pope teach infallibly?
10. Why is the Church able to teach infallibly?

LESSON 27

# Other Things to Know About the Church

## All Must Belong to the Church to Be Saved

Now that we have studied the marks and attributes of the Church we realize that *all are obliged to belong to the Catholic Church in order to be saved.*

The Ark of Noah is a symbol of our Church. Just as only those who remained in the Ark were saved, so also, only those who belong to the Catholic Church will be saved. This means that all who are saved are saved because they are united to the Church whether they know it or not. *When we say, "Outside the Church there is no salvation," we mean that those who through their own grave fault do not know that the Catholic Church is the true Church or, knowing it, refuse to join it, cannot be saved.*

The Holy Father, Pope Pius XII, and the Cardinals of the Sacred Congregation of the Holy Office explained the phrase "Outside the Church there is no salvation" in an official letter in 1949. They wrote, ". . . it is not always required (that one may obtain eternal salvation) that he be incorporated into the Church actually as a member, but it is necessary that at least he be united to her by desire and longing." This desire is defined as a "good disposition of soul whereby a person wishes" to do God's will. Those who live as the voice of conscience tells them to live certainly have this "good disposition."

### The Ark and the Church

Noah's ark is a fascinating symbol for the Church. Just as Noah and his family and all the animals were saved from the flood by remaining inside the ark, so all of us who remain a part of the Church are saved as we travel across the rocky seas of life. Many churches are built to resemble the inside of a ship. The main part of the interior of a church is called the "nave," which is Latin for "ship." Additionally, the flying buttresses of many old cathedrals in Europe are said to resemble oars coming out the side of a ship.

God bestowed a great grace on Cardinal Newman, showing him where to find the truth and giving him the grace to embrace that truth. Many people, however, are not as fortunate as he. They love God and make use of the graces He has given them, but are not members of the true Church. They are deprived of the precious gifts and helps from heaven which one can enjoy only in the Catholic Church. We should, therefore, do all that we can to encourage them to join the Catholic Church. At the same time we must not forget that *they who remain outside the Catholic Church through no grave fault of their own and do not know it is the true Church, can be saved by making use of the graces which God gives them.*

Pray this invocation for the conversion of non-Catholics: "That Thou wouldst vouchsafe to bring back into the unity of the Church all that stray, and to lead all unbelievers to the light of the Gospel, we beseech Thee to hear us, O Lord."

Cardinal Newman is an outstanding convert to the Catholic Faith. He came into the Church as a result of his own study, and of course God's grace. Because he was not able to trace the Church of England back to the time of Christ, he joined the Catholic Church. Newman was famous as a speaker and writer about religion, so his conversion brought many of his followers into the Catholic Church. One of the poems he wrote when he was trying to make up his mind to join the Church is "Lead Kindly Light." Are you familiar with the words of this poem that have also been put to music?

## The Church Is the Mystical Body of Christ

A famous convert who lived many years ago called the Catholic Church the wonderful body of the living Christ. This description of the Church is another way of saying what the great St. Paul said, ". . . He (Christ) is the head of his body, the Church" (Col. 1:18). The human body has many members—arms, legs, eyes, ears, etc.—each distinct and different from the others, yet closely united. Like the body, the Church has many members in its faithful, in all parts of the world, united through baptism with Christ as their Head. As the head guides the human body, so Christ directs the entire Church.

This union between Christ and the members of the Church, and among the members themselves, is much closer than the union between the head and members of the human body, for it is a supernatural union. This explanation helps us to understand that *the Catholic Church is called the Mystical Body of Christ because its members are united by supernatural bonds with one another and with Christ, their Head, thus resembling the members and head of the living human body.*

## We Should Be Worthy Members of the Church

In any club or organization, we are not considered active members if we just belong. We must work hard in every undertaking, be loyal to the leaders, and especially when wearing the uniform try not to do anything to disgrace the club. In this way we are benefiting ourselves and giving a good name to the organization. As good Catholics we, too, must be active workers for the Church. We must take part in the works of the Church and pray for its leaders. Above all, we should thank God for having called us to the Church, and promise to remain faithful always.

The Apostles received the gift of tongues on the first Pentecost. All the people listening to Peter's sermon, although not familiar with his language, understood him as though he were speaking in their own individual language. This miracle showed that the Catholic Church is for all men and nations.

As members of the Church charity places on us the great responsibility of trying to bring others into the Church. By our prayers to the Holy Spirit, our encouragement to non-Catholics, our clear explanation of what the Church teaches, and our own good example, we can help bring souls into the one true fold.

## The Communion of Saints

Toward the end of the Apostles' Creed we use the term "communion of saints." Here the word "communion" means a union or group or society. This expression means that the supernatural bonds of sanctifying grace and charity unite us with Christ and many other souls.

### The Faithful on Earth Are Active Members of God's Family

The souls united in the communion of saints are, first of all, the faithful on earth. They make up the Church Militant. The word "militant" means fighting. This name is given them because all the members are still taking part in a war against the temptations of the world, the flesh, and the devil. We must gain heaven. We, here on earth, belong to the Church Militant. In order to strengthen ourselves, we perform the spiritual and corporal works of mercy, pray for one another, pray for the suffering members of Christ's family, and ask the help of those favored ones who have already reached heaven.

### The Souls in Purgatory Are Suffering Members of God's Family

The second group of souls in the communion of saints are the souls in purgatory, those who have died in the state of grace, but who have to atone for unforgiven venial sins or the punishment due to sin. These souls are unable to help themselves. They depend on the prayers of their friends both on earth and in heaven for release from the pains of purgatory. Their sufferings and trials should be a warning to us and should keep us watchful that we do all in our power to secure heaven for ourselves.

### The Souls in Heaven Are Victorious Members of God's Family

The communion of saints includes also the blessed in heaven. These members have already won heaven, and see God face to face. They pray for the faithful on earth and the souls in purgatory.

Now that we know about the saints in heaven, on earth, and in purgatory we know that: *By "the communion of saints" is meant*

> *"Those in the Catholic Church, whom some rebuke for praying to saints and going on pilgrimages, do not seek any saint as their savior. Instead, they seek saints as those whom their Savior loves, and whose intercession and prayer for the seeker He will be content to hear. For His Own sake, He would have those He loves honored. And when they are thus honored for His sake, then the honor that is given them for His sake overflows especially to Himself."*
>
> —St. Thomas More

*the union of the faithful on earth, the blessed in heaven, and the souls in purgatory, with Christ as their Head.*

### The Members of the Church Can Help One Another Through the Communion of Saints

Since the spiritual bond of sanctifying grace and divine charity unites the members of the communion of saints, they are able to help one another, particularly in their spiritual needs. Many people whom we have never met pray for us every day. In the offertory of each Mass there is a prayer for all the faithful, living and dead. The saints in heaven, particularly those to whom we pray, help us with their prayers. *Through the communion of saints, the blessed in heaven can help the souls in purgatory and the faithful on earth by praying for them.*

Since the blessed have already won their reward, they are best able to help us. They deserve our gratitude and affection, as well as our imitation. We should celebrate their feast days and practice the virtues they exercised while on earth. We should especially love and imitate our patron saints. *The faithful on earth, through the communion of saints, should honor the blessed in heaven and pray to them, because they are worthy of honor and as friends of God will help the faithful on earth.*

When one of our brothers or sisters is ill or in trouble, Mother does all she can to help. Sometimes we may be tempted to complain that the sick or suffering member gets all the attention. Our Holy Mother Church cares for her suffering members in purgatory in just the same way. She shows us how our prayers and good works, which we could offer for ourselves, will also aid her suffering members.

The very best way to help these suffering souls is to have Masses offered for them. In doing this we offer an infinite sacrifice in and through Jesus Christ Himself. In addition, we may also say short indulgenced prayers for the poor souls. Briefly then, *the faithful on earth, through the communion of saints, can relieve the sufferings of the souls in purgatory by prayer, fasting, and other good works, by indulgences, and by having Masses offered for them.*

"Merciful Lord Jesus, grant them everlasting rest."

We must show the same charity to the faithful on earth that we have for the souls in purgatory and the blessed in heaven. Our Lord said to His Apostles, "Love one another." We must not be satisfied with just praying for our fellow men. We must also help them in other ways whenever they need it. We must help not only those whom we like, but all of God's children, remembering that what we do for them we do for Christ. In other words, *the faithful on earth, as members of the Mystical Body of Christ, can help one another by practicing supernatural charity and, especially, by performing the spiritual and corporal works of mercy.*

The communion of saints encourages us to depend on the prayers and good works of the entire Church besides our own prayers and good works. It teaches us how, as healthy, holy members of the Church, we can help other members of Christ's Mystical Body.

### TERMS TO KNOW

- deprived
- spiritual needs
- supernatural bonds
- indulgences
- gift of tongues
- supernatural charity
- Mystical Body
- communion of saints

## FOR ME TO REVIEW

*Catechism Lesson*

**509. Q. Are all bound to belong to the Church?**

A. All are bound to belong to the Church, and he who knows the Church to be the true Church and remains out of it cannot be saved.

**1125. Q. Is it enough to belong to God's Church in order to be saved?**

A. It is not enough to belong to the Church in order to be saved, but we must also keep the Commandments of God and of the Church.

**510. Q. Is it ever possible for one to be saved who does not know the Catholic Church to be the true Church?**

A. It is possible for one to be saved who does not know the Catholic Church to be the true Church.

**1201. Q. What does the communion of saints mean?**

A. The communion of saints means the union which exists between the members of the Church on earth with one another, and with the blessed in heaven, and with the suffering souls in purgatory.

**1202. Q. What benefits are derived from the communion of saints?**

A. The following benefits are derived from the communion of saints: the faithful on earth assist one another by their prayers and good works, and they are aided by the intercession of the saints in heaven, while both the saints in heaven and the faithful on earth help the souls in purgatory.

**1196. Q. Do we not slight God Himself by addressing our prayers to saints?**

A. We do not slight God Himself by addressing our prayers to saints, but, on the contrary, show a greater respect for His majesty and sanctity, acknowledging, by our prayers to the saints, that we are unworthy to address Him for ourselves, and that we, therefore, ask His holy friends to obtain for us what we ourselves are not worthy to ask.

**1197. Q. How do we know that the saints hear us?**

A. We know that the saints hear us, because they are with God, who makes our prayers known to them.

**1385. Q. Can the faithful on earth help the souls in purgatory?**

A. The faithful on earth can help the souls in purgatory by their prayers, fasts, almsdeeds; by indulgences, and by having Masses said for them.

**Questions and Exercises**

1. How did Cardinal Newman discover that the Catholic Church is the one true Church?
2. How are the members of the Church united?
3. Should we take part in the activities of the Church? Why?
4. In what ways can we bring others into the Church?
5. What do we call the union that exists among the members of the Church in heaven, on earth, and in purgatory?
6. How can you be a militant Catholic?
7. What can you do to shorten the time spent in purgatory by yourself, or others dear to you?
8. Do people whom we do not know pray for us? When and how?
9. Why is the Mass the best way of helping the souls in purgatory?
10. What is meant by belonging to the Catholic Church in desire?

## FOR ME TO REMEMBER

1. There is but one true religion, the Catholic religion.
2. Everyone must belong to the Catholic Church, at least in desire, in order to be saved.
3. We should thank God each day for the privilege of being members of His Church, and should encourage others who do not share our privilege of studying the teachings of the Catholic Church.
4. Those who are outside the Catholic Church through no fault of their own are not deserving of blame.
5. People who use all the means they know to attain salvation, and who make use of the graces God has given them, have the desire to become members of the Church even though they are not actually members of it.
6. The term "Mystical Body" refers to the spiritual union which exists between Christ and the members of His Church and the members among themselves.

## FOR ME TO DO

1. Prepare a talk on the communion of saints, showing why it can be called a Royal Family.
2. Explain how we members of the Church Militant are not fighting our battles alone.
3. Make a chart showing the members of the communion of saints in heaven, on earth, and in purgatory.
4. Why is it wrong to say one religion is as good as another?

**CHAPTER 8**

# The Forgiveness of Sins and Life Everlasting

LESSON 28

## The Forgiveness of Sins

### Christ Gave His Church the Power to Forgive Sins

One day while Jesus was traveling through Galilee healing the sick and afflicted, four men brought to Him a paralyzed man lying on a cot. But there was such a large crowd around the house where Jesus was, that the men could not get in through the door. So they made a hole in the flat roof and, let the cot down through it. When Jesus saw how much faith the people had He said to the sick man, "Son, thy sins are forgiven thee" (Mk. 2:5). Some of the Scribes accused Jesus of blasphemy for they knew only God could forgive sins.

Then to prove that He had the power to forgive sins, Christ restored the power of walking to the paralytic.

This took place before Christ instituted the sacrament of Penance and Reconciliation. From earlier lessons we remember that on the evening of His resurrection, Christ said to His Apostles: "Receive the Holy Spirit; whose sins you shall forgive, they are forgiven them; and whose sins you shall retain, they are retained" (Jn. 20:23). Through these words of Christ, penance became a sacrament, and the Apostles were given the power to forgive sins.

## The Church Administers the Sacrament of Penance and Reconciliation

A story from the life of Abraham Lincoln reminds us of the goodness of God in pardoning our sins. One day this great president wanted to pardon a soldier when the cabinet officials thought the soldier should be punished. Lincoln's excuse in signing the pardon was, "You do not know how hard it is to let a human being die when you feel that a stroke of the pen will save him." God also is merciful—infinitely merciful. He is the only One who can forgive sins, and He never loses an opportunity to do so if the sinner is truly sorry. He wanted so much to save us from hell that, besides dying on the cross, He instituted the sacrament of Penance and Reconciliation.

The power of forgiving sins was not to be used only while our divine Lord was on earth. He knew that man would sin and sin again. He gave the power to the Apostles, and they in turn ordained priests to help them. In this way they passed on the power that Christ had given to them. Through all the years since then, the

### The Importance of Frequent Confession

Some people think of the sacrament of Penance and Reconciliation as medicine we take when our souls are sick. And this is a good analogy. It does make our souls healthy again. But that is not the only way to consider this sacrament. Confession does not just purify us of past sins the way medicine keeps us from getting sick, it can also keep us from committing future sins. In that way, we can think of it like vitamins we might take that keep us from even getting sick at all. However, in order for the sacrament to work like this, we must receive it on a regular basis. The Church teaches we must go to confession at least once a year, but if we go 4–6 times a year, the sacrament is much more powerful and helps us remain free of sin.

Church has continued to ordain men to the priesthood, so that they might restore grace to souls that had lost it.

*By "the forgiveness of sins" in the Apostles' Creed is meant that God has given to the Church, through Jesus Christ, the power to forgive sins, no matter how great or how many they are, if sinners truly repent.*

### TERMS TO KNOW

- paralytic
- minister of God
- requisites
- blasphemy

Through the sacrament of holy orders the priests have the power, as ministers of God, to forgive sins in God's name. And we ought to ask God to help us remember always, that our sins can be forgiven, no matter how serious they are. This thought should be a great comfort to us. It should make us thank God for the sacrament of Penance and Reconciliation. One way of showing gratitude is by receiving the sacrament often. For we must not forget that Christ instituted the sacrament of Penance and Reconciliation not only to forgive sins, but also to provide the means of leading a holier life.

When we go to confession, we should prepare ourselves fully for this great sacrament. Do you recall the five things we must do to make a good confession? Every Catholic should know them by heart. They are: first, examine our conscience; second, be sorry for our sins; third, have the firm purpose of not sinning again; fourth, confess our sins to the priest; fifth, be willing to perform the penance the priest gives us.

## FOR ME TO REVIEW

*Catechism Lesson*

**85. Q. Through what means may we obtain the "forgiveness of sins"?**

A. We may obtain the "forgiveness of sins" especially through the sacraments of Baptism and Penance and Reconciliation.

### Questions and Exercises

1. Did Christ institute the sacrament of Penance and Reconciliation?
2. Did Christ give the Apostles the power to forgive sins?
3. Is any sin too great to be forgiven?
4. Is sorrow for sin a necessary condition for forgiveness?
5. Does the sacrament of Holy Orders give priests the power to forgive sins?
6. Does Penance and Reconciliation give grace to those already in the state of grace?
7. Should we be afraid to confess any sin to the priest?
8. Does a daily examination of conscience help us in preparing for confession?
9. Does the penance we say remit all the temporal punishment due to our sins?
10. Should we try to make up in some way for the wrong we do, even though it is not seriously sinful?

## FOR ME TO REMEMBER

1. Christ gave the Apostles the power to forgive sins on the first Easter Sunday night.
2. The best way to thank God for the sacrament of Penance and Reconciliation is to make use of it often.
3. We should make a careful preparation for the reception of this sacrament.
4. No matter how often or how seriously we sin, our sins may be forgiven if we are sorry for them.

## FOR ME TO DO

1. Make a chart showing the most important words connected with the sacrament of Penance and Reconciliation. Be able to explain the terms.
2. Write a letter to a non-Catholic friend explaining why we go to confession.
3. Find a copy of the words of Our Lady of Fatima in regard to the forgiveness of sins.
4. Write an act of thanksgiving for the gift of the sacrament of Penance and Reconciliation.
5. How would you explain the saying, "Despise sin, but not the sinner"?
6. What five things are necessary for the worthy reception of the sacrament of Penance and Reconciliation?

We should frequently receive the sacrament of Penance and Reconciliation.

LESSON 29

# The Resurrection of the Body and Life Everlasting

## The Catholic Church Teaches the Meaning of Death

One day Jairus, an important man of Capernaum, begged Jesus to lay His hands upon his very sick little daughter. While Jesus was on the way to the home, messengers came to tell Jairus that his daughter had died. When our Lord arrived at the home of Jairus there was a great clamor. Jesus went into the house and said, "Why do you make this din, and weep?" Then sending the people outside, He brought the lovely twelve-year-old girl back to life. Imagine how happy and grateful her father was!

Although this event does not tell us what death is, it does give an idea of the sadness a death causes in a family. For this reason very few people like to think about death. When they do, they usually picture it as something very far away. Perhaps it is far away for some of us, but no matter how far off, death is one thing we cannot escape. St. Paul says, ". . . it is appointed unto men to die once" (Heb. 9:27).

At the moment of death we know the soul leaves the body. All the earthly pleasures which our bodies have enjoyed are ended. Our eyes are no longer able to see the beauties which God has created. Our feet no longer are able to carry us. Our hands are not able to feel. Our bodies return to the earth to await resurrection day.

## Death, Though a Punishment for Sin, Is a Blessing

It is true that death is a punishment for sin, but death is also a blessing. If we have been faithful, death is the gateway to heaven.

It means going home to God. Just when or how we will pass through this gateway none of us knows. Only one thing is certain; there will be no escaping it.

## We Must Always Be Prepared for Death

We must keep ourselves ready for the coming of the Master as did the wise virgins in the Gospel. Then we will not fear the sentence that will be passed at death. Holy Mother Church reminds us frequently of death in her favorite prayer to our Lady: "Pray for us sinners, now and at the hour of our death. Amen."

## All Men Will Rise From the Dead

One of the beautiful scenes in the life of our Lord is the restoring of His friend Lazarus to life. The first message to our Lord when Lazarus was dying was, "He whom Thou lovest is sick." Instead of hurrying to Bethany as we would imagine our kind and loving Lord would do, He waited a few days.

When Christ and His disciples finally reached Bethany, they learned that Lazarus was already dead. According to the custom at that time, he had been buried the day he died. Our Lord was sad when He saw the grief of His two friends, Mary and Martha, the sisters of Lazarus. We know that He actually wept. He went to the entrance of the tomb and in a loud voice called, "Lazarus, come forth!" Picture the body beginning to move, sitting up, and finally standing up. Lazarus had been brought back to life. How surprised the people were! How grateful Mary and Martha felt!

One day our bodies, too, will rise from the dead. St. Matthew describes the scene in the Gospel when he says that God "will send forth his angels with a trumpet and a great sound, and they will gather his elect from the four winds, and from one end of the heavens to the other" (Mt. 24:31).

At this summons the resurrection of the body will take place. *By "the resurrection of the body" is meant that at the end of the world the bodies of all men will rise from the earth and be united*

*again to their souls, nevermore to be separated.* The very same body which was ours during life will be restored to us for eternity.

In his epistle St. Paul says, "... we shall all indeed rise, but we shall not all be changed" (1 Cor. 15:51). *The bodies of the just will rise to share forever in the glory of their souls.* This means the body, which during life took part in many actions which were worthy of reward, will share the reward with the soul for all eternity. The body will not feel pain or suffering, and all the blessed will experience great joy and will share perfect peace and love. All the things our hearts desire will be found in heaven. The greatest joy of all will be found in seeing God face to face in heaven and possessing Him as our very own. This happiness will last forever.

At the end of the world the bodies of all men will rise from the earth and be united again to their souls, nevermore to be separated.

*The bodies of the damned will also rise to share in the eternal punishment of their souls.* As the bodies of the just shared in their good works during life, so also did the bodies of the wicked share in their evil pleasure. In death the wicked will be able to feel every form of pain. Even in the midst of dreadful torments, they will live forever.

The resurrection of the body applies to all human beings who have died. It will not apply to the Blessed Mother. At the end of her

**The Four Last Things**

- Death
- Judgment
- Heaven
- Hell

life on earth *by the special privilege of her Assumption, the body of the Blessed Virgin Mary, united to her immaculate soul, was glorified and taken into heaven.* In the year 1950, Pope Pius XII defined this teaching of the Church and declared it an article of faith. He said that at the end of her life on earth Mary was assumed into heaven, body and soul. This means that all Catholics must believe that our Blessed Lady's body and soul, free from any stain of sin or decay, was taken into heaven.

## The Particular Judgment Will Take Place Immediately After Death

What will happen to us after we die? The time immediately after death will be very important for us because our everlasting home will then be decided upon. As soon as the soul leaves the body, God judges us. Every thought, word, and act of our life will flash in review before God and ourselves. Then God will pass upon us an eternal sentence. He will never change it. *The judgment which will be passed on each one of us immediately after death is called the particular judgment.*

Whatever reward or punishment we receive at this particular judgment will be the result of our behavior while on earth. There will be no time to beg for mercy. The sentence of the Judge will be carried out at once. There are three possibilities. *The rewards or punishments appointed for men after the particular judgment are heaven, purgatory, or hell.*

### Purgatory

It is possible that few people will go straight to heaven when they die. Nothing soiled can enter heaven, so it is seldom that even a person whom we consider good escapes purgatory.

When Lucia, one of the children of Fatima, was talking to our Lady, she asked her if two little girls from their village who had recently died, had gone to heaven. Our Lady replied that one of them was in heaven, but that the other little girl would be in purgatory until the end of the world. This private revelation agrees with the teaching of the Church that: *Those are punished for a time in purgatory who die in the state of grace but are guilty of venial sin, or have not fully satisfied for the temporal punishment due to their sins.*

Our wills are so weak that often we do not fight off temptations of the world, the flesh, and the devil. We sometimes wrongly tell ourselves, "Oh, it's only a venial sin," or "I know it is a sin, but I can confess it and be forgiven." Our souls will need to be purified from these sins when we die. The place where they are purified is purgatory.

Sometimes we do not do enough penance for the sins we have committed, especially the more serious sins. We know that the eternal punishment due to these sins is taken away through the sacrament of penance. The penance which we do after confession remits some of the temporal punishment. But it does not always fully make up; there still remains some temporal punishment. In purgatory this punishment is made up.

The rewards or punishments appointed for men after the particular judgment are heaven, purgatory, or hell.

### Hell

One of the things we often hear people speak of as a great evil is a sudden and unprovided death. Perhaps we have never thought too much about this. If we did, we would realize how dreadful it is to die in mortal sin. For, *those are punished in hell who die in mortal sin; they are deprived of the vision of God and suffer dreadful torments, especially that of fire, for all eternity.*

***TERMS TO KNOW***

- corruption
- temporal
- deprived
- assent
- Assumption
- unprovided
- unquenchable

The first part of this answer needs no explanation. On this earth we can only understand in part the beauties of the vision of God. We must accept the words of the saints who have tried to describe them for us. St. Paul tells us that "eye has not seen, nor ear heard, nor has it entered into the heart of man, what things God has prepared for those who love him" (1 Cor. 2:9). St. Stephen, the first martyr of the Church, saw the heavens opened and was encouraged by this wonderful sight. St. John Chrysostom said he would pass through hell-fire to possess God in heaven.

If, however, we have not repented and confessed our mortal sins, we cannot enjoy heaven. Our greatest sorrow will be that through our own dreadful fault we have deserved the awful tortures of hell. We hardly have an idea what the punishment will be like. None of our earthly sufferings are like it. We do know that there is a fire in hell from these words of our Lord: "It is better for thee to enter into life everlasting lame, than, having two feet, to be cast into the hell of unquenchable fire" (Mk. 9:44). If we think of our last end we will be much less likely to sin. "Holy Mary, deliver us from the pains of hell."

### Heaven

If the thought of hell makes us sad, let us turn to a happier thought, heaven. It is a place of perfect and everlasting joy. It will continue for all eternity, and we will never fear losing it.

*Those are rewarded in heaven who have died in the state of grace and have been purified in purgatory, if necessary, from all venial sin and all debt of temporal punishment; they see God face to face and share forever in His glory and happiness.*

All those who have been faithful in this life will have a home there with God, with our Lady, the angels, the Apostles, and all the saints. Our own dear ones, who have died in grace, will be there with us, too, and we will have none of the cares and worries of life to distract us from the beauty of the vision of God.

## The General Judgment Will Take Place Immediately After the General Resurrection

No one knows, except God, where we will be on the last day. Wherever we are, we know that after all the bodies and souls are reunited, there will be another judgment. *The judgment which will be passed on all men immediately after the general resurrection is called the general judgment.* This will be the same sentence that was passed at the particular judgment.

This general judgment may not seem to be necessary to us, since each human being is judged at once after death. But if we recall the lesson of the Providence of God, perhaps we may understand His reason for a general judgment. In this life, good people often suffer great evils while the wicked seem to be well off. At the general judgment God will show to all men His infinite justice, His infinite goodness, His wise management of all things in each individual's life. So *although everyone is judged immediately after death, it is fitting that there be a general judgment in order that the justice, wisdom, and mercy of God may be glorified in the presence of all.*

**Can you explain the difference between the particular judgement and general judgement?**

After death there will be no time for repentance. It is, therefore, good for us to think of death, heaven, and hell. Let us often pray, "From a sudden and unexpected death, deliver us, O Lord."

## The Apostles' Creed Ends With the Word "Amen"

"Amen" is a Hebrew word. Placed at the end of the Apostles' Creed, it means that all those who make that profession of faith agree to all the truths contained in this prayer. If we say the word thoughtfully, it is the same as saying, "So be it." "This I believe." It also means that we are begging for the graces we need to help us live according to what we believe. *By the word "Amen," with which we end the Apostles' Creed, is meant "So it is," or "So be it"; the word expresses our firm belief in all the doctrines that the Creed contains.*

At death our life on earth ends, but if we have lived according to our faith, a greater, fuller life opens for us in heaven. Only then will we really appreciate the words of St. Augustine: "Thou hast made us for Yourself, O Lord, and our hearts are restless till they rest in You."

"Lord, I fear Your justice, I implore Your mercy, deliver me not to everlasting pains. Grant that I may possess You in the midst of everlasting joys."

### FOR ME TO REVIEW

*Catechism Lesson*

**86. Q. What do we mean by the "resurrection of the body"?**

A. By the "resurrection of the body" we mean that the bodies of the dead shall be restored to life, rise again on the last day, and be united to the souls from which they were separated by death.

**1392. Q. In what state will the bodies of the just rise?**

A. The bodies of the just will rise glorious and immortal.

**1393. Q. Will the bodies of the damned also rise?**

A. The bodies of the damned will also rise, but they will be condemned to eternal punishment.

**1374. Q. What is the judgment called which all men have to undergo on the last day?**

A. The judgment which all men have to undergo on the last day is called the general judgment.

**1372. Q. What is the judgment called which we have to undergo immediately after death?**

A. The judgment we have to undergo immediately after death is called the particular judgment.

**1375. Q. Will the sentence given at the particular judgment be changed at the general judgment?**

A. The sentence given at the particular judgment will not be changed at the general judgment, but it will be repeated and made public to all.

**1378. Q. What are the rewards or punishments appointed for men's souls after the particular judgment?**

A. The rewards or punishments appointed for men's souls after the particular judgment are heaven, purgatory, and hell.

**1381. Q. What is purgatory?**

A. Purgatory is the state in which those suffer for a time who die guilty of venial sins, or without having satisfied for the punishment due to their sins.

**1379. Q. What is hell?**

A. Hell is a state to which the wicked are condemned, and in which they are deprived of the sight of God for all eternity, and are in dreadful torments.

**1395. Q. What is heaven?**

A. Heaven is the state of everlasting life in which we see God face to face, are made like unto Him in glory, and enjoy eternal happiness.

**25. Q. What does "Amen" mean?**

A. "Amen" means, "so be it" and expresses a desire that the petition may be granted.

### Questions and Exercises

1. Why must we die?
2. Can anyone escape death?
3. What can we do to be prepared to meet death at all times?
4. Will our bodies and souls be separated at death?
5. When will the particular judgment take place?
6. When will the general judgment take place?
7. Does death mean the beginning of life for everyone?
8. Why do we visit the graves of the dead?
9. What will happen to our bodies and souls on the day of judgment?
10. What faculty that God has given us is going to determine whether we will merit heaven or hell?

### Matching

*Number one to twelve on your paper. After each number write the appropriate letter from the second column.*

| | |
|---|---|
| 1) Virtue of goodness, pity, or kindness | A. just |
| 2) Decay, return to dust | B. mercy |
| 3) Those who have kept God's laws | C. vision |
| 4) Arising to life | D. resurrection |
| 5) Truths, teachings | E. Assumption |
| 6) Having been taken up | F. privilege |
| 7) Right or proper | G. corruption |
| 8) Sight | H. temporal |
| 9) Only for a time | I. doctrines |
| 10) Kept from having | J. deprived |
| 11) Exception, away from common rule | K. preserved |
| 12) Saved | L. fitting |

## FOR ME TO REMEMBER

1. I am certain that I will die.
2. I do not know when or how I will die.
3. I will be judged immediately after death.
4. I will be in heaven or in hell for all eternity. I will not be given another chance.
5. On the last day my body will rise and be united again to my soul.
6. I will be eternally rewarded or eternally punished.

## FOR ME TO DO

1. Discuss some of the following:

   Why do Catholics honor the dead?

   Why do some people remain faithful to God despite great hardships?

   How do things appear at the moment of death?

   How will people feel when they come together for the general judgment?

   Why did Christ describe death as a thief in the night?

   Why does the Holy Scripture say we will not sin if we remember our last end?

2. Locate and write the important fact which is described in each of the following scriptural quotations: (*a*) Hebr. 9:27, (*b*) Apoc. 22:5, (*c*) 1 Cor. 2:9, (*d*) 2 Thess. 1:9, (*e*) Jn. 5:28–29.

# UNIT 4 Our Duties to God

# CHAPTER 9
# Living According to What We Believe

*"I the Lord, am your God, who brought you out of the land of Egypt, that place of slavery. You shall not have other gods besides me. You shall not carve idols for yourselves in the shape of anything in the sky above or on the earth below or in the waters beneath the earth; you shall not bow down before them or worship them. For I, the Lord, your God, am a jealous God, inflicting punishment for their fathers' wickedness on the children of those who hate me, down to the third and fourth generation; but bestowing mercy down to the thousandth generation, on the children of those who love me and keep my commandments.*

*"You shall not take the name of the Lord, your God, in vain. For the Lord will not leave unpunished him who takes his name in vain.*

*"Remember to keep holy the Sabbath day. Six days you may labor and do all your work, but the seventh day is the Sabbath of the Lord, your God. No work may be done then either by you, or your son or daughter, or your male or female slave, or your beast, or by the alien who lives with you. In six days the Lord made the heavens and the earth, the sea and all that is in them; but on the seventh day he rested. That is why the Lord has blessed the Sabbath day and made it holy" (Exod. 20:2–11).*

*In units 1 to 3 we have learned much about God and the three Divine Persons. We have learned of God's great goodness to us.*

*Now, to prove to God that we are grateful, we must:*

*Live according to what we believe.*
*Adore God and Him only.*
*Use His name with reverence.*
*Worship Him as the Church directs.*

We have learned the part which the Holy Spirit plays in the drama of Redemption. We have seen how the third Person of the Blessed Trinity works in the Church and in each soul. We have gained greater knowledge of the divine origin of the Church, of its mission on earth, and of the marks and attributes which point to the Church as the one true Church of Christ. We learned to appreciate our membership in the Church and in the communion of saints, and to understand better the doctrines of the resurrection of the body and life everlasting. We also gained a deeper knowledge of actual and sanctifying grace.

Now we shall see how we can co-operate with these graces by avoiding sin and doing good; how we can lead a Christian life on earth in preparation for the happiness of heaven; how God's laws will guide us to this goal.

We cannot reach heaven safely unless we follow the spiritual road signs, or commandments, which God and His Church have placed along the way.

LESSON 30

# Laws Help Us Live as We Believe

Have you ever stopped to think how very necessary laws, as well as rules and directions are in our daily lives? We could not possibly play games without rules. How could you make a birdhouse, an airplane, or a flower garden without directions? What would your home or community life be like without rules? Imagine, if you can, a busy highway where no one obeyed traffic regulations, or a ball game where everyone made up rules as the game was being played. Laws bring order and peace; laws faithfully observed bring greater security, better regulated lives, and therefore actually more freedom.

As you know, there are certain laws of nature which help the plants and animals to carry out God's plan for them. Flowers and plants grow and provide food and beauty for man; ice and snow melt and become a means of irrigation for crops; soil absorbs moisture and nourishment necessary for the growth of vegetation; the sun and stars shine and furnish light and heat. If any one of these lower creatures were to stop following the laws of nature, confusion would result. We must, therefore, observe the laws of nature in our treatment of these lower creatures in order to help carry out God's plan for them. So also must we observe the laws of nature which govern our bodies. Most of all we must obey the laws which govern our minds and wills and especially the Commandments of God and His Church, in order that we may reach our eternal destiny.

## The Laws of God—A Means of Salvation

Since the very beginning of time, long before anyone had ever heard of the ten commandments, God deeply imprinted on the souls of men the laws which govern human nature. This natural inborn knowledge of right and wrong taught that the highest honor is due to God; that man could not willfully injure himself; that man must do to others as he would have them do unto him. Conscience, or the voice of reason within each of God's human creatures, helped man in choosing good and avoiding evil.

You remember that man's mind became darkened and his will weakened as a result of original sin. So God made His law known to man in words that could not be mistaken. Read the story of the ten commandments in the twentieth Chapter of Exodus, the second Book of the Old Testament. The powerful words used by God in giving these commandments to Moses prove to us that *besides believing what God has revealed, we must keep His law.* Faith alone, therefore, is not enough for salvation. Man must indeed use his intellect to know and believe what God has revealed, but he must also use his will to keep God's law.

God did not mean these commandments merely for the small group of Israelites. He intended that all men should use them as guides to help them live peacefully on earth in such a way as to prepare for union with Him in heaven. We cannot reach this destination safely unless we follow the spiritual road signs, or commandments, which God and His Church have placed along the way. And we cannot keep God's law without His help. This he will give us if we ask Him.

God's first and foremost law commands us to love God above all things, and to please Him each moment of the day by doing the things He wants us to do. You have often heard the expression, "Offer it up." Do you understand the meaning of these words? Do you really make each daily action, whether pleasant or not, an act of love of God?

God demands that we love Him with our whole heart, as He deserves. Loving Him means at least obeying Him. God and His divine will must come first in our affections. We may not love ourselves or any creature more than we love God. True love of God prompts us to wish Him all honor and glory and every good; and to do all in our power to obtain it for Him. Again, true love of God shows itself in action, for our Lord said, "He who has my commandments and keeps them, he it is who loves me" (Jn. 14:21).

Besides loving God, we must love our neighbor as ourselves. This means that we should wish those things for our neighbor that we would like to have for ourselves—happiness and holiness in this life and glory in the next. It means we must help our neighbor if he is in need, in body or in soul. We must treat everyone in the world as Christ would, for all men are our brothers.

## God Reduced His Commandments to Two—Love of God and Love of Neighbor

To have happiness and holiness in this life and glory in eternity we must keep the whole law of God. If we are to do this we must let the advice of our Lord guide us. One day a doctor of the law asked Him which was the greatest commandment of the law. Our Lord answered that it was to love God completely and then to love our neighbor.

God loves us with an infinite love. In return, He demands that we love Him, and that we show this love by obeying His law.

**The two great commandments that contain the whole law of God are: first, Thou shalt love the Lord thy God with thy whole heart, and with thy whole soul, and with thy whole mind, and with thy whole strength; second, Thou shalt love thy neighbor as thyself.**

The whole law of God binds us to love of God, of self, and of neighbor. True love of God, of self, and of neighbor, means among other things: adoration of God; respect for His holy name; observance of Sundays and holy days; obedience; respect for life; purity in thought, word, and deed; justice and truth; observance of Church laws on marriage; and helping our neighbor. We therefore realize that *to love God, our neighbor, and ourselves we must keep the commandments of God and of the Church, and perform the spiritual and corporal works of mercy.*

## FOR ME TO REVIEW

*Catechism Lesson*

**1125. Q. Is it enough to belong to God's Church in order to be saved?**

A. It is not enough to belong to the Church in order to be saved, but we must also keep the commandments of God and of the Church.

**1127. Q.Which are the commandments that contain the whole law of God?**

A. The commandments which contain the whole law of God are these two: 1st, Thou shalt love the Lord thy God with thy whole heart, with thy whole soul, with thy whole strength, and with thy whole mind; 2nd, Thou shalt love thy neighbor as thyself.

### TERMS TO KNOW

- divine origin
- Israelites
- security
- binding
- eternal destiny
- abstinence
- unmistakable

### Questions and Exercises

1. Are laws necessary in our daily life?
2. Are laws necessary in our spiritual life?
3. Do God's laws govern our minds and wills?
4. Does conscience sometimes regulate our actions?
5. Is the story of the Ten Commandments told in the book of Genesis?
6. Did God compose the Ten Commandments only for the Israelites?
7. Should we try to please God every minute of the day?
8. May we love any creature more than we love God?

9. Is the whole law of God contained in the first three commandments?
10. Do we have any opportunities to prove our love of God?

## FOR ME TO REMEMBER

1. Laws are intended to produce order and peace which will bring about freedom and happiness.
2. God's first law is that we love Him above all things; and show our love by obeying His laws.
3. Laws guide us to our heavenly goal.

## FOR ME TO DO

1. The text says that our most important duty in obedience is fulfilled when we obey the laws which govern our minds and wills. Explain what these laws are, why this statement is true and how it applies to us.
2. Which faculty do you use especially in obeying God's laws?
3. How do little acts of mortification enable us to obey God's laws?
4. Draw up a list of commandments which apply to your daily life. Examine your conscience on them each evening.
5. What kind of neighborhood do you live in? Do you give an example of obedience to God's law to your neighbors rather than try to impress them with your beautiful home?
6. Say a special prayer each day to our Lady asking her to help you to be faithful to God's laws. Since she fulfilled the laws not meant for her, ask her to help you obey the laws which were made for you.

LESSON 31

# The Works of Mercy; The Commandments; The Counsels

The laws of God include our performing the works of mercy. In fact on the last day we will be judged on whether we have performed them or not (Mt. 25:31–46).

## The Corporal Works of Mercy

We know that our Lord was kind to everyone in word and deed. He especially sympathized with the poor and suffering, and even performed miracles to relieve their miseries. In this way He clearly showed His love of neighbor through the corporal works of mercy which He performed—that is through the good deeds done for men's bodies. Remember His words: "Amen I say to you, as long as you did it for one of these, the least of my brethren, you did it for me" (Mt. 25:40).

Very often we are able to help our neighbor spiritually through the corporal works of mercy. Because of our kindness, he may open his heart to us and eventually to God.

Since the corporal works of mercy help us serve Christ in this world, it is important that we know them. *The chief corporal works of mercy are seven:*

*1. to feed the hungry;*

*2. to give drink to the thirsty;*

*3. to clothe the naked;*

*4. to visit the imprisoned;*

*5. to shelter the homeless;*

*6. to visit the sick;*

*7. to bury the dead.*

### To Feed the Hungry

This is the first want to be attended to, for without food we die. We can fulfill this first work of mercy by giving food to those who are in need; by giving money to purchase food for the needy; by contributing to societies for funds for this purpose.

Examples: Joseph feeding the Egyptians (Gen. 41:56).
Our Lord and the Multitude (Mk. 8:2).
St. Elizabeth of Hungary whose alms fed the poor.

We can feed the hungry by volunteering at a soup kitchen.

### To Give Drink to the Thirsty

Thirst, like hunger, is a very painful experience. Our Lord promises a reward for even a cup of water given in His name. "For whoever gives you a cup of water to drink in my name, because you are Christ's, amen I say to you, he shall not lose his reward" (Mk. 9:40).

> Examples: The woman at the well (Jn. 4:1–42).
> Rebecca to the servant (Gen. 24:18).
> Christ on the cross: "I thirst" (Jn. 19:28).

### To Clothe the Naked

This is a necessary work if the needy or destitute are to preserve modesty and protect themselves from the cold. We perform this work by giving clothing to the poor, to refugees, and to those stripped of their belongings by floods, hurricanes, or fire; by making garments for those in need, or by contributing to those organizations which help provide these articles.

> Examples: Tabitha at Joppa made garments for destitute widows (Acts 9:36).

St. Martin shared his cloak with a beggar.
St. Catherine of Siena.

These first three corporal works of mercy can be classed as *almsgiving.*

Almsgiving obtains for us remission for venial sins, brings the blessing of God upon us, makes atonement for the temporal punishment due to our sins, and assures eternal merit hereafter. By almsgiving we make friends with the poor; they in turn pray for us, and their prayers have great power with God.

### To Visit the Imprisoned

It is a charity to visit the imprisoned in order to encourage and comfort them. St. Paul tells us to: "Remember those who are in bonds as if you were bound with them" (Hebr. 13:3).

Examples: The Christians visited St. Paul at Jerusalem and Damascus (2 Cor. 11:32–35).
St. Peter Claver visited the slaves.
St. Francis Xavier.

### To Shelter the Homeless

Hospitality is a duty recommended to us by St. Paul when he says: "Let brotherly love abide in you, and do not forget to entertain strangers; for thereby some have entertained angels unawares" (Hebr. 13:1–2). We have many opportunities to shelter the homeless in our care of orphans and displaced persons. Even when we are not actually giving these latter a home, we can treat them in such a way that they will be made to feel at home in our country, where even the language is strange.

Examples: Martha and Mary received our Lord into their home as a guest (Lk. 10:38).
The disciples at Emmaus (Lk. 24:29).
The Great St. Bernard in the Alps.

### To Visit the Sick

The object of the visit to the sick or injured in home, hospital, on the battlefield, or elsewhere is to bring spiritual or temporal relief to the sufferer. We can perform this work of mercy by sympathizing with the sick, by helping them to be patient and resigned; by bringing them food, delicacies, and little comforts; by procuring doctor, nurse, medicine; and by calling the priest to attend to them.

> Examples: Jesus at the pool (Jn. 5:6).
> Damien and the Lepers.
> St. Vincent de Paul
> The priest visiting the sick.

### To Bury the Dead

It is a particularly good and holy work of mercy to provide the dead with decent burial, and to attend funerals or to drop in to pay our respects at the wakes of those with whom we may have associated. St. Augustine says: "We ought to show respect to the bodies of Christian people, because they have been the instruments employed by the soul."

> Examples: The people of Naim (Lk. 7:12).
> Joseph of Arimathea and Nicodemus (Mk. 15:46).

Have you ever read the poem, "How the Great Guest Came" by Edwin Markham, or the story, "Where Love Is There God Is Also," by Leo Tolstoy? Both of these writings help us to see the corporal works of mercy in action.

Daily, God gives us the opportunity to perform some one or more of the corporal works of mercy. Consider the many opportunities that may arise for you to spread the kingdom of God on earth. Perhaps your companions forgot their lunches; you could share your sandwiches and milk with them; you can contribute to collections requested by the bishop in order to help bear the expense of the clothing, food, and medical needs of the orphans and the homeless; perhaps you could write a letter to, or visit a sick friend personally.

## The Spiritual Works of Mercy

The corporal works of mercy, which care for the wants of the body, are very good and necessary. But the spiritual works of mercy, which concern the soul, are even more important. Jesus did not merely cure the sick and feed the hungry. He also made every effort to relieve the spiritual needs of the people. He performed the greatest work of mercy when He redeemed man by His suffering and death on the cross. Again He is our Model.

Next to concern for our own salvation, is the need to help our neighbor attain his eternal happiness. When we realize that the chief likeness to God is not in the body but in the soul which is spiritual, and free, and immortal, it makes it easier for us to carry out the command of God to help our neighbor save his soul. In what better way can we do this than through the spiritual works of mercy? Do you know them?

*The chief spiritual works of mercy are seven:*

1. *to admonish the sinner;*
2. *to instruct the ignorant;*
3. *to counsel the doubtful;*
4. *to comfort the sorrowful;*
5. *to bear wrongs patiently;*
6. *to forgive all injuries;*
7. *to pray for the living and the dead. Let us explain each one.*

### To Admonish the Sinner

We can understand the value of this great work of mercy if we recall the words of St. James: "He ought to know that he who causes a sinner to be brought back from his misguided way, will save his soul from death, and will cover a multitude of sins" (James 5:20). We perform this work of mercy by kind but firm words, by good example, by wise zeal, and by prayer.

Examples: The thief on our Lord's right hand (Lk. 23:42).
St. Paul at Athens (Acts 17:22).
Elias and the false prophets (3 Kings 18:21–39).

### To Instruct the Ignorant

Ignorance is often the source of such evils as missing Mass, neglecting the sacraments, or doing things to excess. We can be helpful by answering doubts and difficulties, by directing persons to hear sermons and catechism instructions, by lending or recommending good books, and by wise and charitable correction.

> Examples: Our Lord in the parables—New Testament.
> St. Peter, after Pentecost (Acts 2:14).

### To Counsel the Doubtful

This work of mercy calls for gentleness and kindness. We can often lighten the mental strain of our neighbor by giving advice to him in his temporal or spiritual trials and difficulties. Sometimes a kind word or gentle act is all that is needed to help those who are in doubt to see what God expects of them. Sometimes we can bring or direct a person to a priest.

> Examples: Christ to the rich young man (Mt. 19:21).
> Gamaliel to the Council (Acts 5:35).

### To Comfort the Sorrowful

Our own experience shows us how great a charity is this work of mercy. We may practice it toward others by showing sympathy to them in their trials, encouragement in their difficulties, and by kindness in time of trouble and sorrow.

> Examples: Our Lord and Magdalen (Lk. 7:48).
> Joseph and his fellow prisoners (Gen. 40:7).
> The widow's son (Lk. 7:13).

### To Bear Wrongs Patiently

By this work of mercy we help both our neighbor and ourselves. Our good example of cheerfulness and patience when unjustly accused or treated or when things are difficult encourages our neighbor, and at the same time merits a reward for ourselves.

> Examples: Our Lord in His Passion (Lk. 23:34).
> David, being stoned (2 Kings 16).
> St. Joseph on the flight into Egypt (Mt. 2:13).

### To Forgive all Injuries

This is the lesson taught by our Lord on Calvary. Christ prayed to His heavenly Father to forgive His executioners. "Father, forgive them, for they do not know what they are doing" (Lk. 23:34). The true Christian loves all men, even those who reproach and persecute him. We too, because of our love of God, should forgive all injuries; not once but as many times as necessary, as our Lord told St. Peter (Mt. 18:21–22).

> Examples: Our Lord on the Cross (Lk. 23:34).
> Joseph and his brothers (Gen. 45:5).
> St. Stephen (Acts 7:60).

### To Pray for the Living and the Dead

The conversion of a soul may at some time or other depend on our prayers. We must pray for the pope and the Church, for our parents, relatives and friends, for bishops and the clergy, for civil leaders, and for the holy souls in purgatory. To be able to help our deceased relatives by prayer should be a comfort and a consolation to us.

> Examples: Our Lord for His disciples and the entire Church (Jn. 17:9–23).
> Moses for his people (Exod. 32:11).
> St. Augustine for his mother.

*Everyone is obliged to perform the works of mercy, according to his own ability and the need of his neighbor.* This does not mean that we neglect our own salvation in order to aid our neighbor. The phrase "according to his own ability" tells us that each must do what he is able to do. "According to the needs of his neighbor" indicates that one need not always evenly distribute his charity, but should regulate it according to the condition of the neighbor in question. The help or good example we give to our companions may make a difference in the conduct of some boy or girl, not only now, but also in later life.

But then we must not think of helping our neighbor only so far as these seven corporal and seven spiritual works of mercy are concerned. *All the ordinary deeds done every day to relieve the corporal or spiritual needs of others are true works of mercy, if done in the name of Christ,* that is, to please Christ, or to show our love for Him. Let us use every opportunity to practice the beautiful virtue of charity. Often repeat this prayer:

"All for Thee, Most Sacred Heart of Jesus," especially when performing a good deed.

## The Ten Commandments

You will remember that our Lord said there are two great commandments: (1) to love God; (2) to love our neighbor as ourself. The Ten Commandments are included in these two commandments. Three of the ten commandments tell us of our duties to God directly. The other seven commandments tell us of the duties we owe directly to our neighbor and to ourselves.

Did you notice the repetition of one particular word in each of the first three commandments? What is that word? It is the word "Lord." In the first, the Lord; in the second, the Lord's name; in the third, the Lord's day. The word "Lord" does not appear in any of the remaining commandments. The repetition of this word not only directs our thoughts to God but also shows us that the work commanded by these three commandments tends directly toward the honor and glory of God. These first three commandments are an explanation of the first great commandment; the

**The commandments of God are these ten:**

1. I am the Lord thy God; thou shalt not have strange gods before Me.
2. Thou shalt not take the name of the Lord thy God in vain.
3. Remember thou keep holy the Lord's day.
4. Honor thy father and thy mother.
5. Thou shalt not kill.
6. Thou shalt not commit adultery.
7. Thou shalt not steal.
8. Thou shalt not bear false witness against thy neighbor.
9. Thou shalt not covet thy neighbor's wife.
10. Thou shalt not covet thy neighbor's goods.

last seven commandments are an explanation of the second great commandment.

God in His infinite goodness and love has given us these ten commandments to guide the actions of our whole life; every minute of every day. There is nothing that He, our Creator and our Redeemer, has not done for us to help us to gain heaven. Truly, He is our dear Father and closest Friend. Knowing this, *we should not be satisfied merely to keep the commandments of God, but should always be ready to do good deeds, even when they are not commanded.* Generous lovers of God do not measure their generosity. They give themselves wholeheartedly to a life of good deeds.

## "If Thou Wilt Be Perfect"

The young man who had asked Christ what he must do to gain eternal life was told by our Lord to keep the commandments. When he replied that he had kept the commandments since youth, Christ answered: "If thou wilt be perfect, go, sell what thou hast, and give to the poor, and thou shalt have treasure in heaven and come, follow me" (Mt. 19:21). By these words, Christ invited this rich man to a life of perfection. Do you know what

*There the angel of the LORD appeared to him as fire flaming out of a bush.[a] When he looked, although the bush was on fire, it was not being consumed.*

EXODUS 3:2

that means? Christ was asking this young man to spend his life for God in a manner far more perfect than that required by the commandments.

In order to follow such a high calling, or vocation, *our Saviour especially recommends the observance of the evangelical counsels—voluntary poverty, perpetual chastity, and perfect obedience.* These three evangelical, that is gospel counsels are like words of advice. To follow this advice and take the three vows of poverty, chastity, and obedience is especially pleasing to our Lord, and will help us to serve Him in a more perfect manner.

Voluntary poverty means giving up earthly possessions.

Perpetual chastity means giving up the right to marriage and promising to remain pure in soul and body.

Perfect obedience means fulfilling the commands of appointed superiors as making known the will of God to us.

To you also, our Lord says: "Keep the commandments if you wish to serve Me and to save your soul." Perhaps He is also saying: "Come, follow Me, through the practice of the three vows." Men and women in religious life live in full these evangelical counsels. Those who choose marriage can still practice these counsels in part according to their state in life. Memorize the ten commandments not only for the sake of reciting them, but for the sake of living them. Often say the prayer: "Jesus, teach me who You want me to be."

***TERMS TO KNOW***

- corporal
- perpetual
- chastity
- brethren
- refugees
- evangelical
- destitute
- temporal
- meritorious
- remission
- spiritual
- works of mercy
- admonish
- atonement
- counsel
- excess
- instruct
- doubtful
- conversion
- ignorant
- voluntary
- poverty
- perfection
- obedience

## FOR ME TO REVIEW

*Catechism Lesson*

**819. Q. Which are the chief corporal works of mercy?**

A. The chief corporal works of mercy are seven: To feed the hungry, to give drink to the thirsty, to clothe the naked, to ransom the captive, to harbor the harborless, to visit the sick, and to bury the dead.

**813. Q. Which are the chief spiritual works of mercy?**

A. The chief spiritual works of mercy are seven: To admonish the sinner, to instruct the ignorant, to counsel the doubtful, to comfort the sorrowful, to bear wrongs patiently, to forgive all injuries, and to pray for the living and the dead.

**820. Q. How may we briefly state the corporal works of mercy?**

A. We may briefly state the corporal works of mercy by saying that we are obliged to help the poor in all their forms of want.

**1130. Q. Which are the commandments of God?**

A. The commandments of God are these ten:

1. I am the Lord thy God, who brought thee out of the land of Egypt, out of the house of bondage. Thou shalt not have strange gods before me. Thou shalt not make to thyself a graven thing, nor the likeness of any thing that is in Heaven above, or in the earth beneath, nor of those things that are in the waters under the earth. Thou shalt not adore them, nor serve them.
2. Thou shalt not take the name of the Lord thy God in vain.
3. Remember thou keep holy the Sabbath day.
4. Honor thy father and thy mother.
5. Thou shalt not kill.

6. Thou shalt not commit adultery.
7. Thou shalt not steal.
8. Thou shalt not bear false witness against thy neighbor.
9. Thou shalt not covet thy neighbor's wife.
10. Thou shalt not covet thy neighbor's goods.

### Questions and Exercises

1. What motive should we have for all our good deeds?
2. How are we to observe the commandments?
3. How did Christ perform the spiritual and corporal works of mercy?
4. Why should we visit the sick? The imprisoned?
5. What was Jesus' greatest work of mercy?
6. What is almsgiving? What does it do for us?
7. Give some examples of Christ's spirit of forgiveness.
8. In what ways did Christ practice obedience to God's laws?

### Matching

*Match the following spiritual and corporal works of mercy, on your own paper.*

| | |
|---|---|
| 1. To feed the hungry | A. Sending clothing to needy families |
| 2. Give drink to the thirsty they may be doing | B. Reminding our friends of the wrong |
| 3. Shelter the homeless | C. Not excusing ourselves when we are accused of doing something we did not do |

| | |
|---|---|
| 4. Clothe the naked hard-working man | D. Getting a glass of water for a |
| 5. Visit the imprisoned | E. Paying a visit to a classmate who was in an accident |
| 6. Visit the sick | F. Giving advice to someone not well instructed in our religion |
| 7. Bury the dead | G. Sending food to children whose father is unemployed |
| 8. Admonish the sinner | H. Paying a visit to someone who is in jail |
| 9. Instruct the ignorant | I. Explaining the teachings of our Church to those who do not know them |
| 10. Counsel the doubtful | J. Offering a Mass for a deceased relative or friend |
| 11. Comfort the sorrowing | K. Attending a funeral |
| 12. Bear wrongs patiently | L. Giving a home to refugees from other countries |
| 13. Forgive all injuries | M. Consoling those who are in trouble |
| 14. Pray for living and dead | N. Excusing those who have hurt our feelings |

## FOR ME TO REMEMBER

1. The Ten Commandments are our guides on the way to heaven.
2. The Ten Commandments of God are summarized in the law of charity.
3. The Ten Commandments express God's will for us.
4. The two great commandments are: (1) love of God; (2) love of our neighbor.
5. The first three commandments are an explanation of the first great commandment of God.

6. The spiritual and corporal works of mercy help us gain merit for heaven.
7. The lives of Christ and the saints give us examples of the practice of the spiritual and corporal works of mercy.

## FOR ME TO DO

1. Draw two tables of stone. On the first print: *God,* I–III. On the second print: *Self and Neighbor,* IV–X. Under each list what belongs there.
2. Look up the story of the Ten Commandments in the Bible. Plan a short talk to the class, telling what book of the Bible the Commandments are contained in, and why they are there, and how they were given.
3. Make a chart of the corporal works of mercy. Show how Christ exemplified each one—and how you can practice each one.
4. Explain what is meant by performing the spiritual and corporal works of mercy with the right motive.
5. How can the help you give to others throughout the day bring you closer to Christ?

## In God's Service

*Lord God, whose we are and whom we serve, help us to glorify you this day, in all the thoughts of our hearts, in all the words of our lips, and in all the works of our hands, as becomes those who are your servants, through Jesus Christ our Lord. Amen.*

# CHAPTER 10
# The First Three Commandments: Love of God

LESSON 32

## The First Commandment: We Must Worship God

Thus far this year we have learned about God, Father, Son, and Holy Spirit. Now we shall study in detail each of the first three commandments of God. They tell us our duties to God. The first commandment is: *I am the Lord thy God; thou shalt not have strange gods before Me.*

### What the First Commandment Commands

Did a friend of yours ever try to call you away while you were playing a good game of baseball? What did you do? Suppose that instead of a friend, your father came all the way over to the ball field and told you to come home at once. Why would you stop playing at once when your father called? Your father has authority over you; he has the right to punish you, and you know for your own good that you had better obey.

Our Father in heaven wanted His family on earth to live in peace and good order. He, therefore, gave man the Ten Commandments. God knows that it is hard to obey laws, but He also knows that it is much harder to live in a world where there are no laws.

To show how necessary it is for us to observe His laws God introduced the very first commandment by reminding us who He is. "I am the Lord thy God." What thoughts come to your mind as you think over these words? The little word "I" tells us that there

is only one God. The word "Lord" means more than "master." It means the one from whom all have existence.

God, we learned, is the Supreme Being, infinitely perfect, who made all things and keeps them in existence. Therefore, the very first words of the first commandment remind us that He who gives us the laws is our Creator and Preserver. They help us to realize how important it is to obey God's laws. They remind us that we must not only acknowledge God as our Lord and Creator but that we must worship and honor Him in a special way.

The second part of the first commandment says: ". . . thou shalt not have strange gods before Me." What is meant by strange gods? What pictures have you seen of strange gods in geography books or movies? Buddha? A mummified animal? Strange gods, we may say, are false gods, or any creature adored in the place of the one true God. The pagans worship the sun, moon, stars, and animals. This is idolatry and is sinful. These things have no power to help us. God alone can answer our prayers. He alone has a right to supreme worship as the

## The "strange gods" of today

When we read the Bible or history books, we hear about pagan cultures worshiping false gods, those who supposedly control the sea or the wind or the sun. Or think of the golden calf from the book of Exodus. It's tempting to think that we would never engage in sacrilegious behavior like this, but "strange gods" can come in many forms. Today, our society tends to "worship" certain kinds of technology, like phones or computers, or in some cases we worship other people, like celebrities and politicians. It may not be worship in the explicit form of the word, but anytime we place all our time, focus, energy, and happiness in something like this, it can become a god. As children, you have to be careful not to place sports, video games, or anything else above God. God must always be the center of our lives.

Creator and Preserver of all things. The catechism explains it this way: *By the first commandment we are commanded to offer to God alone the supreme worship that is due Him.*

## How We Worship God

In order to understand how to give God supreme worship, let us think about our parents. How do we honor and please them? Our fathers and mothers are pleased and happy when we listen to them and believe what they tell us. Moreover, they are glad when we come to them with our troubles. Why? We show that we trust them. We show our love for our fathers and mothers by respect and obedience, and by making little sacrifices to do things for them. So too *we worship God by acts of faith, hope, and charity, and by adoring Him and praying to Him.*

### Faith

Faith helps us to observe the first commandment. We give God supreme worship by believing Him because He is infinite truth. We believe as unchangeably true all that He has revealed and we believe it on His own word. Christ worked great miracles for those who had faith in Him and He also praised them highly.

"And wherever He went, into village or farm or town, they laid the sick in the market places, and entreated him to let them touch but the tassel of his cloak; and as many as touched him were saved" (Mk. 6:56). We too can show our faith in God by doing the things which faith demands of us; by making acts of faith often; and by professing our faith whenever God's honor demands it.

In order to have this belief we must do certain things. *Faith obliges us, first, to make efforts to find out what God has revealed.* We can do this by studying our religion and finding out as much as we can about it. *Second, faith obliges us to believe firmly what God has revealed.* As soon as we know the truth we must believe it. It is good for us to say the prayer recorded in St. Mark 9:23: "I do believe; help my unbelief." *Third, faith obliges us to profess our faith openly whenever necessary.*

All of us have shown our faith openly many times. We have done so when we prayed reverently in church or at home; when we went to church on Sunday; when we bowed our heads on hearing the name of Jesus. Christ has promised to claim us as His own before His Father in heaven for our open profession of faith.

There are times when it is absolutely necessary that we profess our faith openly. These are the occasions when God's honor requires it, or the good of our neighbor demands it. Can you think of such instances? The lives of the early martyrs or modern martyrs have many examples.

Since a Catholic must worship God by faith he must guard it carefully. How? The introduction of this book discusses this matter. We can, however, summarize it here. A *Catholic can best safeguard his faith by making frequent acts of faith, by praying for a strong faith, by studying his religion very earnestly, by living a good life, by good reading, by refusing to associate with the enemies of the Church, and by not reading books and papers opposed to the Church and her teaching.* You might discuss each point.

### Sins Against Faith

The first commandment forbids sins against faith. Few Catholics after being instructed in their religion go so far as to doubt or deny any of the Church's teachings. Even those unfortunate persons who leave the Catholic Church, usually do not do so because of difficulties concerning theological doctrine. The bad example of some persons in the Church, a failed marriage, the desire for worldly success, or some other unworthy motive often tempts them.

Joan is a sad example of a girl who was thus tempted. Educated in Catholic schools, a member of the parish study club, and active in receiving the sacraments, one would not expect Joan to do what she did. However, when the time came to break off company with a young man who spared no words in condemning the Church and its teachings, Joan was weak. She "loved" herself and the man more than she loved God. She unwisely renounced her faith. Joan committed the sin of apostasy—or complete rejection of the truths of the Catholic faith.

Unbelief or lack of faith is the sin of infidelity. Those people commit it who know the truths of faith and deliberately refuse to accept them.

An instructor in a Catholic college acted against faith in another way. He taught that all who are not members of the Catholic Church would go to hell. This is against that teaching of the Church which explains that: "They who remain outside the Catholic Church through no grave fault of their own and do not know it is the true Church, can be saved by making use of the graces which God gives them." The teacher, in this case, refused to give up his wrong belief even after the Church explained it to him; he was a heretic. His sin is called heresy. Heresy is willingly refusing to believe one or more truths of the Catholic faith.

*Indifferentism* is a common sin against faith. It is the sin of those who act or speak as if all religions were equally good, or who say that you can believe what you choose to believe. Parents can commit the sin of indifferentism if they do not take care that their children receive sufficient religious instruction, for instance, if they allow them to go to non-Catholic summer Bible schools or the like. Many times the priest warns people about indifferentism when he commands parents whose children are in public schools to send them to instruction classes.

Briefly, then, answering the question how a Catholic sins against faith, we may say: *A Catholic sins against faith by apostasy, heresy, and indifferentism.*

### Hope

Hope helps us to observe the first commandment. We worship God by hope, that is, by expecting from Him eternal salvation and all the helps that are necessary to obtain it: pardon for our sins, and divine grace, the means of obtaining eternal life. *Hope obliges us,* therefore, *to trust firmly that God will give us eternal life and the means to obtain it.* We can strengthen our confidence in God by saying often: "Heart of Jesus, I put my trust in Thee."

Christ wants us to remember that when we hope we are placing our trust in God who is an all-powerful and all-good Father. Christ said if we ask the Father anything in His name He will give it to us. For what may we hope? Because we are made of soul and body, we may hope for everything we need for soul and body.

### Understanding Hope

Sometimes today we think that hope is when we wish for something to happen that may not actually end up happening, like our team winning the game or getting the last slice of cake. But the virtue of hope is different than this modern connotation. This kind of hope is founded in a confident trust that what God promises will take place without a doubt, it just has not happened yet. So we hope for heaven, not because we hope it is true that it exists—it does exist because God tells us—but we hope for it because we long to go there one day. This is a subtle but important distinction.

### Sins Against Hope

Just as there are sins against faith, so too, there are sins against hope. *The sins against hope are presumption and despair.*

We have learned that grace is necessary for salvation. Anyone, therefore, who thinks or acts as if he could be saved without the help of God commits the sin of presumption. A second way of sinning by presumption is by expecting to get to heaven without making proper use of the means God wants us to use. Some of the means we must use are prayer and the reception of the sacraments. Presumption, then, is one kind of sin against hope. *A person sins by presumption when he trusts that he can be saved by his own efforts without God's help, or by God's help, without his own efforts.*

When Judas hanged himself he committed a sin against hope. What was the sin he had committed? Despair. A *person sins by despair when he deliberately refuses to trust that God will give him the necessary help to be saved.* Judas' sin of despair was the direct opposite of the sin of presumption. He did not have enough hope. Judas was completely discouraged. He abandoned all hope of forgiveness from Christ. He forgot that Christ had called him a friend even while he was sinning. He forgot that Magdalen had sinned and had been forgiven. No matter how bad things are or will become we must never give up hope. No matter how sinful we are, the merciful Christ wants us to hope in Him. Christ rewarded the thief who showed his trust to Him in almost his last breath on the cross (Lk. 23:43). Not to hope in God is a grave sin against so loving and forgiving a Father. God is nearest when the night is darkest. Remember Job!

***TERMS TO KNOW***

- atheist
- acknowledge
- elevation
- apostasy
- pagans
- exposed
- infidelity
- preserver
- condemning
- heretic
- unchangeable
- sacrilege
- presumption
- superstition
- indulgence
- despair
- entreated

## Charity

Charity helps us to observe the first commandment. Charity means love. When we speak of charity as a way of worshiping God, we do not mean feelings and words, but we mean essentially loving God with our heart and our will. We love God with our wills when we at least keep His commandments. A person who has not broken a commandment seriously and is free from mortal sin is worshiping God by charity, at least in the first and lowest degree. If he is keeping all the commandments then he also loves his neighbor. Why? Because he is not only observing the first three

commandments which concern his duties to God directly, but also the last seven which pertain to his neighbor. *Charity obliges us to love God above all things because He is infinitely good, and to love our neighbor as ourselves for the love of God.*

The more we love God, the more carefully we fulfill His commands. Even small children have loved God so much that they performed all their actions out of love for God. This is perfect love of God. Name some children saints who even gave up their lives for God. Say often throughout the day: "My God, I love You."

## Sins Against Charity

There are many sins against charity. However, *the chief sins against charity are hatred of God and of our neighbor, envy, sloth, and scandal.*

Every sin is, in a way, an offense against charity because, by sinning, we choose some pleasure or created thing in place of God's wishes or commands. A mortal sin is a complete turning away from God. The worst mortal sin is hatred of God. Hate means to wish evil to, and to be happy at misfortune falling upon the one hated. Those who hate God wish or even try to cause evil to befall God and rejoice when grievous sins are committed. Hate is the sin that is found in hell just as charity is the virtue that is found in heaven.

*Hatred of one's neighbor* consists in wishing him harm and rejoicing at his ill fortune. If this involves deliberately wishing a serious evil, it is a grave sin.

Sometimes people, and even children, are jealous of the good things that others have. People might be jealous of their neighbor's car or home. Children are sometimes sad if others get better marks in school, or have toys which they do not have. Charity requires us to be happy with our neighbor over the good things he has. If we are jealous, we commit the sin of *envy.*

*Sloth* is another sin against charity. To be slothful is to be sad in the presence of spiritual goods. Sloth makes us neglect our duties toward God and neighbor, either out of laziness or too much business. A father who does not support his family through laziness is slothful. A person who neglects his prayers for a long time through laziness is also slothful. A person who is anxious to accomplish too much in a day may also be in a state of sloth. If we sometimes feel a dislike for the things of God, like prayer, the sacraments, or the study of religion, let us beg our Blessed Mother, who was the most diligent of God's creatures, to give us a love for them. A little prayer we can say to her is: "O Mary, make me to live in God, with God, and for God."

### Understanding Sloth

The sin of sloth can be misunderstood. It does not simply mean being lazy. While being lazy is a bad thing, the sin of sloth specifically refers to being spiritually lazy. It means we do not care about spiritual things. A person can work very hard at school or at his job and still suffer from sloth because he does not care to read Scripture, or pray, or go to Mass.

*Scandal* is another sin against charity. Scandal is any act, word, or criticism which causes another to sin or which weakens another's strength against sin. Our Lord said it were better that a person be drowned rather than give bad example or scandal to others. How do we sometimes, perhaps, scandalize our younger brothers and sisters? Our younger brothers and sisters are quick to imitate our behavior at home, in church, or in public. They have a right to expect us to use decent language, to obey promptly, and in general, to live according to the commandments of God and of His Church. They look up to us and try to be like us. We must give them good example—always.

Thus we see that to keep the first commandment we must not only pray the acts of faith, hope, and charity, but must also grow in these virtues. By faith we believe in God; by hope we confidently trust that God will give us the help we need to save our souls; and by charity we love and reverence God and keep His commandments.

## Superstition and Sacrilege

The sins against the three theological virtues are not the only sins forbidden by the first commandment. *Besides the sins against faith, hope, and charity, the first commandment forbids also superstition and sacrilege.*

*Superstition* is a sin against the first commandment because through it either one gives God a worship that is not suited to Him as the Supreme Being or gives a creature the worship that belongs to God.

Some of us may have seen others giving creatures the worship due to God alone. For instance those who carry a rabbit's foot, or a four-leaf clover because they actually believe it will protect them, commit the sin of superstition. How about black cats and walking under ladders?

Others commit this sin by believing that certain words or actions have magical powers. They sin whether they say the words and do the actions themselves or whether they go to other persons who use them. They call these words or actions spells. Some foolishly superstitious people believe that human beings can fortell the future from the lines of a person's hand, tea leaves, constellations of stars, or playing cards.

Would Catholics who believed that certain prayers or the wearing of certain scapulars or medals would guarantee their eternal salvation even without a good and devout life be guilty of superstition?

To believe in dreams is also superstition. It is likewise superstitious to go to spiritists who falsely claim they can contact people who have died.

How, then, does a person sin by superstition? *A person sins by superstition when he attributes to a creature a power that belongs to God alone, as when he makes use of charms or spells, believes in dreams or fortunetelling, or goes to spiritists.*

*Sacrilege* is the next sin against the first commandment we shall study. *A person sins by sacrilege when he mistreats sacred persons, places, or things.*

You know some holy persons who are consecrated to God's service. It is a sacrilege to deliberately strike or ill-treat a bishop, priest, or other person dedicated to God. It was a great sacrilege for the communists when they tortured and imprisoned bishops, priests, and sisters in countries behind the Iron Curtain. Do you know of any such cases?

What are some holy places that you have seen? It is wrong to break into or rob or improperly use churches, chapels, altars, and cemeteries. In Russia, communists have turned churches into club houses. They have destroyed statues and altars. Even in our own country at one time a group of people desecrated Catholic cemeteries by breaking the crosses and Christian monuments. To deliberately steal, break, or destroy important property belonging to the Church can be a sacrilege.

In the Old Testament we read about King Balthazar, who at a banquet used sacred vessels stolen from the Temple in Jerusalem. God was so angry about the disrespect shown to these sacred vessels that the same night He permitted the king to be slain by an enemy and his nation conquered. The sin King Balthazar committed is called sacrilege.

Adoration and prayer help us to observe the first commandment. We must adore God as our Creator. This means we must acknowledge both in our mind and in our conduct that we depend entirely upon Him. It means that we desire to do His will in all things because He is the Supreme Being and when we know His will we do it. This little prayer will serve as a reminder: "Teach me, O Lord, to do thy will, for thou art my God" (Ps. 142:10).

Perhaps the easiest way to worship God is by prayer, a loving raising of our minds and hearts to God. Our prayers and acts of worship reveal the love for God that is in our hearts. They keep us mindful that God is always with us and help us behave, as we should in His presence. They show that we realize that God is the Supreme Being and Creator of all things.

The greatest prayer and the highest form of worship that we

can offer to God is the Holy Sacrifice of the Mass. We ought to learn all we can about the Mass, and to assist at it whenever we can. The blessings of the Mass will stay with us throughout the day.

Now we have learned what we mean when we say that *we worship God by acts of faith, hope, and charity, and by adoring Him and praying to Him.* This worship must be given both in mind and in behavior. An example might help us to understand better. A watch or clock has inside machinery and an outside face with hands which tell time. Can we tell time if we have only the inner works? Can we tell time if we have only the face and hands? No. In the same way worship of God must come from our hearts, and it must show in our words, our actions, and our entire conduct.

## FOR ME TO REVIEW

*Catechism Lesson*

**1140. Q. What is the first commandment?**

A. The first commandment is: I am the Lord thy God: thou shalt not have strange gods before me.

**1143. Q. How does the first commandment help us to keep the great commandment of the love of God?**

A. The first commandment helps us to keep the great commandment of the love of God because it commands us to adore God alone.

**1144. Q. How do we adore God?**

A. We adore God by faith, hope, and charity, by prayer and sacrifice.

**1164. Q. How does a person sin against faith?**

A. A person sins against faith: 1st, By not trying to know what God has taught; 2nd, by refusing to believe all that God has taught; 3rd, by neglecting to profess his belief in what God has taught.

**1182. Q. Which are the sins against hope?**

A. The sins against hope are presumption and despair.

**1188. Q. How do we sin against the love of God?**

A. We sin against the love of God by all sin, but particularly by mortal sin.

**472. Q. What mortal sins are opposed to faith?**

A. Atheism, which is a denial of all revealed truths, and heresy, which is a denial of some revealed truths, and superstition, which is a misuse of religion, are opposed to Faith.

**1183. Q. What is presumption?**

A. Presumption is a rash expectation of salvation without making proper use of the necessary means to obtain it.

**1185. Q. What is despair?**

A. Despair is the loss of hope in God's mercy.

### Questions and Exercises

*Write 1 to 15 on a paper and after each number write the letter of the sentence which fits it best.*

| | |
|---|---|
| 1. atheist | A. One who abandons his belief in the Church |
| 2. apostate | B. The greatest of the theological virtues |
| 3. heretic | C. Belief in dreams |
| 4. pagan | D. Admit openly |
| 5. faith | E. Expecting to be saved without God's help |
| 6. hope | F. Belief in the truths God has revealed |
| 7. love | G. Laziness or over activity |
| 8. infidelity | H. One who does not believe in God |
| 9. indifferentism | I. Trust in God's promises |
| 10. presumption | J. Loss of hope in God's mercy |
| 11. despair | K. One who refuses to believe some of the truths God has revealed |
| 12. superstition | L. Lack of faith |
| 13. sacrilege | M. One who worships false gods |
| 14. sloth | N. The belief that all religions are equally good |
| 15. profess | O. Mistreatment of a blessed object |

## FOR ME TO REMEMBER

1. We must worship God because He is the Supreme Being who made all things and keeps them in existence.
2. We worship God by faith, hope, charity, prayer, adoration.
3. The highest form of worship is the holy sacrifice of the Mass.
4. We are bound to profess our faith openly when God's honor or our neighbor's good requires it.

5. We cannot attain salvation without God's help.
6. No matter how seriously we have sinned, God will forgive us if we are sorry.
7. The worst mortal sin is hatred of God.
8. To keep the first commandment we must not only pray the acts of faith, hope, and love, but we must also grow in these virtues.

## FOR ME TO DO

1. Find places in the Old Testament where the worship of false gods is mentioned.
2. Compose original acts of faith, hope, and love. In them, tell God some special thing you will do to show your faith, hope, love.
3. Explain why the sacrifice of the Mass is the highest form of worship.
4. Discuss the ways and means you have of worshiping God.
5. List the occasions during the day when you openly profess your faith.
6. How could you sin through presumption?
7. Explain indifferentism.
8. What examples from the life of Christ will comfort us if we feel our sins are too great to be forgiven?
9. Give some examples of how we can show our love of God in our everyday actions.
10. How can we show our love for our neighbor?

LESSON 33

# The First Commandment Permits Us to Honor the Saints

We have learned what it means to worship God. Now we are ready to learn more about the respect due to some very special friends of God—the saints.

## Honor Given Saints Differs From Honor Given God

Let us first pay a visit to the home of a boy we shall call Terry. If Terry really loves his dad, how will he act toward him? He will always be very respectful and obedient. Now suppose that Terry's dad invites a relative or a dear friend of his to spend some time in his home. How would Terry's dad want him to act toward that person? Would he expect Terry to show the same love for his friend as he did toward his father? Why not? He knows Terry feels closer to him because he is his father. The same is true when we consider the respect we owe the saints. *The first commandment does not forbid us to honor the saints in heaven, provided we do not give them the honor that belongs to God alone.*

Now let us suppose Terry's dad invites his friend, Mr. Smith, to live at his home for a long time. Terry spends more and more time with Mr. Smith because he has shown great interest in Terry. Gradually, Terry begins to realize how kind the man is. Terry also notices that his dad is pleased with the liking he shows for Mr.

When we pray to the saints we ask them to offer their prayers to God for us.

Smith. It is one way of approving his dad's choice of friends. In like manner, *we honor the saints in heaven because they practiced great virtue when they were on earth, and because in honoring those who are the chosen friends of God we honor God Himself.*

Terry has been watching Mr. Smith very closely. He notices that he has many good qualities. Terry has often watched his actions and listened to his conversation. Before long Terry finds himself walking, talking, and thinking in the same way as Mr. Smith. What is Terry doing? He is paying Mr. Smith a compliment by imitating him. This is one way in which we, too, honor the saints. In fact, imitating their holy lives is the best way to honor them and to please God.

One day Terry got into a fist fight with one of his comrades. Although Terry did his best, he returned home with visible signs of what had happened. On entering the back door he came face to face with Mr. Smith. Terry offered a hurried explanation, followed by a petition to help him break the news gently to his father.

Often when we get into a bout with sin and come limping home with a spiritual "black eye," we make use of the saints in somewhat the same way Terry made use of Mr. Smith. *When we pray to the saints we ask them to offer their prayers to God for us.*

After Terry had explained to Mr. Smith what had happened, he left to attend to his "battle wounds" confident that his hero would be able to intercede for him. Why did he place such trust in his friend? He knew Mr. Smith was a good friend of his father. Furthermore, Mr. Smith had shown that he loved Terry and therefore, Terry felt sure he would not disappoint him. We place even greater confidence in the saints, and with good reason for *we know that the saints will pray for us because they are with God and have great love for us.*

Reliquary of St Agatha's arm in Palermo Cathedral, Sicily Saint Agatha of Sicily (died ca. 251), patron saint of martyrs, wet nurses, fire, earthquakes, and eruptions of Mount Etna.

## How We Honor the Relics of Saints

The time finally came for Mr. Smith to leave Terry's home. Before leaving, he gave Terry a picture of himself, a fishing pole and line which he had used, and a football. Terry cherished these possessions very highly because they were a constant reminder of his good friend. He was also determined to keep them for a long time. We can call these objects relics because the word "relics" means things left from the past. Just as Terry respected the articles given him by Mr. Smith, but in a much more reverent way, *we honor relics because they are the bodies of the saints or objects connected with the saints or with our Lord.*

Let us pause now and review the three ways of honoring the saints. *We can honor the saints: first, by imitating their holy lives; second, by praying to them; third, by showing respect to their relics and images.*

Some non-Catholics object to our having statues and pictures of saints in our homes or churches. But *the first commandment forbids the making or the use of statues and pictures only when they promote false worship.*

In the city of Ephesus in Asia Minor, silversmiths made miniature temples—small likenesses of the wonderful Temple of Diana, the goddess of all Asia. Use of these souvenirs encouraged the worship of Diana, therefore, they promoted false worship which is forbidden by the first commandment. When some of the Ephesians became Christians through the preaching of St. Paul, the silversmiths began to lose their trade so they caused trouble for the saint.

Now let us get back to Terry to help us understand another point. Terry's father told him that Mr. Smith had met with a serious accident. Upon hearing this news, Terry went at once to his own room. When his father came up, he found a solemn-faced Terry gazing admiringly at a picture of Mr. Smith. He was showing his respect before a picture of a very dear friend. Terry is not the only one who shows respect, in this way, for a friend.

We do the very same thing in our religious life. For *it is right to show respect to the statues and pictures of Christ and of the saints, just as it is right to show respect to the images of those whom we honor or love on earth.* They often suffered hardships for the love of God and made many sacrifices in order to spread His kingdom.

That God Himself approves devotion to images and relics may be learned from the following incidents. First, the body in the prophet's tomb coming to life. "And Eliseus died, and they buried him. And the rovers (robbers) from Moab came into the land the same year. And some that were burying a man, saw the rovers, and cast the body into the sepulcher of Eliseus. And when it had touched the bones of Eliseus, the man came to life, and stood upon his feet" (Kings 13:20–21). In the Acts of the Apostles we find a story of how the handkerchiefs of St. Paul were taken to the sick and healed them (Acts 19:11–12).

These examples concern happenings of the Old and New Testaments. We can, however, find that even today God does wonderful things through objects which have been used by His special friends. These incidents prove that God Himself honors the bodies of His saints and regards even objects that have touched them, as holy.

### Veneration vs. Worship

To explain our relationship with the saints and the Blessed Mother, we should understand the difference between the word "veneration" and "worship." Worship is what we give to God. But veneration means to show reverence for, to honor and respect, and this is what we give to Mary and the saints. We honor and respect them, but we do not worship them, and they do not want our worship! In addition to venerating them and learning from their heroic sanctity, we ask for their intercession before God. Just as we ask our brothers and sisters here on earth to pray for us and our family, so too can we ask the saints in heaven.

We Catholics know that God alone works miracles and wonders. And if a miracle is worked through some relic, we know it is God who worked it, not the relic itself. So it is not superstition when we keep and honor some piece of bone from a saint, something that has touched his body, or an article that has been used by him. We do not adore and serve these things. We only venerate them, that is, show special respect toward them. We adore God alone. *We honor Christ and the saints when we pray before the crucifix, relics, and sacred images because we honor the persons they represent; we adore Christ and venerate the saints.* The honor we give to God is different from and much greater than the honor we give to the saints.

Non-Catholics seem to have a hard time understanding our veneration of the saints and their relics and images. Suppose a non-Catholic friend of yours would accuse you of praying to a statue, a crucifix, or a picture. How would you answer him? You could say: *We do not pray to the crucifix or to the images and relics of the saints, but to the persons they represent.*

The images and pictures serve only as a help to keep our attention on what we are doing. We place them in our churches and classrooms, to remind us of our heavenly friends just as we keep heirlooms or place the pictures of living, or especially of dead parents on our desks or dressers at home. We love our parents and like to have them near us even if only in this way. The pictures help us to look up to our parents, to respect them, and to be like them. This is the reason why we say that we do not pray to a crucifix or an image or relic of a saint.

## Summary of the First Commandment

The first commandment is: "I am the Lord thy God; thou shalt not have strange gods before Me." This commandment obliges us to give to God alone the supreme worship that is due Him. We do this by acts of faith, hope, and charity, and by adoring Him and praying to Him. All thoughts, words, deeds, or omissions that are contrary to these acts by which we worship God, are forbidden by this commandment. The following sins are the chief sins against the first commandment: infidelity, apostasy, heresy, indifferentism, taking part in non-Catholic worship, presumption, despair, hatred of God, hatred of our neighbor, sloth, envy, scandal, superstition, and sacrilege. We adore God and venerate the saints. We do not pray to the images or relics of God or His saints, but rather do we pray to the persons that they represent.

### TERMS TO KNOW

- intercede
- confident
- miniature
- false worship
- venerate
- imitating
- petition
- approving
- cherished
- relics

## FOR ME TO REVIEW

*Catechism Lesson*

**1196. Q. Do we not slight God Himself by addressing our prayers to saints?**

A. We do not slight God Himself by addressing our prayers to saints, but, on the contrary, show a greater respect for His majesty and sanctity, acknowledging, by our prayers to the saints, that we are unworthy to address Him for ourselves, and that we, therefore, ask His holy friends to obtain for us what we ourselves are not worthy to ask.

1198. Q. **Why do we believe that the saints will help us?**

A. We believe that the saints will help us because both they and we are members of the same Church, and they love us as their brethren.

1204. Q. **Does the first commandment forbid us to honor relics?**

A. The first commandment does not forbid us to honor relics, because relics are the bodies of the saints or objects directly connected with them or with our Lord.

1211. Q. **Does the first commandment forbid the making of images?**

A. The first commandment does forbid the making of images if they are made to be adored as gods, but it does not forbid the making of them to put us in mind of Jesus Christ, His Blessed Mother, and the saints.

1212. Q. **How do we show that it is only the worship and not the making of images that is forbidden by the first commandment?**

A. We show that it is only the worship and not the making of images that is forbidden by the first commandment, 1) Because no one thinks it sinful to carve statues or make photographs or paintings of relatives or friends; 2) because God Himself commanded the making of images for the temple after He had given the first commandment, and God never contradicts Himself.

1213. Q. **Is it right to show respect to the pictures and images of Christ and His saints?**

A. It is right to show respect to the pictures and images of Christ and His saints, because they are the representations and memorials of them.

**1215. Q. Is it allowed to pray to the crucifix or to the images and relics of the saints?**

A. It is not allowed to pray to the crucifix or images and relics of the saints, for they have no life, nor power to help us, nor sense to hear us.

**1216. Q. Why do we pray before the crucifix and the images and relics of the saints?**

A. We pray before the crucifix and the images and relics of the saints because they enliven our devotion by exciting pious affections and desires, and by reminding us of Christ and of the saints, that we may imitate their virtues.

### Questions and Exercises

1. Does the first commandment forbid us to honor the saints?
2. May we give the saints greater honor than we give God?
3. Do we honor God in honoring the saints?
4. Are we forbidden to pray to the saints?
5. Do the saints love us?
6. Do we adore Mary and the saints?
7. Do we pray to the crucifix?
8. Can we ask the saints to obtain favors from God for us?
9. Should we have religious pictures in our homes?
10. Are parts of the bodies of saints called relics?

## FOR ME TO REMEMBER

1. I can best honor the saints by imitating their holy lives and heroic virtues.
2. When I venerate, or honor, the saints in a special way, I honor God Himself.
3. Our devotion to the saints must not be as great as our devotion to God.
4. We do not *pray* to images; we pray to the persons they represent.
5. Religious pictures and objects remind us of Christ and the saints and should be evident in every home.

## FOR ME TO DO

1. Make a list of the ways in which saints are honored in your parish church; in your home.
2. What are relics?
3. How can the saints help us?
4. Of what value is it to have crucifixes and religious pictures in our homes?
5. Plan a program in honor of one of the saints.
6. How can one violate the first commandment?
7. List the names of several saints and tell in what way or ways you would like to imitate them.
8. How would you explain to a non-Catholic friend the presence of a crucifix in your bedroom?
9. If you could choose several religious pictures or objects for your home, what would you choose? Why?
10. What does the first commandment forbid?

*"Those in the Catholic Church, whom some rebuke for praying to saints and going on pilgrimages, do not seek any saint as their savior. Instead, they seek saints as those whom their Savior loves, and whose intercession and prayer for the seeker He will be content to hear. For His Own sake, He would have those He loves honored. And when they are thus honored for His sake, then the honor that is given them for His sake overflows especially to Himself."*

*—St. Thomas More*

LESSON 34

# The Second Commandment

The second commandment of God is: Thou shalt not take the name of the Lord thy God in vain.

Let us now expand our knowledge about the second commandment. What do you already know about the second commandment?

*By the second commandment we are commanded always to speak with reverence of God, of the saints, and of holy things, and* as we shall study later, we are also commanded *to be truthful in taking oaths and faithful to them and to our vows.*

One of a person's most prized possessions is his name. His name tells who he is. To praise a man is to connect praise with his name. The names of two great Americans will never be forgotten. George Washington will always be remembered as he who was "First in war, first in peace, and first in the hearts of his countrymen." For Americans, the name of Abraham Lincoln will never die as long as there are school children and lovers of freedom to appreciate him and to realize what he and his famous speech have meant to mankind: ". . . That this nation under God shall have a new birth of freedom; and that government of the people, by the people, and for the people shall not perish from the earth."

Again if a man is not upright or sincere, his name is not upheld or revered. Such are the names of Judas Iscariot—traitor to the divine Master—and that of Benedict Arnold—traitor to his country. You know the story of their wrong deeds and you also know how little regard men have for them.

If we consider the name of a man so precious, think of how we should respect and reverence the name of God and of holy persons or things.

## Honor to God's Name

When a person is important to us, his name also becomes important. We honor our parents when we uphold and respect their names. We keep illustrious and alive our nation's heroes and leaders by writing songs and poems about them, and by erecting monuments and public buildings in their honor.

Think of the cities in our country named after saints and the schools and institutions honored by the names of famous or saintly people. What is the name of your parish? You revere that name. You will always be respectful and loyal to it. You would not like to hear that name dishonored.

And yet we hear people using the sacred name of God or the Holy Name of Jesus Christ in an insulting manner. Even Christians do this sometimes, thoughtlessly of course, for the most part. Let us remember that the reverent use of God's name brings blessings. Jesus Himself said: ". . . if you ask the Father anything in my name, he will give it to you" (Jn. 16:23). In suffering, that name will be our consolation, and in death, our salvation.

### The Church and the Holy Name of Jesus

The Church grants us many favors and rich indulgences for reverently repeating our Redeemer's name. It would be well to learn some of the following prayers and say them often. "Blessed be the most holy name of Jesus without end." "Blessed be the name of the Lord." "Eternal Father, by the most precious blood of Jesus Christ, glorify His most holy name, according to the desires of His adorable Heart."

> *"The sweet Name of Jesus produces in us holy thoughts, fills the soul with noble sentiments, strengthens virtue, begets good works, and nourishes pure affection. All spiritual food leaves the soul dry, if it contain not that penetrating oil, the Name Jesus."*
>
> *—St. Bernard of Clairvaux*

The Church bestows the sacraments and other blessings in and through the Holy Name: "I absolve thee, in the name of the Father, and of the Son, and of the Holy Spirit." The Bible tells us of miracles worked in His name. St. Peter cured the lame man at the temple gate saying: "In the name of Jesus Christ of Nazareth, arise and walk" (Acts 3:6). Holy Scripture reminds us that: "There is no other name under heaven given to men by which we must be saved" (Acts 4:12). The Bible again tells us that ". . . at the name of Jesus every knee should bend of those in heaven, on earth and under the earth" (Phil. 2:10).

Accordingly, let us show reverence for God's name by using it thoughtfully and respectfully in prayer, and by bowing our heads when we hear it mentioned. By honoring the holy name of God here on earth we merely do what the angels and saints will do for all eternity in heaven.

> Have you heard of the good old lady who told the priest who had come to visit her that she was worried about what to say to God when she stood before Him in heaven. The priest advised her to bow her head and repeat the words she had so often spoken here on earth: "Praised be Jesus Christ!" He assured her that she would not have to wait long before the whole heavenly court would chime in with that glorious and thrilling answer to her words: "Forever and ever. Amen!" So it will be with us. If we honor His holy name here on earth, we have every reason to hope that God will call us to join in honoring His name in heaven.

Not only must we praise God and speak of Him with profound respect, but we must also speak with reverence of the Blessed Virgin, the angels, the saints, the Church and everything that pertains to her service, our Holy Father, the pope, our bishops and priests, and all members of religious orders and societies. As we have learned before, the saints are special friends of God, and we honor God when we honor them. We honor God also when we speak with reverence of any person or thing pertaining to God or consecrated or dedicated to His service. Never fail to tip your hat to a priest or religious wherever you meet them.

## Proper Oaths

There are times when we may use God's name outside of prayer; as for instance when we take an oath. *An oath is the calling on God to witness to the truth of what we say.* "The Lord, your God, shall you fear; him shall you serve, and by his name shall you swear" (Deut. 6:13).

It is lawful at times to take an oath. In other words, swearing that a thing is true by asking God to confirm what we say can be permitted. An oath is a guarantee of truthfulness; it is useful in having our word accepted in important matters which concern the glory of God or the good of our neighbor or of ourselves. If, however, we take an oath for some small or unimportant thing we do wrong. And if we take an oath to do that which is wrong, or impossible, we likewise do wrong. However we are not obliged to keep such an oath; on the contrary we may never do something wrong even if we have taken an oath to do so. Such an oath does not bind.

An oath reverently and properly taken is a meritorious act of divine worship; otherwise it is sinful.

The obligation to fulfill a promise made under oath is grave or light depending on the seriousness of that which is promised.

We must be careful not to treat an oath lightly. We cannot take an oath on a slight pretext. Sometimes we hear boys and girls say "Cross my heart," and even grownups say: "I'm telling the truth, so help me God!" This is seldom a true oath. We might call it a speech mannerism, that is, a way of talking which has become more or less a habit. As such it might be allowed. But it is not permitted to take an oath for a slight reason. *To make an oath lawful, three things are necessary: first, we must have a good reason for taking an oath; second, we must be convinced that what we say under oath is true; third, we must not swear, that is, take an oath, to do what is wrong.*

In our courts it is necessary at times to take oaths. Some day you may be a witness in a court of law and be required to raise your right hand and take an oath and say: "I swear to tell the truth, the whole truth, and nothing but the truth, so help me God." When a person is commanded by lawful authority to take an oath and he tells the truth, God is not offended. He is pleased because He is honored. Such oaths honor God because we call upon Him as all-knowing and all-truthful.

But suppose the witness tells a lie, for instance by saying that he saw what he knows he did not see, or by falsely naming some innocent person (perhaps someone he does not like) as the one guilty of the crime. In either case, this witness is asking God, who is Truth itself, to confirm his untruthfulness. Such false swearing is more than an ordinary lie. It is a mortal sin of perjury. Under oath, even a little lie is a serious matter. *A person who deliberately calls on God to bear witness to a lie commits the very grievous sin of perjury.*

To take an oath without sufficient reason, or to swear rashly, is ordinarily a venial sin but can be mortal if it is the occasion of scandal.

Very often the sin of perjury is the result of bribery. Someone bribes a witness (offers him a reward, usually money) to tell a lie. Perhaps the one who asks him to do this attempts to escape a jail sentence or to throw the blame on another—sometimes an innocent victim. It is a mortal sin for any man to bribe a witness to lie while under oath, no matter what the reward or benefit might be. Resolve never to take a false oath no matter what you might get for your action. Resolve never to lie under oath.

Government officials are often obliged to take oaths. An official calls on God to witness his promise to fulfill his office conscientiously. The president of the United States, the members of his cabinet, judges, senators, and representatives take such an oath by which they pledge themselves to be loyal to their country, its people, and to the duties entrusted to their care. We must always remember that taking an oath is no mere routine, matter-of-fact, everyday affair, but a serious religious act. It is something to be done prudently and carried out faithfully.

## Lawful Vows

A vow is not the same as an oath. A *vow is a deliberate promise made to God by which a person binds himself under pain of sin to do something that is especially pleasing to God.* A vow is an act of divine worship by which we acknowledge God's supreme dominion. It is a promise voluntarily made to God alone, to perform some good action.

A vow renders the good action more acceptable to God. As a result we can make more progress in virtue. A vow is a promise made of our own free will; no one is bound or can be compelled to make one. "If thou wilt not promise, thou shalt be without sin" (Deut. 23:22). A vow made under force is not valid, that is, it does not bind.

What we promise by vow must be possible and morally good. The promise must be pleasing to God; not anything wrong, as in the case of one of the judges of Israel, Jephte. Before going to battle he vowed to the Lord that if he were victorious, he would offer as a holocaust whoever should first come out of the doors of his house. His only daughter came to meet him, and she was sacrificed (Judges 11:30–40). Such a vow is not only foolish but also displeasing to God and should not be made or fulfilled. It is a sin to make such a vow. It is also a sin to keep such a vow.

Usually we promise something that we are not obliged to do—a pilgrimage, for instance; but we may also promise something which we are obliged to do anyway—for example, to observe the fasts of the Church, to keep the holy days, to be temperate in eating and drinking. In this case failure to keep one's promise is a twofold sin.

The owner of a factory, whose only child was dangerously ill, vowed before God that if she recovered, he would never have work done on Sundays and holy days. He was then doubly bound to observe the holy days. She got well and he kept his word.

There are different kinds of vows. Some are private vows made by individuals privately. Such vows are often made by a person when in trouble or affliction or as an act of thanksgiving. Often such vows are accompanied by a condition. The person makes a kind of bargain with God. Jacob promised to make an offering of part of his possessions to God provided He brought him back prosperously to his father's house (Gen. 28:20–22). We should never make a vow hastily or before seeking the advice of a priest or confessor, however. We must remember that a vow brings responsibility. We must do what we vow under pain of sin.

## Evangelical Counsels

**Those who live the consecrated life take vows of chastity, poverty, and obedience. These are known as the evangelical counsels.**

In the present day many persons, in illness or affliction, promise to visit some place of pilgrimage, to make an offering to some church, to give a statue, to give an offering for a mission baby, or to fast on certain days, and the like. These can be simple promises or they can be vows, depending on the intention.

Some vows are public and officially accepted by the Church. Such are the vows of religion, or the vows taken by those especially who wish to dedicate themselves to the service of God. Poverty, chastity, and obedience are the three vows taken by religious. They are very useful, for by them an individual entirely gives up the world, in order to serve God better. These vows are most pleasing to God, for those who take them enter into the religious state and consecrate not only all they do, but their very selves to God. Such vows bring great blessings. They both bind and help a person to lead a life of perfection in Christ.

***TERMS TO KNOW***

- upright
- heavenly court
- oath
- meritorious
- sacred
- profound
- witness
- deliberate
- perjury
- rashly
- bribery
- dominion
- voluntarily
- vow
- consecrate
- affliction

A vow is an act of religion and is something good like prayer. However, just as we are forbidden to take an oath about an unimportant thing, so also are we forbidden to make a vow about something unimportant.

We should keep a promise made to God; to do otherwise would be sinful. Whether it would be a mortal or a venial sin to break a vow would depend on the vow itself, and the intention a person had in making it.

Remember, one should never make a vow without consulting a confessor. A vow carries with it responsibilities. It must be made only after careful thought. We must fulfill the promise we make. "It is much better not to vow, than after a vow not to perform the things promised" (Eccles. 5:3–4).

## FOR ME TO REVIEW

*Catechism Lesson*

**1217. Q. What is the second commandment?**

A. The second commandment is: Thou shalt not take the name of the Lord thy God in vain.

**1219. Q. What are we commanded by the second commandment?**

A. We are commanded by the second commandment to speak with reverence of God and of the saints, and of all holy things, and to keep our lawful oaths and vows.

**1221. Q. What is an oath?**

A. An oath is the calling upon God to witness the truth of what we say.

**1222. Q. How is an oath usually taken?**

A. An oath is usually taken by laying the hand on the Bible or by lifting the hand towards heaven as a sign that we call God to witness that what we are saying is under oath and to the best of our knowledge really true.

**1223. Q. What is perjury?**

A. Perjury is the sin one commits who knowingly takes a false oath; that is, swears to the truth of what he knows to be false. Perjury is a crime against the law of our country and a mortal sin before God.

**1232. Q. What is a vow?**

A. A vow is a deliberate promise made to God to do something that is pleasing to Him.

**Questions and Exercises**

1. How does the Church use the Holy Name?
2. What should we do when the Holy Name is mentioned?
3. Outside of prayer, when may we take God's name?
4. What do we do when we take an oath?
5. What are the conditions for making an oath lawful?
6. Can civil authorities demand that we take an oath?
7. Are we ever forced to make vows? Explain your answer.
8. What was wrong with Jephte's vow?
9. Give some examples of vows that have been made and kept.
10. What are the three vows taken by religious? What do they mean? What is their value?

## FOR ME TO REMEMBER

1. The Holy Name of God is worthy of the highest respect.
2. Oaths and vows are serious matters; they should not be taken lightly.
3. To tell a lie while under oath is called perjury.
4. In making a vow we promise to do something especially pleasing to God.

## FOR ME TO DO

1. Look up vows in the *Catholic Encyclopedia.* Prepare a talk to give to your family.
2. How is perjury committed? Give some examples.
3. Look up the regulations of the Holy Name Society. How do the members expressly obey the second commandment?
4. Gather information on the feast of the Holy Name. Report on it.
5. Compose a prayer in honor of the Holy Name. In it promise greater reverence and respect for this sacred name.
6. If you hear God's name is used irreverently, plan in some way to correct this evil.
7. If someone whom you could not correct spoke irreverently of God, what prayer might you say to help atone for it?
8. How could you decide how seriously you had sinned in breaking a vow?
9. How can we show respect for God's name by our actions?
10. Explain what is meant by a deliberate promise?

LESSON 35

# What the Second Commandment Forbids

Besides improper oaths and vows, the second commandment also forbids blasphemy, profanity, and cursing.

*Blasphemy is insulting language which expresses contempt for God, either directly or through His saints and holy things.* It is said to be against God, but it may be indirect at times as when an utterance is made against the saints or sacred things. This is indirect blasphemy because of their close relationship with God.

### TERMS TO KNOW

- blasphemy
- contemptuous
- willful
- contempt
- profanity
- scandal
- dedicated
- irreverent
- penalties

Let us see how a person could be guilty of such an offense. People usually commit the sin of blasphemy because they are dissatisfied with something God has sent them—such as sickness, poverty, lack of talent, failure, and the like. As a result they complain against God, and actually hate Him, or are contemptuous (scornful) toward Him. We should never complain or murmur about what happens, but rather take everything, good as well as bad, as coming from the hand of God for our own or others' spiritual or bodily welfare. "Do all things without murmuring" (Phil. 2:14). God knows what is best for us. Let us trust and thank Him for everything we have.

Loss of temper and lack of faith lead people to say things which they do not mean. At times they take the name of God in vain. *By taking God's name in vain is meant that the name of God or the holy name of Jesus Christ is used without reverence; for example, to express surprise or anger.* Surely you could give many examples of the use of profane language. Perhaps you have heard it used in an exciting baseball game, or by a boy who thinks it sounds big or smart.

Sometimes blasphemy is confused with taking God's name in vain, or as it is also called, *profanity.* They are different, however. Blasphemy shows willful hate or contempt for God, the saints, and holy things, while profanity is irreverent use of holy names. Profanity is committed by using the name of God without just cause, thoughtlessly, through habit, impatience, surprise, or merely to emphasize a point. The use of God's name is profane when it does not honor God, or help our neighbor or ourselves.

The sinfulness of profanity or using the name of God in vain, depends upon how deliberate it is, and the irreverence we intend toward God, or the scandal we might give by it. *It is a sin to take God's name in vain; ordinarily, it is a venial sin.* It can become serious and a mortal sin when there is deliberate and intentional contempt of God or His holy name.

*Cursing* is another sin against the second commandment. *Cursing is the calling down of some evil on a person, place, or thing.* The calling down of some evil can be good or bad. In certain cases it is lawful and sinless as when a judge sentences a criminal in court, or when God Himself decrees penalties against sinners. But then there are times when it is unlawful and sinful, for example: "Hope you break your leg!" or "Go to the devil!" Here we do not wish good but misfortune and harm to our neighbor. Such conduct is uncharitable. Cursing is a venial sin when it is due to thoughtlessness, but it is a mortal sin when the evil wished is serious—when we really wish serious evil to some person, place, or thing.

Whenever we hear a person indulge in blasphemy, profanity, or cursing, let us quietly say a little prayer to Jesus to ask Him to forgive this person who has spoken so carelessly. Pray every day that you may not fall into these sins. God, to whom we owe everything and to whom we should utter only words of gratitude and praise, is insulted by them.

## Summary of the Second Commandment

The second commandment is: "Thou shalt not take the name of the Lord thy God in vain."

This commandment obliges us always to speak of God, of the saints, and of holy things with respect and reverence.

We honor God in a special way when the oath we take is lawful.

We honor God, also, when we keep the vow we make to God.

But we dishonor God: (1) by taking His name in vain; (2) by blasphemy, which is using insulting words about God, or the saints, or holy things; (3) by cursing, that is, wishing evil on any creature of God; (4) by taking an unlawful oath; and (5) by not keeping a vow we may make.

## FOR ME TO REVIEW

*Catechism Lesson*

**1218. Q. What do you mean by taking God's name in vain?**

A. By taking God's name in vain I mean taking it without reverence, as in cursing or using in a light and careless manner, as in exclamation.

**1241. Q. What is blasphemy, and what are profane words?**

A. Blasphemy is any word or action intended as an insult to God. To say He is cruel or find fault with His works is blasphemy. It is a much greater sin than cursing or taking God's name in vain. Profane words mean here bad, irreverent or irreligious words.

**Questions and Exercises**

1. What do the words "in vain" mean?
2. Why should we try to control our tempers?
3. Is it a venial sin to take God's name in vain?
4. How can you help others overcome the habit of cursing?
5. Why is blasphemy such a serious offense against God?

## FOR ME TO REMEMBER

1. Blasphemy and profanity are not the same things. Blasphemy shows willful hatred while profanity shows irreverence.
2. Prayer will help overcome the habit of blasphemy, profanity, or cursing.

## FOR ME TO DO

1. What could you do or say if you heard one of your friends talking in a shocking way and often using the Holy Name without necessity?
2. Suppose you were heard to use the name of God thoughtlessly when your teammate failed to make second base. How would you make good the wrong you have done?
3. A pedestrian runs into the path of the taxi in which you are riding. The taxi driver utters a shocking and cursing remark. What could you say or do to repair this wrong?
4. Recite the Divine Praises as an act of reparation for the sins against the second commandment committed this day all over the world.
5. Can such expressions as "God never sends me anything good," "Why must it always happen to me?" "What good does it do to pray anyway?" be grievously sinful?
6. A certain boy, when engaged in excited play, constantly uses expressions which appear to be swearing, such as, "So help me," or "Honest to God I'm right." Would you say he expressed an oath?
7. A lady always says, "Oh my God." She promises her confessor that she will do better but her conduct has not improved. What have you to say about this?
8. If on your way home from school today you hear God's name used irreverently, what could you do?
9. Discuss the reverence the Church shows at Mass for the name of God, of our Lord, Mary, and the saints.

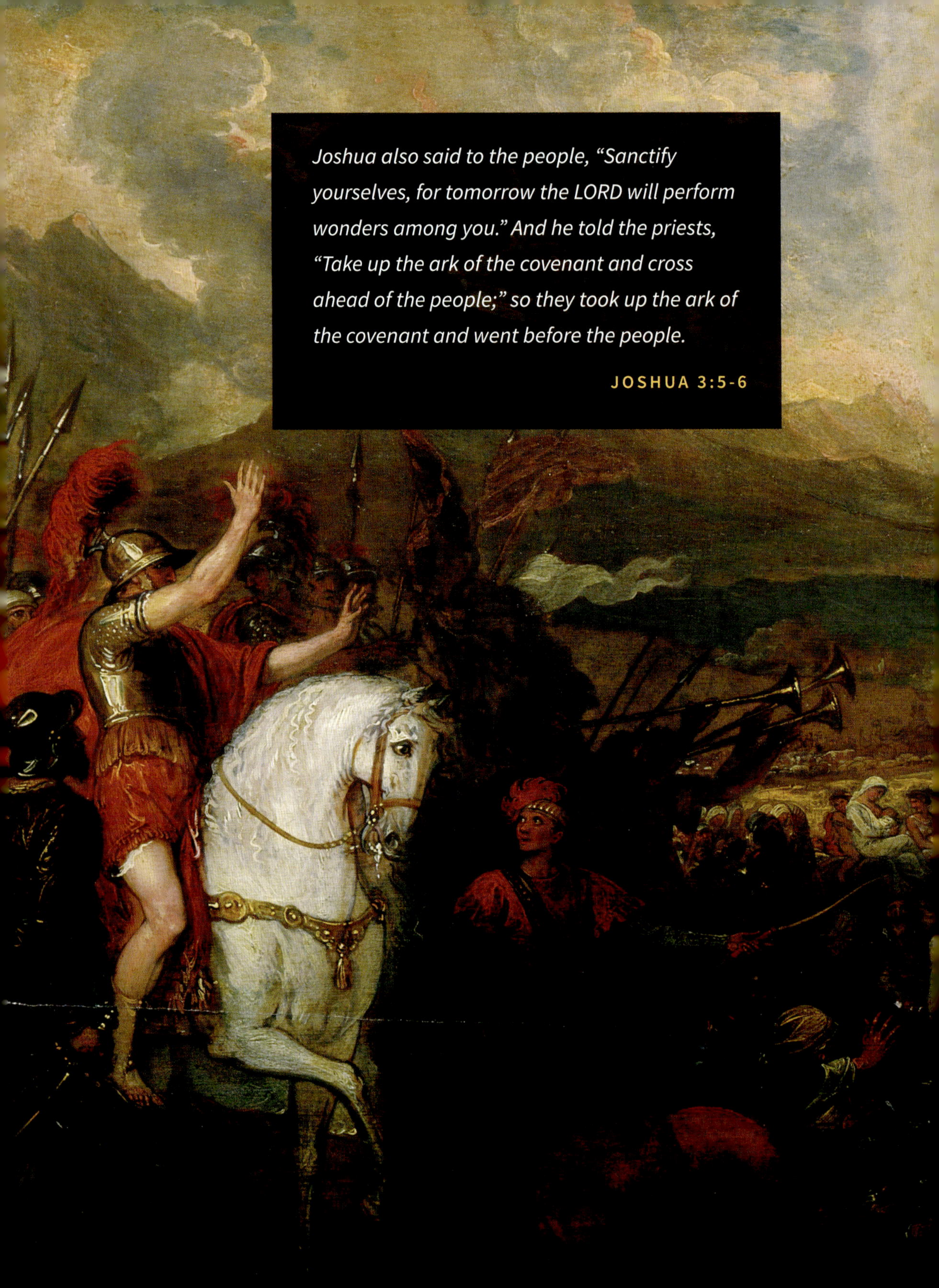

*Joshua also said to the people, "Sanctify yourselves, for tomorrow the LORD will perform wonders among you." And he told the priests, "Take up the ark of the covenant and cross ahead of the people;" so they took up the ark of the covenant and went before the people.*

JOSHUA 3:5-6

LESSON 36

# The Third Commandment

The third commandment of God is: Remember thou keep holy the Lord's day.

## Worship of God

Every man's conscience tells him that he is obliged to worship God. He should, however, not only worship God by himself alone, but in public and with others. There never has been an age in which men have not publicly worshiped God. History records that men everywhere, even in pagan lands, have regularly set aside certain hours or days or seasons for public worship. You have no doubt read how the Muslims, at certain hours every day, turn toward Mecca, the birthplace of Mohammed, and pray. Are we as faithful in saying the Angelus?

All our time belongs to God, as the Psalmist says: "Yours is the day, and yours is the night" (Ps. 73:16). God gave us the seven days of the week but He asks us to return one of them to Him as a token of our gratitude. By special command the Lord appoints the portion of time He wants from us when He says: "Remember to keep holy the Sabbath day. Six days you may labor and do all your work, but the seventh day is the Sabbath of the Lord, your God" (Exod. 20:8–10).

The observance of this day of rest recalls God's rest after the work of creation, the rest of Christ in the tomb, and prefigures our rest with God in eternity. God meant it to teach consideration to those who hire others; and to remind us not only to take care of our own needs but to give particular attention to the worship we owe God. Perhaps that is why God started this commandment with the word "Remember." Men sometimes become so wrapped up in their own interests that they forget God. The Sabbath, therefore, gives man an opportunity to worship God, to rest from his labors, and to experience in a small measure, the unending rest and joy of heaven.

## Observance of the Sabbath

The third commandment, as God gave it to the Jewish people, named the seventh day of the week, that is, the sabbath, as the special day of worship. God Himself laid down detailed rules as to the manner in which this day was to be observed (Exod. 20:8–11). Many Jews still keep Saturday holy to the Lord. We Christians, however, observe Sunday as the Lords day.

Using the power given to her by her divine Founder, the Catholic Church chose the first day of the week to replace the Sabbath of the Jews and determined just how Christians were to sanctify it to the Lord. The Church did not retain the various restrictions prescribed for the Sabbath among the ancient Jews; but all Catholics are obliged to attend Mass and to abstain from servile work.

The glorious events of Easter Sunday and Pentecost Sunday sanctified the first day of the week, so the Apostles spoke of it as the "Lord's Day" and kept it holy. We find in the Apocalypse that St. John the Apostle mentions the first day of the week as the "Lord's Day" (Apoc. 1:10). The Acts of the Apostles, which were written by St. Luke, and the First Epistle of St. Paul to the Corinthians speak especially of the "first day of the week" (Acts 20:7; 1 Cor. 16:2).

The Apostles, under the guidance of the Holy Spirit, made the change. The following are among the reasons: (1) the work of creation began on the first day of the week. (2) Our Lord rose from the dead on a Sunday. (3) The Holy Spirit came down upon the Apostles on Sunday. (4) The Apostles received the power to forgive sins on Sunday. (5) The Church was solemnly and gloriously launched on its work on a Sunday. Two of these reasons ought to be particularly remembered: *The Church commands us to keep Sunday as the Lord's day, because on Sunday Christ rose from the dead, and on Sunday the Holy Spirit descended upon the Apostles.*

We should give God the first day of the week. So we go to Mass, say our prayers, and do other good things on Sunday and know that we are doing right. Sunday observance brings down God's favor and blessings upon us. It gives us a special opportunity to thank God the Father who created us, God the Son who redeemed us, and God the Holy Spirit who sanctifies us.

There are many ways of worshiping God. When we are in the state of grace and have the intention of doing so we can make our every prayer, work, and play an act of worship. But, *by the third commandment we are commanded to worship God in a special manner on Sunday, the Lord's day.* The "special manner" consists in this that *the Church commands us to worship God on Sunday by assisting at the Holy Sacrifice of the Mass.*

## Assistance at Mass

To take part in the Mass is the greatest act of religion we can offer to God. Certainly you know why. The Catholic Church teaches us that in the Mass the body, blood, soul, and divinity of Jesus Christ are offered as a sacrifice to the heavenly Father under the appearance of bread and wine. This act represents anew the offering of the Sacrifice of the Cross by Christ to God the Father.

When we assist at Mass we give God the best possible gift. We give Him the very gift by which Christ told us He wished to be remembered and which pleases His Father best. At the Last Supper when our Lord offered the first Mass, He took the bread, blessed it and gave it to His Apostles saying: "Take and eat; for this is my body." In like manner He took the wine and gave it to His Apostles saying: "All of you drink of this; for this is my blood of the new covenant, which is being shed for many unto the forgiveness of sins" (Mt. 26:26–28).

After this our Lord told His Apostles to do the same thing in remembrance of Him. In these words our Lord gave the Apostles and their successors the power to say Mass. In these words Jesus told us that the way He wanted to be remembered was by the Holy Sacrifice of the Mass.

To fulfill our obligation of assisting at Mass we must be actually present, inside the church if possible, so that we can see or hear the priest and follow the parts of the Mass. However, when attendance at Mass is heavy, presence in the vestibule or sacristy might be permitted. Even though we may not be able to enter a church because of its overcrowded condition, we can still hear Mass provided we are part of the congregation assisting at the Holy Sacrifice and are able to follow the Mass. A person who is separated by a considerable distance from the worshipers certainly is not present at Mass. Is a person whose body is present at Mass but whose mind and will are miles away really present?

Since attendance at Mass is the way God wishes us to honor Him, the duty to hear Mass on Sundays and holy days of obligation rests upon all Catholics who have reached the use of rea-

After this our Lord told His Apostles to do the same thing in remembrance of Him. In these words our Lord gave the Apostles and their successors the power to say Mass.

son and are above seven years of age and who are not lawfully excused. Deliberately to miss Mass on a Sunday or holy day of obligation, without just cause, or to miss a considerable part of the Mass, is a grave sin. To come a little late is a venial sin. To come quite a bit late and to leave quite a bit early could be a grievous sin.

We must hear an entire Mass from beginning to end; that is, from the priest's entrance into the sanctuary till his departure into the sacristy. One is considered to have missed Mass if one is not present for all the three principal parts of the Mass: the Offertory, the Consecration, and the Communion.

Just being present at Mass is not enough. We must know what is going on. It will help to keep our attention from wandering if we remember that assisting at Mass is the same as if we stood at the foot of the cross when our Lord was crucified. We should not act like those who mocked Christ and laughed at Him. Rather we will want to join with the Blessed Virgin to adore our Lord, to offer Him our love, to thank Him, to beg His forgiveness, to ask His grace, and to offer ourselves to God with our suffering Saviour.

### Reasons Excusing From Attending Mass

Because the obligation to assist at Mass is grave, no light reason, such as a slight headache, a short distance from church, or inability to be dressed in the newest or latest styles, is sufficient for staying away from Sunday Mass. Those who on every slight pretext excuse themselves from their obligation of hearing Mass on Sunday in addition to committing many serious sins will gradually slip into religious carelessness and indifference, perhaps even losing their faith.

A grave inconvenience to oneself or to another excuses one from the obligation. You have no doubt experienced or read about heavy snowfalls that crippled transportation or prevented the use of buses or other public vehicles. Perhaps in icy weather you have heard the warning over radio or television cautioning owners of private cars to remain off the highways. Very bad weather is certainly an excuse.

Other excusing causes may be illness, old age, or infirmity, a long distance from the church, unusual difficulties of transportation; a call of duty as in the case of a doctor, nurse, fireman, policeman, or other public welfare workers; or charity to a friend or neighbor. We should be sturdy Christians, nonetheless, and not let anything but really serious causes interfere with our hearing Mass on Sundays or days of obligation.

### TERMS TO KNOW

- public worship
- observance
- restrictions
- prescribed
- right intention
- deliberately
- consideration

## FOR ME TO REVIEW

*Catechism Lesson*

**1242. Q. What is the third commandment?**

A. The third commandment is: Remember thou keep holy the Sabbath day.

**1243. Q. What are we commanded by the third commandment?**

A. By the third commandment we are commanded to keep holy the Lord's day and the holy days of obligation, on which we are to give our time to the service and worship of God.

**1245. Q. How are we to worship God on Sundays and holy days of obligation?**

A. We are to worship God on Sundays and holy days of obligation by hearing Mass, by prayer, and by other good works.

### Questions and Exercises

1. What great events have made Sunday an important day in the Catholic Church?
2. Why does God want us to observe Sunday as a day of rest?
3. Who changed the Sabbath from Saturday to Sunday? Why?
4. Why does the Church command us to worship God by hearing Mass?
5. Must we be present in the church to fulfill our Sunday obligation?
6. What reasons might exempt us from Sunday Mass?
7. With what words was the priesthood established?
8. In what other ways besides hearing Mass should we keep Sunday holy?

## FOR ME TO REMEMBER

1. It is not enough to just "go to Mass." We must also take part in it.
2. We must worship God both publicly and privately.
3. Holy Mass is the greatest act of worship man can offer God.
4. The three principal parts of the Mass are: Offertory, Consecration, and Communion.
5. We cannot fulfill our Sunday obligation by hearing Mass on radio or television.
6. Sunday is a day of rest, and provides us with the opportunity to give thanks to God for all His goodness to us.

## FOR ME TO DO

1. Aunt Mary insists on your staying home from Sunday Mass. She is old and often feels quite ill. May you stay home if there is no other Mass? What reason can you give for your answer?
2. A boy who was out late Saturday night sleeps halfway through Sunday Mass. Has he fulfilled his obligation of hearing Mass? Why?
3. Mass is being shown on TV so you decide not to go to church this Sunday. Have you fulfilled your obligation?
4. Why do many Catholics look at the Host and whisper, "My Lord and my God" at the elevation of the Mass?
5. The third commandment says, "Remember thou keep holy the Sabbath." How can you explain to your Jewish neighbor the Christian practice of observing Sunday rather than Saturday as the Sabbath.
6. The Mass is the most perfect act of worship man can offer God. Why? Are any other good works recommended to help us keep Sunday holy?
7. How do you help at home to make it easier for your mother to keep holy the Lord's day?
8. May a person be excused from hearing Mass on Sunday? For what reasons?
9. Read and discuss the prayers of the Canon of the Mass which follow the consecration.

LESSON 37

# The Third Commandment Forbids Unnecessary Work on Sunday

The third commandment does not merely command us to attend Mass on Sunday. It commands more than that. *By the third commandment of God all unnecessary work on Sunday is forbidden.* But what is to be understood by this kind of work? *Servile Work is that labor which distracts us from true spiritual leisure and rest.*

How clearly does the wisdom of God show forth in this commandment? He not only sets aside Sunday as a day of worship, but by so doing He gives man a chance to rest. Man lays down his usual tasks and is able to spend some time socially with his family and friends. Jesus said to the Pharisees: "The Sabbath was made for man, and not man for the Sabbath" (Mk. 2:27).

Painting, playing music, attending a garden, going on a walk—these activities are enjoyable in their own right. Paying our taxes, doing homework, buying and selling, putting in hours for our usual weekly job—these tasks prevent us from the joy of the Lord's Day.

## When Work Might Be Permitted

There are times, however, when Sunday labor is permitted. Necessity may be the reason. Have you heard the story of the man who was engaged in the trucking business? On Saturday afternoon a customer requested that he haul a cargo of fish which was expected late Saturday night. It would mean working Sunday morning. The Catholic truck driver did not want to take on the job saying that he had to attend Mass and did not accept or do Sunday work. When the fish dealer explained that his cargo would spoil if he waited until Monday, the trucker consented,

### TERMS TO KNOW

- servile
- urgent
- re-create
- physically
- piety
- obliged
- mentally
- functions

saying: "I will not ask my men to work, my two sons and I will haul the fish." Here we have a valid excuse for Sunday labor. If the fish had not been hauled, the customer would have suffered considerable loss.

The Church permits the performing of necessary work in order that the blessings of God may not be lost. She teaches, therefore, that it is lawful to cut and to gather in crops if they are in danger of being destroyed. Urgent work may also be permitted if life and property are endangered by floods, fires, storms, tornadoes, accidents, or the like. Railroad, bus, and air lines must be kept in operation. Policemen, firemen, nurses, hospital attendants, bakers, caretakers of ball parks, golf courses, and bathing beaches must be allowed to work.

Charity offers a second excuse for work. Caring for the sick or digging a grave would come under this head. Religion permits servile work which directly renders honor to God. Janitors who take care of church furnaces on Sunday and ring the bell for the various services, perform works of piety toward God. The honor of God will require the preparation of the altar and vestments for Mass. Church functions held on Sunday always necessitate a certain amount of work.

Work for our own need is lawful and may be performed on Sunday when it cannot be performed conveniently on another day. Such work as caring for livestock, cooking, dishwashing, and the like are works of necessity, and may be performed on Sundays and holy days of obligation. *Servile Work is allowed on Sunday when the honor of God, our own need, or that of our neighbor requires it.* ". . . it is lawful to do good on the Sabbath" (Mt. 12:12). Can you think of examples?

Sunday, for the child who loves God, is not only a day of rest; it is a day to rejoice, a day set aside and entirely different from the rest of the week. It is a day that helps us to turn to God, to see Him in all the joy and peace around us and to adore and thank Him as He deserves. It is a day to re-create ourselves in body and soul.

"Amen. Blessing and glory and wisdom and thanksgiving and honor and power and strength to our God forever and ever. Amen." (Apoc. 7:12).

## FOR ME TO REVIEW

*Catechism Lesson*

**1252. Q. What is forbidden by the third commandment?**

A. The third commandment forbids all unnecessary work and whatever else may hinder the due observance of the Lord's day.

**1255. Q. Is work on Sunday ever lawful?**

A. Work is lawful on Sundays when the honor of God, the good of our neighbor, or necessity requires them.

### Questions and Exercises

1. What kind of work is forbidden on Sunday?
2. Name some occasions on which you might perform work.
3. What is meant by work?
4. Are holy days to be observed the same as Sunday?
5. Is mowing the lawn on Sunday a violation of the third commandment?

## FOR ME TO REMEMBER

1. Sunday is a day of religion, rest, and rejoicing.
2. Necessity, charity, and religion are sufficient excuses for work on Sunday.

## FOR ME TO DO

1. The mother of a large family attends at the bedside of her sick husband all week. The laundry has piled up. May she do it on Sunday?
2. A farmer and his family were just ready to start for Mass on Sunday morning when they noticed that a heavy storm was threatening. In order to save his crops the farmer went out into the field and ordered his hired man to do the same. They all missed Mass. Were they justified in doing so? Give reasons for your answer.
3. Is it true that rest from work on Sunday benefits those who keep the Sabbath? Explain.
4. Make a chart showing the three types of work.
5. Should a storekeeper close his store on Sunday? Why?
6. Getting to Mass, and getting there on time.

# Prayers

## The Sign of the Cross

In the name of the Father, and of the Son, and of the Holy Spirit. Amen.

## The Lord's Prayer

Our Father who art in heaven, hallowed be Thy name; Thy kingdom come; Thy will be done on earth as it is in heaven. Give us this day our daily bread; and forgive us our trespasses as we forgive those who trespass against us; and lead us not into temptation, but deliver us from evil. Amen.

## The Hail Mary

Hail Mary, full of grace, the Lord is with thee; blessed art thou among women, and blessed is the fruit of thy womb, Jesus. Holy Mary, Mother of God, pray for us sinners, now and at the hour of our death. Amen.

## Glory Be to the Father

Glory be to the Father, and to the Son, and to the Holy Spirit. As it was in the beginning, is now, and ever shall be, world without end. Amen.

## The Apostles' Creed

I believe in God, the Father Almighty, Creator of heaven and earth; and in Jesus Christ, His only Son, Our Lord; who was conceived by the Holy Spirit, born of the Virgin Mary, suffered under Pontius Pilate, was crucified, died, and was buried. He descended into hell; the third day He arose again from the dead; He ascended into heaven, and sits at the right hand of God, the Father Almighty; from thence He shall come to judge the living and the dead. I believe in the Holy Spirit, the Holy Catholic Church, the communion of saints, the forgiveness of sins, the resurrection of the body, and life everlasting. Amen.

## The Confiteor

### Ordinary Form

I confess to almighty God
and to you, my brothers and sisters,
that I have greatly sinned
in my thoughts and in my words,
in what I have done,
and in what I have failed to do;
through my fault, through my fault,
through my most grievous fault;
therefore I ask blessed Mary ever-Virgin,
all the Angels and Saints,
and you, my brothers and sisters,
to pray for me to the Lord our God. Amen

### Extraordinary Form

I confess to Almighty God,
to blessed Mary ever Virgin,
blessed Michael the Archangel,
blessed John the Baptist,
the holy Apostles Peter and Paul,
and to all the saints
that I have sinned exceedingly
in thought, word, and deed,
through my fault,
through my fault,
through my most grievous fault.
Therefore, I beseech blessed Mary ever Virgin,
blessed Michael the Archangel,
blessed John the Baptist,
the holy Apostles Peter and Paul,
and all the saints,
to pray for me to the Lord our God. Amen.

## Morning Offering

O Jesus, through the Immaculate Heart of Mary, I offer Thee my prayers, works, joys and sufferings of this day for all the intentions of Thy Sacred Heart, in union with the Holy Sacrifice of the Mass throughout the world, in reparation for my sins, for the intentions of all our relatives and friends, and in particular for the intentions of the Hold Father. Amen.

## The Angelus

V. The angel of the Lord declared unto Mary.
R. And she conceived of the Holy Spirit.

Hail Mary, full of grace! the Lord is with thee; blessed art thou among women, and blessed is the fruit of thy womb, Jesus. Holy Mary, Mother of God, pray for us sinners, now and at the hour of our death. Amen.

V. Behold the handmaid of the Lord.
R. Be it done unto me according to thy word.

Hail Mary, etc.

V. And the Word was made flesh.
R. And dwelt among us.

Hail Mary, etc.

V. Pray for us, O holy Mother of God.
R. That we may be made worthy of the promises of Christ.

*Let Us Pray*
Pour forth, we beseech Thee, O Lord, Thy grace into our hearts, that we to whom the Incarnation of Christ, Thy Son, was made known by the message of an angel, may by His passion and cross be brought to the glory of His resurrection, through the same Christ Our Lord. Amen.

## Regina Coeli

*(Said during Eastertide, instead of the Angelus)*

Queen of heaven, rejoice, Alleluia.
For He whom thou didst deserve to bear, Alleluia.
Hath risen as He said, Alleluia.
Pray for us to God, Alleluia.
V. Rejoice and be glad, O Virgin Mary! Alleluia.
R. Because Our Lord is truly risen, Alleluia.

*Let Us Pray*
O God, who by the resurrection of Thy Son, Our Lord Jesus Christ, have vouchsafed to make glad the whole world, grant, we beseech Thee, that, through the intercession of the Virgin Mary, His Mother, we may attain the joys of eternal life. Through the same Christ Our Lord. Amen.

## Hail, Holy Queen

Hail, Holy Queen, Mother of Mercy; hail, our life, our sweetness, and our hope! To thee do we cry, poor banished children of Eve; to thee we do send up our sighs, mourning and weeping in this vale of tears. Turn, then, most gracious advocate, thine eyes of mercy toward us; and after this our exile, show unto us the blessed fruit of thy womb, Jesus. O clement, O loving, O sweet Virgin Mary!

## An Act of Faith

O my God, I firmly believe that Thou art one God in three Divine Persons, Father, Son, and Holy Spirit; I believe that Thy Divine Son became man, and died for our sins, and that He will come to judge the living and the dead. I believe these and all the truths which the Holy Catholic Church teaches, because Thou hast revealed them, who canst neither deceive nor be deceived.

## An Act of Hope

O my God, relying on Thy almighty power and infinite mercy and promises, I hope to obtain pardon of my sins, the help of Thy grace, and life everlasting, through the merits of Jesus Christ, my Lord and Redeemer.

## An Act of Love

O my God, I love Thee above all things, with my whole heart and soul, because Thou art all-good and worthy of all love. I love my neighbor as myself for the love of Thee. I forgive all who have injured me, and ask pardon of all whom I have injured.

## An Act of Contrition

O my God, I am heartily sorry for having offended Thee, and I detest all my sins, because of Thy just punishments, but most of all because they offend Thee, my God, who art all-good and deserving of all my love. I firmly resolve, with the help of Thy grace, to sin no more and to avoid the near occasions of sin.

## The Blessing Before Meals

Bless us, O Lord, and these Thy gifts, which we are about to receive from Thy bounty, through Christ Our Lord. Amen.

## Grace After Meals

We give Thee thanks for all Thy benefits, O Almighty God, who livest and reignest forever; and may the souls of the faithful departed, through the mercy of God, rest in peace. Amen.

# The Mysteries of the Rosary

## The Five Joyful Mysteries

1. The Annunciation
2. The Visitation
3. The Birth of Our Lord
4. The Presentation of Our Lord in the Temple
5. The Finding of Our Lord in the Temple

## The Five Luminous Mysteries

1. The Baptism of Our Lord in the Jordan
2. The Wedding Feast at Cana
3. Our Lord's Proclamation of the Kingdom of God
4. The Transfiguration of Our Lord
5. The Institution of the Eucharist

## The Five Sorrowful Mysteries

1. The Agony of Our Lord in the Garden
2. The Scourging at the Pillar
3. The Crowning With Thorns
4. The Carrying of the Cross
5. The Crucifixion and Death of Our Lord

## The Five Glorious Mysteries

1. The Resurrection of Our Lord
2. The Ascension of Our Lord into Heaven
3. The Descent of the Holy Spirit Upon the Apostles
4. The Assumption of Our Blessed Mother into Heaven
5. The Coronation of Our Blessed Mother in Heaven

The Immaculate Conception with the Fifteen Mysteries of the Rosary

# Answer Key

## CHAPTER 1

### LESSON 1

1. Godlike living gives glory to God. If others know we are performing our actions because we love God they are performing our actions because we love God they will more easily realize how truly great and good He is, and we will thus increase His glory.
2. It is hard to imagine what our home in heaven will be like, for St. John says, "Eye hath not seen, ear hath not heard, nor has it entered into the mind of man what great things God has in store for those who love Him." We will possess everything we could desire, without anything we could dislike.
3. The Church instructs us in the ways of good conduct, advises us when we need help. The Church decides what is expected of Catholics under certain circumstances and offers correct remedies when difficulties arise.
4. The Apostles' Creed is an important prayer because it contains a summary of the chief truths God has made known to man.
5. Reason and Revelation both prove there is a God.
6. Revelation means that God has made known to us certain truths in a special way.
7. We can make our faith stronger by practicing it and by begging God frequently to strengthen it.

8. In our daily life we use the gift of faith believing all that God has revealed about himself through His Church and by accepting all disappointments and pleasures as coming from God. We can do many things to prove we believe in God and our religion.
9. Yes.
10. We can learn to know God by praying to Him, by seeing His goodness in all things He gives us, by listening to sermons and instructions, by good reading and by hard, regular study.
11. To prove our love for God we can obey His laws and do things that are hard for love of Him. We can practice virtue and the works of mercy.
12. The best way to serve God is to do all our ordinary actions out of love for Him.
13. Any creature; God keeps all things in existence by His almighty power.
14. (a) Make a visit to a church. Talk to God and ask Him to guide you as His faithful subject.

    (b) Say your grace before and after meals more fervently, realizing these gifts come from the great God.

    (c) Offer some little trial in reparation to Him.
15. Dear God, help me to use my home as a means of pleasing God. Do not let me do anything that will detract from its sacredness. Guide all of us living here in the way of truth.
16. Jesus spoke of His heavenly Father's kingdom to His followers. In all His actions He showed great respect and reverence for God. He gained the grace to help us know, love, and serve God.

17. God made everything for the use of His creatures. Sharing those we have with others and thus trying to please God because we love Him is a good proof of our love of God.
18. We should love the Church because it is the chief means God has given us to attain union with Him in heaven. Besides this we know it is the one true Church, and Christ's Mystical Body on earth
19. We can prove we believe in God by making the Sign of the Cross, tipping our hats or bowing our heads when we pass a Catholic Church, by refusing to eat meat on Friday during lent, obey the Ten Commandments which God gave us, and in many other ways.
20. The word Creed means belief. In this Unit it means the summary of all our beliefs.

## LESSON 2

1. Infinitely perfect means absolutely perfect, completely perfect, perfect without any limits.
2. The state of grace means at least freedom from mortal sin, it means God dwelling in our souls with His divine life giving our souls supernatural life.
3. We can thank God for watching over us by never doing anything we would be ashamed to have Him see us do.
4. God shows His mercy by everything He has done but especially by forgiving our sins when we are sorry for them.
5. 1-H, 2-A, 3-J, 4-G, 5-I, 6-E, 7-C, 8-F, 9-B, and 10-D

## LESSON 3

1. Reason proves there is a God: first, by showing that the world around us could not have come into existence by

itself; second, by showing us that there is someone greater than man who will reward good deeds, and punish the evil.

2. In addition, divine public revelation shows us that there is a God.
3. We must believe all that God has revealed because He is Truth itself, He knows all things, He cannot deceive or be deceived.
4. God made known His truths in the Old Testament through the patriarchs and prophets.
5. Conscience tells us that our good deeds will be rewarded and our bad deeds punished by someone greater than man.
6. Some people have not been properly instructed; some are proud to admit there is a Supreme Being; sinners want to believe there is no God.
7. Yes
8. No
9. Supernatural revelation is made up of the truths God has made known to us in Sacred Scripture and Tradition.
10. Yes

## LESSON 4

1. a
2. a
3. a
4. a
5. c
6. c

7. c
8. b
9. a
10. a

## CHAPTER 2

### LESSON 5

1. Angels are like God in that they are pure spirits.
2. The angels are like man in that they have intellect and free will; they are different from man in that they have no bodies.
3. Wisdom, power, holiness (sanctifying grace).
4. Because God made them above any of His other creatures; they resemble God more than any other creature.
5. By calling on them frequently to help us; by listening for their voice.
6. No
7. An occasion of sin is any person, place, or thing that might tempt us to commit sin.
8. From God, our Lady, the saints; especially from the reception of Holy Communion.
9. 1. Angles, 2. Men, 3. Pure, 4. Bodies, 5. Free will, 6. Wisdom, 7. Power, 8. Holiness, 9. Faithful, 10. Sinned, 11. Faithful, 12. Eternal, 13. Heaven, 14. See, 15. Love, 16. Adore, 17. Praying, 18. Messengers, 19. Guardian, 20. Praying, 21. Protecting, 22. Advising, 23. Faithful, 24. Hell, 25. Bad, 26. Devils, 27. Tempting, 28. Bad, 29. Ourselves, 30. Persons, 31. Things, 32. Resist, 33. Sin, 34. Ask.

## LESSON 6

1. Yes
2. Yes
3. Yes
4. No
5. Yes
6. Yes
7. No
8. Yes
9. No
10. Yes

## LESSON 7

1. Yes, it is spiritual because it has no body or material parts, and immortal because it will never die.
2. Body, soul, intellect, will, home, family, grace, virtues, gifts.
3. Intellect and will, etc.—natural. Sanctifying grace, etc.—supernatural.
4. To test their love and obedience. Yes.
5. God the Son is the Son of God by nature; we are adopted sons of God because we are His adopted children through the sacrament of baptism.
6. Gave them intellect and free will and the divine life of grace.
7. Because He loved them—Because He loves us.
8. Our love for Him.

# CHAPTER 3

## LESSON 8

1. Yes; Yes
2. We share in Adam's punishment because Adam is the father of the human race, and as his children, we share in his punishment.
3. "I will renounce Satan, and all his work, and all his empty promises."
4. We must earn our bread by the sweat of our brow.
5. We should show how greatly sin offends God and how ungrateful we have been in being so thankless to such a loving Father.
6. God is just in punishing us because He did not take away any of the gifts which belong to our human nature by only those extra gifts which make us special children of God.
7. By the Immaculate Conception we mean that our Lady was conceived without the stain of original sin.
8. 1854
9. Obedience and humility.

## LESSON 9

1. Because grace helps us to avoid sin, strengthens against temptation, and makes us more pleasing to God.
2. Make an act of contrition and, if the sin was serious, resolve to go to confession as soon as possible.
3. In the Mass and the sacraments.
4. We will receive temporal punishment for venial sins.

5. We can atone for venial sins by prayer, acts of mortification, helping the poor, performing spiritual and corporal works of mercy.
6. We should confess venial sins because any sin offends God, no matter how slight: and if we humbly confess our failures, grace will be increased and the sin removed.
7. Yes, because all sin offends God who is so good.
8. To commit sin
9. God loves purity of soul. When in the state of grace our good acts gain supernatural merit. An imperfect motive might be fear that we might die while not in the state of grace and thus merit hell.
10. Because if we do, God will bless our day and night and keep temptation from us or help us overcome it.
11. Deadly. Because mortal sin kills the life of grace in us.
12. Two: mortal and venial.
13. Sanctifying grace.
14. Yes
15. Occasions of sin.
16. No
17. Prayer, frequent reception of sacraments, cultivation of good habits and practices.
18. Sloth
19. Covetousness
20. It may lead us to commit mortal sin.

**Fill in the Blank**

1. Thought.
2. Desire.
3. Word.
4. Action.
5. Omission.
6. Mortal.
7. Venial.
8. Grievous.
9. Less.
10. Deprive.
11. Sanctifying.
12. Forgiven.
13. Confession.
14. Deprives.
15. Sanctifying.
16. Supernatural.
17. Less.
18. Mortal sin.
19. God's.
20. Purgatory.

**Matching**

A-2

B-3

C-1

D-4

E-6

F-3

G-6

H-1

I-4

J-3

K-3

# CHAPTER 4

## LESSON 10

1. God realized that man is weak compared with the angels. God loved man so much He wanted to give him a chance to get to heaven.
2. Because He is both God and man.
3. God wanted man to realize the great need for the Redeemer; He wanted man to realize how dependent he is on God; He wanted man to understand the great dignity of the one who had been offended.
4. The people in the Old Testament had to believe in God's promises and follow their consciences in the worship of God.
5. To help them keep faithful and to remind them of their great need for a Redeemer.

## LESSON 11

1. Annunciation Day
2. Jesus Christ
3. Two
4. Incarnation
5. Yes
6. Bethlehem
7. St. Joseph
8. Magnificat
9. Humility, poverty, obedience, etc.
10. Gabriel
11. 3
12. Divine
13. He is without sin
14. David's
15. They obeyed the command of Caesar

## LESSON 12

1. Saviour
2. Circumcision
3. Presentation
4. Purification
5. Simeon: Great confidence in God. Anna: Pray Thy kingdom come.
6. Magi
7. Do the work God wants us to do; obey parents.

8. Prayer, penance, fasting
9. Receive Christ into our hearts as Simeon received Him in his arms. Do penance as our Lord did. Pray and do good to others like Him.

## LESSON 13

1. Through His sufferings and death on the cross.
2. Jesus chose poor men, uneducated and unskilled.
3. When He was about 30—at His baptism.
4. John the Baptist, in the Jordan River.
5. The heavens opened and the Holy Spirit came down upon Jesus in the form of a dove. The voice of Father said, "This is My beloved son, in whom I am well pleased."
6. The devil told Jesus to change stones to bread, to cast Himself down from the pinnacle of the Temple, and finally to worship him (Mt. 4:1-11).
7. To show us we cannot expect to go through life without temptations.
8. Prayer and the sacraments.
9. Galilee—Capharnaum.
10. By means of parables, telling stories about things with which the people were familiar.
11. The Holy Eucharist, His death, Resurrection, and the Church.
12. Faith.
13. Same as No. 11, as well as the prophecies from the Old Testament.

# CHAPTER 5

## LESSON 14

1. D
2. H
3. A
4. E
5. I
6. B
7. F
8. J
9. C
10. G

## LESSON 15

1. No
2. No
3. Yes
4. Yes
5. When we do things without thinking of the consequences we are like Peter. When we are afraid to defend the Church or its leaders for we might lose some place of honor.
6. No
7. Yes
8. Yes
9. Yes
10. Yes

## LESSON 16

1. By keeping in the state of grace. Then any deed that we perform for love of God is rewarded.
2. By the offering we make of ourselves—and of money.
3. Ourselves.
4. It is offered to God.
5. The Mass
6. Because it is Christ's sacrifice renewed.
7. Christ though the priest.
8. Using the missal—keeping united to Christ.
9. He is God—He had ordained them priests.
10. By offering Himself to us in Holy Communion.

## LESSON 17

1. Limbo
2. Tomb
3. Holy Scripture
4. Easter Sunday
5. Mary Magdalen
6. His divinity
7. Those who have been faithful.
8. Greatest—Christ rose through His own power.
9. To instruct His Apostles and to prove He had risen.
10. Through Christ's power

## LESSON 18

1. Holy Spirit—Third Person of the Blessed Trinity
2. Mount of Olives
3. 40 days
4. Ascension
5. Kind and Judge
6. Mighty and majestic
7. So that the honor of God may be made known; a so that all men will receive their just reward or punishment.
8. "Come ye blessed of my Father, possess you the kingdom which is prepared for you."
9. He rose from the midst of His Apostles and ascended into heaven.
10. That Christ went to prepare a place for us in heaven.

# CHAPTER 6

## LESSON 19

1. Yes
2. The Holy Spirit brings us grace and keeps us more closely united to God.
3. The Holy Spirit helps us make important decisions, helps us in important undertakings and keeps us pleasing to God.
4. Christ mentioned the Holy Spirit when He instructed the Apostles to baptize "In the name of the Father, and of the Son, and of the Holy Spirit."

5. God the Holy Spirit dwells in our souls through grace and in this way makes us temples of God.
6. The Holy Spirit dwells in us through grace.
7. As our advocate, the Holy Spirit asks favors for us, defends, protects, and assists us.
8. The Nicene Creed states, "I believe...in the Holy Spirit, the Lord and Giver of Life; who proceeds from the Father and the Son, who together with the Father and Son is adored and glorified."
9. The Holy Spirit is a spirit. His works are entirely spiritual. Since the work of the Holy Spirit takes place within our souls, it is hard to see His effects and hence a test of faith to believe in Him and His work.
10. "God the Holy Spirit, accept my humble thanks for your great gift of grace. May I never lose an opportunity to increase the store of grace in me, and may I quickly regain the state of grace if I ever have the misfortune to lose."

## LESSON 20

1. God gives us grace to help us keep from sin and to enable us to gain merit for all our acts.
2. In order to know our sins so that we may confess them completely.
3. Yes, because His grace enables us to recall facts we may otherwise have forgotten.
4. Prayer and the sacraments.
5. To keep in the state of grace always or to restore sanctifying grace as soon as possible if we have the misfortune to commit mortal sin.

6. The opportunity may not come again. Once we refuse, it is easier to refuse a second time.
7. To obey promptly and cheerfully; to say morning and night prayers, to study when we would rather play.
8. He would not give up his earthly possessions and follow our Lord.
9. No; Adam and Eve, Lucifer, people who fall into sin.
10. It helps us conquer evil and do good.

**Sanctifying Grace or Actual Grace**

1. S
2. S
3. A
4. S
5. A
6. A
7. S
8. A
9. A
10. A
11. S
12. S
13. S
14. S
15. S
16. A

**Matching**

1. F
2. I
3. H
4. E
5. B
6. A
7. J
8. A
9. C
10. D
11. A
12. G

## LESSON 21

1. Prayer which comes from the heart is most pleasing to God.
2. The simplest kind of prayer is just talking to God, or offering everything we do as a prayer.
3. Yes, because prayer is the lifting up of our minds and hearts to God and we do this when we recall God's presence.
4. To increase sanctifying grace in our soul.
5. The Holy Eucharist gives grace through the merits Christ earned on the cross. Because this sacrament is the Body and Blood of Christ it gives grace in fullest measure.
6. Yes. Sanctifying grace does not dwell in the soul in the state of mortal sin.

7. The Mass: By assisting at it properly, i.e., as at a renewal of Calvary.
8. Yes, because we strengthen our will every time we overcome ourselves, and thus gain grace.
9. Try always to use and never refuse or abuse grace.

## LESSON 22

1. We partake of the nature of God through sanctifying grace.
2. Faith is the foundation stone of all the virtues. If we do not believe we cannot live a Christian life.
3. We should develop our faith by using it—that is by making frequent acts of faith, and by praying for a strong faith.
4. Hope is a supernatural virtue when it springs from grace. Hope is a natural virtue when it is based on natural motives.
5. When we trust that God will give us the grace to reach heaven.
6. Heaven is the fulfillment of all our hopes.
7. We mean that we must love our neighbor even as we love ourselves. If we really love God we will love everything He has created.
8. Christ prayed for His enemies and we as Christians are supposed to imitate Christ. All are God's children.
9. Everyone in the world.
10. Love of God.

## LESSON 23

1. By mortal sin.
2. Use them
3. Wisdom—correct sense of values, e.g., choosing to go to daily Mass.

   Understanding—using the help of God's grace to understand our religion.

   Counsel—obeying our parents' advice; avoiding occasions of sin.

   Fortitude—going without meat on Friday—Communion fast, resisting temptation.

   Knowledge—learning the things we need to do to get to heaven.

   Piety—studying our lessons for love of God.

   Fear of the Lord—having great respect for God's power and justice.
4. The Holy Spirit
5. So that he can lead others to the one true fold, and defend it when necessary.
6. They strengthen our will so that we can fight against greater temptations.
7. Obedience, humility, prudence, silence.
8. Knowledge and doing God's will will get us to heaven. Nothing else is necessary if we wish to gain eternal life.
9. Prayerfully doing all we do for love of God.
10. Not letting anything bother us. We can obtain it by accepting all that happens as the will of God, or at least permitted by Him for good.

11. Not thinking or caring too much of our earthly possessions.
12. If we do not lead a good life we shall be punished when we die.

**Matching**

1. G
2. A
3. D
4. E
5. B
6. C
7. E

## LESSON 24

1. The virtues have to do with our conduct. If our conduct is good we are good citizens.
2. No, because everyone must have certain rules of conduct, whether Catholic or not.
3. When they spring from the grace of God.
4. The moral cardinal virtues are hinges on which all the other moral virtues hang.
5. We give God what is due Him.
6. Giving to the poor, sharing with friends.
7. Not complaining when things go wrong. Putting up with rain when we want sun. Keep trying even when things go wrong.
8. She was your age when first tempted.
9. Giving God the worship that belongs to Him.

# CHAPTER 7

## LESSON 25

1. The Catholic Church is the one true Church of Christ.
2. In order to belong to the Catholic Church a person must be baptized, believe in the teachings of the Church, and submit to her authority.
3. Christ compared the Church with the things the people knew and understood in order to make it possible for them to understand better what the Church is.
4. Because the Church is necessary to help us get to heaven.
5. The Church guides and directs us and advises us—through the priests, bishops, pope—when we are in trouble or danger, and gives us the means of obtaining the grace necessary to obtain heaven
6. Third, the Holy Spirit.
7. The pope.
8. The Church needs the laity as well as the clergy and religious.
9. The laity can join parish groups or clubs, help in all parish undertakings, and lead lives that will give good example.
10. The priests and bishops have a great responsibility. They too are human and in great need of God's help in all their work.
11. Tongues of fire.

**Matching**

1. C
2. B
3. D

4. A
5. E

**Fill in the Blank**

1. temples
2. confirmation
3. Father
4. Son
5. Father
6. Son
7. tongues of fire
8. instituted
9. life
10. Church

## LESSON 26

1. The Church is one because it has only one visible head; all members offer the one same sacrifice; the teachings of the Church are the same all over the world.
2. Martin Luther broke away from the Catholic Church and started the Lutheran Church. The present-day Lutheran Church does not recognize the pope as the one true head of the Church.
3. The members of the Church are united in faith, worship, and government; that is, in what the Church teaches for our belief, in the sacrifice that is offered, and in the rulers of the Church.

4. The pope
5. Assist at Mass, receive the sacraments, perform good works.
6. Catholic means that the Church teaches the same truths through all the ages, all over the world. Since this is what our Church does, it is appropriately called Catholic.
7. The Catholic religion is the one true religion because it is the only one that was founded by Christ.
8. Christ gave authority to Peter when he said, "Upon this rock I will build my Church."
9. The guidance of the Holy Spirit keeps the Church from making a mistake
10. Doctrines of faith and morals
11. No
12. Be faithful to its laws, pray and receive the sacraments often, cooperate with its leaders.
13. A General Council is a meeting of the pope and all the bishops in the world held to clarify some teaching, explain some doctrine, or determine a certain course of action.

**Matching**

1. G
2. A
3. F
4. B
5. A
6. D

7. D
8. C
9. E
10. A

## LESSON 27

1. Through study and reading Cardinal Newman discovered that his church could not be traced back to the time of Christ. Hence he joined the Catholic Church.
2. The members of the Church are united in faith and in sacraments, by supernatural bonds, under one head.
3. Yes, because the Church needs the help of all its members, in order to carry on its work.
4. By good example, by praying for them, by explaining things to them.
5. Communion of Saints.
6. Militant means fighting, so if we fight off the attacks of the Devil and other temptations we are militant Catholics.
7. Assist at Mass, pray, offer frequent prayers and acts of mortification.
8. Yes. In the Mass, which offers to God Almighty the prayers of His divine Son and all the members of His Mystical Body.
9. There is a special remembrance for the dead in the Canon of the Mass.
10. Belonging to the Church in desire means that a person wishes to belong to the one true Church founded by Christ, but for some good reason is not able to join.

# CHAPTER 8

## LESSON 28

1. Yes
2. Yes
3. No
4. Yes
5. Yes
6. Yes
7. No
8. Yes
9. No
10. Yes

## LESSON 29

1. Death is a punishment resulting from Adam's sin.
2. No. "It is appointed to all men once to die."
3. Keep in the state of grace.
4. Yes
5. Immediately after the death of each individual.
6. At the end of the world.
7. Yes—of eternal life.
8. To show respect for our faithful departed, whose bodies will rise again on the Last Day.
9. They will be reunited.
10. Intellect and will.

**Matching**

1. B
2. G
3. A
4. D
5. I
6. E
7. L
8. C
9. H
10. J
11. F
12. K

# CHAPTER 9

## LESSON 30

1. Yes
2. Yes
3. Yes
4. Yes
5. No
6. No
7. Yes
8. No

9. No
10. Yes

## LESSON 31

1. Love of God—His honor and glory.
2. With great generosity toward God.
3. Our Lord was kind to everyone in word and deed.
4. Because they are God's afflicted creatures and need our encouragement.
5. Death on the cross for us.
6. Giving money or help to the poor or needy. It gains added grace and helps remit the temporal punishment due to sin.
7. His forgiveness of those who had put Him to death: of those who had talked about Him; Judas; Peter.
8. Worship of God. Respect of parents, civil authority.

**Matching**

1. G
2. D
3. L
4. A
5. H
6. E
7. K
8. B
9. I

10. F
11. M
12. C
13. N
14. J

# CHAPTER 10

## LESSON 32

1. H
2. A
3. K
4. M
5. F
6. I
7. B
8. L
9. N
10. E
11. J
12. C
13. O
14. G
15. D

## LESSON 33

1. No
2. No
3. Yes
4. No
5. Yes
6. No
7. No
8. Yes
9. Yes
10. Yes

## LESSON 34

1. The Church uses the Holy Name with reverence and respect.
2. Bow our heads.
3. In taking oaths.
4. Ask God to be witness that what we are saying is true.
5. An oath is lawful when taken in the proper manner, for some serious reason, when we know what we are saying is true, or when what we promise to do is not wrong.
6. Yes
7. No, because a vow is a deliberate and free promise. It must be well thought over and consented to.
8. Jephte's vow was wrong because he had no right to take a human life.

9. Sisters, priests, brothers. Lay people who vow not to marry. Blessed Virgin Mary, St. Joseph. Married people who vow to remain faithful to each other.
10. Poverty—to give up the right to use and have property.
11. Chastity—to give up all the rights of the married state, and to live a completely chaste and pure life.
12. Obedience—obeying the commands of our lawful superiors.

## LESSON 35

1. "In vain" means without necessity, or to no purpose.
2. Anger may lead us to sin.
3. Yes
4. Good example. Telling them the harm they do, correcting them each time they curse, teaching them a prayer to say instead.
5. Blasphemy shows hatred or contempt towards God.

## LESSON 36

1. Easter, Pentecost
2. So that we can better honor Him, and regain our strength.
3. The Apostles changed the Sabbath from Saturday to Sunday because of the great events that had taken place on Sunday.
4. Assistance at Mass is the highest form of prayer we can offer.
5. Yes
6. Sickness, charity, work
7. "Do this in remembrance of Me."
8. Quiet relaxation and recreation, reading, praying.

## LESSON 37

1. Unnecessary
2. Sickness, charity, support of family.
3. Servile Work is that labor which distracts us from true spiritual leisure and rest.
4. Yes
5. Yes, unless you cannot reasonably expect to do it on another day.

# Image Credits

Front cover Jesus of Nazareth, King of the Jews (colour litho) / European School, (20th century) / European / Bridgeman Images; (front cover, spine, and back cover) Background pattern © Antares Light, Shutterstock.com

pXI Conversion on the Way to Damascus, Caravaggio (1571–1610), oil on canvas, Santa Maria del Popolo, Rome, [Public domain], via Wikimedia Commons

pXIII hands in pray pose. pencil drawing © s_oleg, Shutterstock.com

pXIV-XV New bible sitting below a stack of antique bibles © Gordo25, Shutterstock.com

pXVI-1 The Holy Trinity, fresco, 1738–9, Luca Rossetti da Orta, St. Gaudenzio Church at Ivrea (Torino), Italy [Public domain], via Wikimedia Commons

p2-66 The Creation of Adam, fresco, (1475–1564) Michelangelo, [Public domain], via Wikimedia Commons

p2-3, 48-49, 74-75, 100-101, 134-135, 176-177, 236-237, 276-277, 294-295, 318-319 Christ and Saint John the Baptist in Hagia Sophia (mosaic) / Byzantine, (13th century) / Hagia Sophia, Istanbul, Turkey / Bridgeman Images

p6-7 Gates of Paradise © VladisChern, Shutterstock.com

p8 Old paper scroll © SimoneN, Shutterstock.com

p13 Holy Trinity © Zvonimir Atletic, Shutterstock.com

p15 The Divine Comedy, Paradiso, Canto 31: The saintly throng form a rose in the empyrean (rose celeste)—by Dante Alighieri (1265-1321), 1885 (engraving) / Dore, Gustave (1832-83) / French / Bridgeman Images

p16-17 Jesus Christ Statue © Marc Bruxelle, Shutterstock.com

p18-19 Savaoph, God the Father, 1885-96 (oil on canvas) / Vasnetsov, Victor Mikhailovich (1848-1926) / Russian / Tretyakov Gallery, Moscow, Russia / Bridgeman Images

p23 First day of creation, Genesis / Schnorr von Carolsfeld, Julius (1794-1872) / German / Bridgeman Images

p24 God the Father, Cima da Conegliano, c. 1510–1517, oil on canvas, Courtauld Institute of Art, described at URL: http://www.artandarchitecture.org.uk/images/gallery/d8c9dc7d.html, The Courtauld Institute of Art, Somerset House, Strand, London, WC2R 0RN, UK, [Public domain], via Wikimedia Commons

p29 Good Shepherd, Bernhard Plockhorst (1825–1907), originally published before 1923 in UK and USA., [Public domain], via Wikimedia Commons

p30-31 Apostle John the Theologian on the island of Patmos. 2012. Canvas, oil. 70 x 50. Artist A.N. Mironov / Creative Commons (CC), via Wikimedia Commons

p31 God Creating the Land Animals, Antonio Tempesta (Italy, Florence, 1555-1630), [Public domain], via Wikimedia Commons

p32 The Last Supper (oil on panel) / Macip, Vicente Juan (Juan de Juanes) (c.1510-79) / Spanish / Prado, Madrid, Spain / Bridgeman Images

p35 Immaculate Conception Catholic Church (Port Clinton, Ohio)—stained glass, St. Patrick / Creative Commons (CC), via Wikimedia Commons

p36 Text of "Our Father" prayer with Trinity in central column (God the Father, dove of the Holy Spirit, Jesus) and Biblical and symbolic scenes in left and right columns., Fridolin Leiber (1853–1912), [Public domain], via Wikimedia Commons

p37 Vector drawing of a Dove in flight © Natsmith1, Shutterstock.com

p40 Photo of prayer card of the Holy Trinity, IndianaJones8856, / Creative Commons (CC), via Wikimedia Commons

p44-45 Statue of the Holy Trinity on the top of the Holy Trinity Column in Olomouc, the Czech Republic, Jan Kameníček, [Public domain], via Wikimedia Commons

p46 Ceiling fresco in the Russian orthodox church of the Holy Trinity (photo) / Bridgeman Images
p47 The Annunciation to the Shepherds (coloured engraving) / English School, (19th century) / English / Bridgeman Images
p49 The Angels in the Planet Mercury, illustration from 'The Dore Gallery', published c.1890 (digitally enhanced image) / Dore, Gustave (1832-83) (after) / French / Bridgeman Images
p50 The Guardian Angel, protecting boy, girl and doll fishing (chromolitho) / English School, (20th century) / English / Bridgeman Images
p52 The Temptation of Christ (coloured engraving) / English School, (19th century) / English / Bridgeman Images
p56-57 The angel at the Sepulchre / English School, (20th century) / English / Bridgeman Images
p58 Angelo Del Beato Angelico (colour litho) / Italian School, (20th century) / Italian / Bridgeman Images
p61 The Creation (coloured engraving) / German School, (19th century) / German / Bridgeman Images
p69 The Garden of Eden / colour lithograph / Watt, John Millar (1895-1975) / British / Bridgeman Images
p70 The expulsion of Adam and Eve from the Garden of Eden / colour lithograph / English School, (19th century) / English / Bridgeman Images
p77 Adam and Eve expelled from Paradise (colour litho) / Raphael (Raffaello Sanzio of Urbino) (1483-1520) (after) / Italian / Bridgeman Images
p78 Virgin Mary Statue © Ryzhkov Sergey, Shutterstock.com
p80-81 Expulsion of Adam and Eve from Paradise (colour litho) / Bridgeman Images
p88 Close up prayer's hand pray in church © Nattapat.J, Shutterstock.com
p97 The banishment from Paradise (coloured engraving) / German School, (19th century) / German / Bridgeman Images
p98-99 Jesus Christ on throne in his glory © Vuk Kostic, Shutterstock.com
p100-101 Christ showing his Sacred Heart. Colour lithograph., This file comes from Wellcome Images, a website operated by Wellcome Trust, a global charitable foundation based in the United Kingdom / Cropped image / Creative Commons (CC), via Wikimedia Commons
p102 Crucifixion At Sunrise—Empty Tomb With Shroud, © Romolo Tavani, Shutterstock.com
p103 Sunset with a reflection in the lake, © Aleksei Marinchenko, Shutterstock.com
p104 Noah's ark 3D rendering, © Adao, Shutterstock.com
p107 Marble statue of Jesus Christ, © Kamira, Shutterstock.com
p108 The Angel with Wonderful News (gouache on paper) / Uptton, Clive (1911-2006) / English / Bridgeman Images
p111 Christmas nativity scene of Joseph and Mary holding baby Jesus, © mastapiece, Shutterstock.com
p112 Visitation (detail), Franz Anton Maulbertsch (1724–1796), fresco, Collection : Vác Cathedral [Public domain], via Wikimedia Commons
p113 Clipboard with a pen, © rCarner, Shutterstock.com
p114-115 The Wise Men journeying (colour litho), English School / (19th century) / English / Bridgeman Images
p121 Nativity / colour lithograph / Lawson, John (19th century) / English / Bridgeman Images
p122 Presentation in the Temple / English School, (19th century) / English / Bridgeman Images

p124 Gold Frankincense and myrrh © marilyn barbone, Shutterstock.com
p126 Twelve Year Old Jesus in the Temple © Zvonimir Atletic, Shutterstock.com
p128 Wedding at Cana © Zvonimir Atletic, Shutterstock.com
p129 The temptation of Christ / engraving by Gustave Dore—later colouring / (1832-83) / French / Bridgeman Images
p130 The marriage in Cana (coloured engraving) / German School, (19th century) / German / Bridgeman Images
p131 Holy communion chalice with wine and bread © ALEX S, Shutterstock.com
p133 Pencil and notebook © Be Good, Shutterstock.com
p135 Jesus is laid in the tomb © Zvonimir Atletic, Shutterstock.com
p136 Closeup of jesus crucified on the cross © Jorge A. Bohorquez, Shutterstock.com
p137 Palm leaves © drpnncpptak, Shutterstock.com
p138-139 Crucifixion, Andrea Previtali (–1528), oil on canvas, Collection: Gallerie dell'Accademia [Public domain], via Wikimedia Commons
p140 Jesus institutes the Holy Eucharist (coloured engraving) / German School, (19th century) / German / Bridgeman Images
p145 6th Stations of the Cross, Veronica wipes the face of Jesus © Zvonimir Atletic, Shutterstock.com
p147 12th Stations of the Cross, Jesus dies on the cross © Zvonimir Atletic, Shutterstock.com
p151 Holy bread rite during the Catholic Mass © Fabio Lotti, Shutterstock.com
p153 Preparation for the first Holy Communion © PhotoRK, Shutterstock.com
p155 Monstrance © Zolnierek, Shutterstock.com
p156 Window w02 depicting the Harrowing of Hell (stained glass) / French School, (13th century) / French / Tours Cathedral, France / Bridgeman Images
p157 Easter Jesus Christ rose from the dead © VladisChern, Shutterstock.com
p158 Jesus Christ is Risen © Rachata Sinthopachakul, Shutterstock.com
p160-161 Jesus Christ, The Resurrection (colour litho) / French School, (19th century) / French / Bridgeman Images
p162 Resurrection of Lazarus (colour litho) / French School, (19th century) / French / French / Bridgeman Images
p163 The Resurrection of Christ (colour litho) / Illustration from Katholische Familienbibel / Bridgeman Images
p167 The Ascension of Christ (colour litho) / German School, (20th century) / German / Bridgeman Images
p169 Lamb of God Lion and Cross © Atomazul, Shutterstock.com
p173 Jesus Christ, The Ascension (colour litho) / French School, (19th century) / French / Bridgeman Images
p174-175 Detail of the painting of the interior of the dome depicting the Holy Trinity, 1663-65 (fresco) / Mignard, Pierre (1612-95) / Photographer: Clement Guillaume / French / Eglise Notre-Dame-du-Val-de-Grace, Paris, France / Bridgeman Images
p176 Depiction of the Christian Holy Spirit as a dove, by Gian Lorenzo Bernini, in the apse of Saint Peter's Basilica, c. 1660, Dnalor 01 / Creative Commons (CC), via Wikimedia Commons
p179 Holy Spirit symbol © Thoom, Shutterstock.com
p181 Baptism of Jesus by John the Baptist / English School, (19th century) / English / (Nelson, 1871) / Bridgeman Images
p187 Open hands in prayer © Jacob_09, Shutterstock.com
p190-191 The sending of the Holy Spirit (coloured engraving) / German School, (19th century) / German / Bridgeman Images
p197 Monstrance © dvande, Shutterstock.com

p198 Girl hands praying to God © narikan, Shutterstock.com
p204 Great was the day, the joy was great ... (coloured engraving) / English School, (19th century) / English / Bridgeman Images
p206 Presentation of Jesus in the Temple (Presentazione di Gesù al Tempio), by Giotto, 1303-1305, 14th century (fresco) / Giotto (Giotto di Bondone) (c.1266-1337) / Italian / Scrovegni (Arena) Chapel, Padua, Italy / Bridgeman Images
p211 Jesus Christ in the Garden Of Olives (colour litho) / French School, (19th century) / French / Bridgeman Images
p213 Vatican City silver coin, bust of pope Pius XI © Yaroslaff, Shutterstock.com
p214 White pearl in shell © Tish1, Shutterstock.com
p216 Boy praying on the Mount © Deer worawut, Shutterstock.com
p220-221 The Sermon on the Mount (coloured engraving) / German School, (19th century) / German / Bridgeman Images
p225 Scene from the life of Jesus (coloured engraving) / French School, (19th century) / French / Bridgeman Images
p228 Strong man child showing bicep muscles © Brian A Jackson, Shutterstock.com
p236 St. Peter's Basilica © Vladimir Sazonov, Shutterstock.com
p238 Interior of the Catholic Church, Islington (engraving) / English School, (19th century) / EnglishJesus Teaching (gouache on paper) / Bridgeman Images
p240 Holy Trinity Catholic Church (Trinity, Indiana)—stained glass, Holy Spirit as a dove, Nheyob, Creative Commons (CC), via Wikimedia Commons
p243 Statue of St. Peter © thaagoon, Shutterstock.com
p244 Portrait de Saint Thomas More, mort à Tower Hill (Londres) en 1535, Transferred from fr.wikipedia to Commons by Bloody-libu using CommonsHelper, Gwengoat at French Wikipedia, Creative Commons (CC), via Wikimedia Commons
p249 Jesus Teaching (gouache on paper) / Bridgeman Images
p251 The Holy Spirit © BrankaVV, Shutterstock.com
p253 Saint Luke Catholic Church (Danville, Ohio)—stained glass, crown of thorns & nails, Nheyob, Creative Commons (CC), via Wikimedia Commons
p255 Sending out the Twelve Apostles (engraving) / English School, (19th century) / English / Bridgeman Images
p258-259 The Exhortation to the Apostles, illustration from 'The Life of Our Lord Jesus Christ' (watercolour over graphite on paper) / Tissot, James Jacques Joseph (1836-1902) / French / Brooklyn Museum of Art, New York / Bridgeman Images
p267 Cardinal Newman (engraving) / English School, (19th century) / English / Bridgeman Images
p280 Silhouette of woman kneeling and praying © asiandelight, Shutterstock.com
p283 Resurrection of Lazarus © Renata Sedmakova, Shutterstock.com
p285 Fresco painted by Giorgio Vasari in the dome of the cathedral of Florence, Italy © BlackMac, Shutterstock.com
p292-293 Deuteronomy: Frontispiece in which God makes the Laws, from the 'Nuremberg Bible (Biblia Sacra Germanaica)' (coloured woodcut) / German School, (15th century) / German / Bridgeman Images
p295 The Ten Commandments (colour litho) / English School, (19th century) / English / Bridgeman Images
p297 Two stone tablets with the ten commandments inscribed on them © Inked Pixels, Shutterstock.com
p302 Feeding the poor © addkm, Shutterstock.com
p310-311 The Burning Bush (coloured engraving) / German School, (19th century) / German / Bridgeman Images

p317 Christ riding into Jerusalem / colour lithograph / English School, (20th century) / English / Bridgeman Images
p320 Little girl in prayer © PUWADON SANG, Shutterstock.com
p325 Icon of Jesus © Jaroslav74, Shutterstock.com
p329 Belshazzar's Feast c.1636-38 (oil on canvas) / Rembrandt Harmensz. van Rijn (1606-69) / Dutch / National Gallery, London, UK / Bridgeman Images
p331 Christus Pantocrator—Artistic representation of Jesus Christ God, the second divine Person of the Most Holy Trinity (Cathedral of Cefalù, c. 1130.), Andreas Wahra, GNU-free documentation licence, Creative Commons (CC), via Wikimedia Commons
p334-335 Saint george riding white horse fighting dragon © TSV Creative, Shutterstock.com
p336 Reliquary of St Agatha's arm in Palermo Cathedral, Sicily / Photographer: Martin Norris / Bridgeman Images
p343 Christ carrying the Cross (chromolitho) / European School, (19th century) / European / Bridgeman Images
p344 Portrait of Abraham Lincoln © timyee, Shutterstock.com
p355 Icon of Christ © Jaroslav74, Shutterstock.com
p360-361 Joshua passing the River Jordan with the Ark of the Covenant, Benjamin West (1738–1820), oil on panel, 1QFKub9RpoHOHg at Google Cultural Institute, [Public domain], via Wikimedia Commons
p365 Bronze picture of the Last Supper © Kozlik, Shutterstock.com
p374 The Virgin in Prayer, 1640-50 (oil on canvas), Sassoferrato, Il (Giovanni Battista Salvi) (1609-85) / Italian, Bridgeman Images
p377 Rosary © StockPhotosArt, Shutterstock.com
p381 The Immaculate Conception with the Fifteen Mysteries of the Rosary (oil on canvas), Cabrera, Miguel (1695-1768) (circle of) / Mexican, Photo © Christie's Images / Bridgeman Images